362.73   Siblings in adoption
          and foster care.
SIB

$49.95

DATE			

Siblings in Adoption and Foster Care

Siblings in Adoption and Foster Care

*Traumatic Separations and
Honored Connections*

EDITED BY

DEBORAH N. SILVERSTEIN
AND
SUSAN LIVINGSTON SMITH

Foreword by Adam Pertman

PRAEGER

Westport, Connecticut
London

Library of Congress Cataloging-in-Publication Data

Siblings in adoption and foster care : traumatic separations and honored connections /
    edited by Deborah N. Silverstein and Susan Livingston Smith.
        p. cm.
    Includes bibliographical references and index.
    ISBN 978–0–313–35143–3 (alk. paper)
1. Adopted children—Family relationships. 2. Foster children—Family relationships. 3.
Brothers and sisters. I. Silverstein, Deborah, 1947– II. Smith, Susan Livingston.
HV875.S54   2009
362.73085′5—dc22   2008033668

British Library Cataloguing in Publication Data is available.

Library of Congress Catalog Card Number: 2008033668
ISBN: 978–0–313–35143–3

First published in 2009

Praeger Publishers, 88 Post Road West, Westport, CT 06881
An imprint of Greenwood Publishing Group, Inc.
www.praeger.com

Printed in the United States of America

The paper used in this book complies with the
Permanent Paper Standard issued by the National
Information Standards Organization (Z39.48–1984).

10 9 8 7 6 5 4 3 2 1

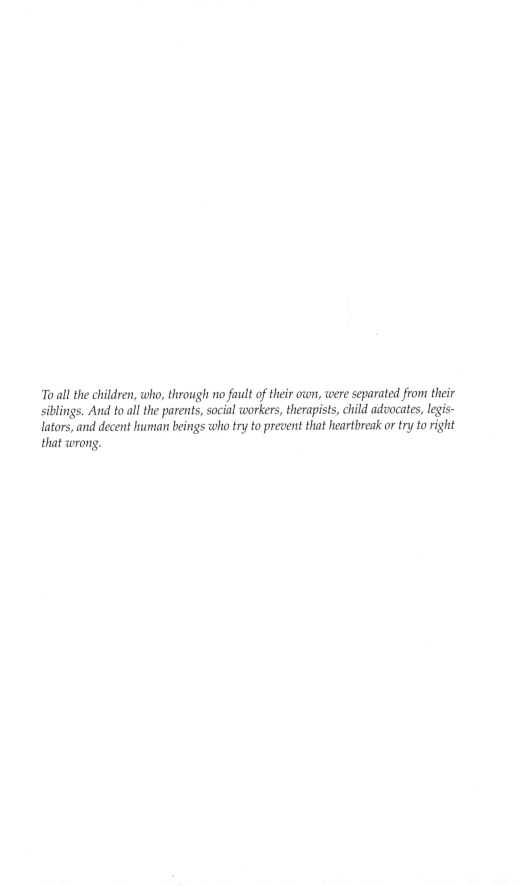

To all the children, who, through no fault of their own, were separated from their siblings. And to all the parents, social workers, therapists, child advocates, legislators, and decent human beings who try to prevent that heartbreak or try to right that wrong.

Contents

Foreword

As the head of an organization that conducts research, I feel compelled to begin this foreword by extolling the inestimable virtues of research. It provides knowledge we never had before; it shatters myths and offers insights; and perhaps most important (when we're paying attention), it empowers us to make better decisions both in our personal lives and in our society. Sometimes, it even serves the simple but vital function of affirming the obvious.

This thoughtful, challenging book accomplishes all of those objectives and, in so doing, strives for a lofty yet achievable goal—to help reshape policies and practices in our country so that they better serve the tens of thousands of foster and adopted children each year who are deprived of relationships with their brothers and sisters.

It turns out that sibling connections are significant, a stark affirmation of the obvious that runs through virtually all the studies cited between these covers. More pointedly, a growing body of research makes it increasingly clear that separating siblings can have detrimental effects on them, while maintaining their bonds can yield developmental, psychic, and social benefits.

All those conclusions seem so intuitively evident that one might reasonably ask whether they need to be stated at all. They do indeed, as evidenced by the simple fact that thousands of siblings are placed into different families every year; are often not enabled to see their brothers and sisters even when it is possible to do so; are sometimes not even told there are boys and girls out there to whom they are related; and, in a reality that is more difficult to accept, are placed into these sorts of situations without serious consideration of whether there might be a better alternative.

I have no doubt that the vast majority of professionals try very hard to make the optimal decisions they can for the sake of the children they serve—and I know that it breaks their hearts whenever they come to the conclusion that separating siblings is the "right" thing to do. Furthermore, the hard reality is that there are times when taking that excruciating step is indeed the best available option.

Generations of secrecy and shame have undermined many aspects of adoption and foster care, however, and nowhere is this simple truth more evident than in policies and practices relating to siblings separated by the child-welfare system. What I mean is this—too often, decisions are made as a result of myths and misinformation rather than on the basis of sound knowledge about the implications of the actions being contemplated.

So, for example, brothers and sisters are sometimes separated because it is perceived that sibling rivalry will have detrimental effects. Those of us who grew up with siblings know this can indeed happen (though it certainly didn't lead anyone to think I should live in a different home from my brothers and sister). But research and experience also teach us that this complex relationship has benefits, such as helping children learn to deal with conflict in a safe and supportive environment, while the removal of a sibling, in and of itself, can have traumatic consequences. Similarly, siblings are sometimes separated out of the belief that it is the best way to provide focused attention to the special needs of one of the children. Again, the potentially deleterious offsetting effects of the split itself may not be sufficiently taken into account; at least as important to consider is that singular attention for children with needs can distort their sense of self and belonging or can possibly be overwhelming. A better answer (while admittedly one that can be more difficult to achieve) is to recruit, prepare, and support families who can effectively care for the children in question *and* their brothers or sisters.

The good news is that more than half the states now address sibling placement as an important consideration, and research on this subject is growing in both quantity and quality. Opportunities for training and education, including conferences such as the one that led to this cutting-edge book, are becoming more available and better utilized; and, according to a story in the *New York Times*, "there is a growing awareness [among mental health professionals] that the interplay between siblings exerts a powerful life-long force." (Rosenthal 1992) Best of all, on the ground, practices in adoption and foster care are clearly headed in the direction of applying that awareness.

All this is happening even though keeping sibling groups intact, or at least in contact, can be complicated, vexing, or just plain hard work for the foster parents, the adoptive parents, the social workers, and the other adults in the picture. It is happening because the repercussions of separation can be even more complicated, vexing, and difficult *for the children.* The rewards of doing the right thing are ultimately enormous for everyone involved.

The research is still insufficient, though it is vital to point out that a growing body of it nearly all points in the same direction. But this is not only about research. Yes, we need more research to bolster best policies, laws, and practices—but we don't need a 10-year longitudinal study to understand what we see with our own eyes every single day: that siblings love each other, support each other, drive each other crazy, give each other strength, tease and fight with each other, and, in many families, provide the only constancy and stability in their lives. Sometimes, siblings even help one another survive.

One more related point—we should not only be learning about siblings, but also from them. According to the same *New York Times* article cited above, a greater number of former foster children are searching for their siblings than for their birth parents; more broadly, we know that in some adoption reunion registries, more people also are looking for their brothers and sisters than their biological mothers or fathers. I wonder if we can figure out what this might mean?

Again, in real life, protecting sibling relationships can obviously be difficult for an array of reasons—from safety issues to geographic limitations to the large size of some families—but dispelling myths and gaining reliable information is imperative if we are to serve the best interests of the children entrusted to our care. The research clearly indicates that for boys and girls who have experienced serious difficulties in their lives—which describes virtually every child touched by adoption and foster care—sibling relationships can be protective, can promote resilience, and can offer a host of other quantifiable and intangible benefits.

Chapter by chapter, this book builds the case for doing the right thing, however complicated that may be. It shatters myths, provides insights, states the obvious, and empowers us to make better decisions. All we need to do is pay attention.

Adam Pertman
Executive Director
Evan B. Donaldson Adoption Institute
Author, *Adoption Nation*

Preface

In March 2006, Kinship Center, The Evan B. Donaldson Institute, and The Berger Institute for Work, Family and Children at Claremont McKenna College joined together to present a two-day conference "Biology and Beyond: Siblings in Foster Care and Adoption." The conference was both well attended and well received. The seeds for this book were sown at that time. Many of the contributors to this book were featured presenters at the conference and agreed to have those materials included. Others suggested that the editors, Deborah N. Silverstein and Susan Livingston Smith, contact organizations or individuals who were not part of the conference to write for this book. The sponsoring organizations, the presenters, and the audience all agreed that the topic of siblings separated by adoption and foster care has received too little attention and that there is a widespread lack of agreement about the definition of the term "sibling," a dearth of ethical practice guidelines about keeping siblings who might be separated by adoptive or foster-care placement connected, and a general lack of responsiveness to the concerns that have already been expressed. This book sets out to remedy, at least in part, some of those disturbing occurrences.

Siblings in Adoption and Foster Care draws together some of the leading thinkers, researchers, and educators in the child-welfare arena to explore the issue from many angles and to offer a variety of perspectives and recommendations. The book contains 12 distinct chapters from Diane F. Halpern's general overview of the complexity of the topic, to Smith's review of the current research. Several chapters, Mary Anne Herrick and Wendy Piccus, Sharon Roszia and Cynthia Roe, Susan Thompson

Underdahl, and Carol Biddle and Carol J. Bishop give the reader insight into the personal experiences of separated siblings; while David Brodzinsky, Michael Trout, and Margaret Creek offer a clinical view. Silverstein and Smith review several programs that seek to minimize the potential negative impact of separating siblings. William Wesley Patton, as he so often does, melds together the legal rights and ramifications of sibling separations. Finally, Jerica M. Berge, Kevin M. Green, Harold Grotevant, and Ruth McRoy report on their research into siblings in open adoption. The hope is, as songwriter Stephen Sondheim wrote, there is "something for everyone."

Acknowledgments

The authors wish to thank Kinship Center and The Evan B. Donaldson Institute, most specifically, Carol Biddle and Adam Pertman respectively, for their encouragement of this project. Further, each of us has the benefit of supportive husbands who listened to the ideas and took a wide berth around us as we worked to bring this manuscript together.

Deborah: I would like to acknowledge the strong support of my coworkers in the Kinship Center offices in Santa Ana, California, who encouraged me, especially Melissa Dodson, Allison Davis Maxon, Sharon Roszia, and Del Stewart. What a wonder it has been to learn from and with them! The commitment of Kinship Center to maintaining sibling connections whether the children can live together or not is one of the best examples of putting ethical principles into quality practice that I have ever seen, and this has touched me deeply. Finally, I would like to acknowledge my own sister, Blaze, who has taught me from the day she was born what true siblingship means.

Susan: I would like to acknowledge my research partner over the past 25 years, Jeanne Howard, whose constant availability for shaping ideas and passion for doing the right thing in serving children has provided tremendous support for my ongoing work. And posthumously, thank you to my big brother, Bill, who provided much nurturance to me as a child.

Further, we appreciate the support of our editor Debbie Carvalko at Praeger for her support and keen eye.

List of Abbreviations

AAP	Adoption Assistance Program
ADHD	Attention Deficit Hyperactivity Disorder
AKN	Adoptive Kinship Network
ASFA	*Adoption and Safe Families Act*
Cal. Welf.	California welfare
CTB	Camp To Belong
CWLA	Child Welfare League of America
DC	"dual contact"
KSSP	Kinship Support Services Program
MC	"mixed contact"
Md. Fam. Law Code	Maryland Family Law Code
MTARP	Minnesota Texas Adoption Research Project
N.H. Ann. Stat., Tit. XII	New Hampshire Annals of Statistics, Title XII
N.J. Rev. Stat.	New Jersey Revised Statute
NRCFCPPP	National Resource Center for Family Centered Practice and Permanency Planning
NSCAW	National Survey of Child and Adolescent Well-Being
N.Y. Dom. Rel. Law	New York Domestic Relations Law
WS DSHS	Washington State Department of Social and Health Services

Full, Half, Step, Foster, Adoptive, and Other: The Complex Nature of Sibling Relationships

Diane F. Halpern

If a society is known by how well it treats those who are most vulnerable, then, as a society, we should be ashamed. Despite the hard work of many caring individuals, our response to children with "broken families" or no families at all is a national tragedy. If you are familiar with the face of foster care in the United States, then you already know that many children, through no fault of their own, are placed in multiple settings as they move through childhood—10 or more is not unusual. Like criminals who have served their sentences, they will be released on their own with little money and dim prospects for meaningful employment when they "age out" of the system, which is usually at age 18. With multiple changes in family settings and schools, even the brightest foster child is unlikely to be on track for higher education or to leave the system with sufficient workplace skills. It is against these grim realities for "kids in care" that we consider the role of siblings, and ask tough questions about possible benefits of keeping kids from the same family together.

There are a large number of children involved in foster care, and every indication is that the numbers are increasing. Intuitively, it seems that children who have suffered multiple losses in their lives should be placed together with siblings with whom they have positive affectional bonds. A defensible philosophy is that siblings—broadly defined as any two children that have sibling-like relationships—should always be placed together, but the reality of foster care does not provide unlimited options and rarely is an ideal philosophy realized for children in care. One reason we serve these children so poorly is that there are so many of them and the resources available cannot meet the tremendous need. According to a 2005 publication (Hegar), 65 to 85 percent of foster children in the United States are in sibling groups. Siblings are more likely to be separated in foster care when they are older and when they are further apart in age. Sibling groups often span ages from older teens to infants when they enter foster care, and they often have special needs. Any combination of these factors makes the placement of multiple siblings in the same home more unlikely because too few families are willing to take a special needs child and multiple siblings, and the larger the sibling group, the more difficult it is to place them together.

The *Adoption and Safe Families Act* of 1997 requires timely placement of children—obviously a good idea, but what is best for a large sibling group? Which siblings should be placed together when there is no single family that will take them all? How long should you wait while looking for a family who will take a larger family group? Critics argue that the only acceptable answer is to search harder for a foster family that will accept all of the children in a sibling group, refusing to answer tough questions about separation and the real scarcity of such placements, a stance that is of little use for a harried worker who is facing the reality of too few families who are willing to accept large groups of siblings. Before addressing the realities of contemporary care, however, we need to consider the theoretical underpinnings of the belief that siblings are best served when they stay together in foster care.

DEFINING WHO IS A SIBLING

If you are familiar with contemporary issues in foster care, then you may be surprised to learn that the word "sibling" is not generally known to nonprofessionals. It is useful to keep this basic idea in mind because professionals can easily alienate the people they most want to help by using language that is perceived to be affected. I once used the word "sibling" at a community event and then had to define it. For the rest of the evening, I was repeatedly asked why I could not just say "brother and sister" like everyone else. This embarrassing event serves as a reminder that academics and professional counselors can easily be out of touch with the community they are trying to serve.

In thinking about the question, "What is a sibling?" consider each of the possibilities below and, for each, decide if the relationship that is being described fits your definition of a sibling:

- Two people with the same biological parents
- Two people who have one biological parent in common

- Two people, who have lived in the same family, but have no biological ties to anyone else in the family
- Two people who are biological cousins and are being raised by their grandmother
- Two people whose parents are married to each other, but they have no biological relationship
- Two people who were conceived with sperm from the same anonymous donor

These various possible relationships test the limits of what it means to be a sibling. The usual dictionary definition includes only the first two examples, reserving the term sibling for people with at least one biological parent in common. But the dictionary definition does not take into account the socioemotional meaning of sibling, especially in the lives of children who have so many other losses in their lives that the sibling relationship may be their only lasting relationship. The usual dictionary definition also ignores the reality of contemporary families, which do not fit some idealized mold of a traditional two-parent family. The third example of two people with no biological ties living in the same family may be the prototypical family for foster children, who often claim foster siblings as the people to whom they are most closely attached. The example of biological cousins being raised by a grandmother is only one example from among many in which an assortment of other distant biological relationships are functional siblings because they are raised together. The fifth example is well-known in contemporary step-families where parents marry and bring their children from earlier unions with them into the new family. The last category is still controversial. Can two people conceived from the same sperm donor, anonymous or not, be called siblings? There are socioemotional and legal implications to how we define a sibling. New means of conception which now include egg donors, sperm donors, "birth mothers" who are neither the egg donor nor the mother who raises the child, and so on will continue to stretch our thinking about which relationships qualify as siblings. Do children have a right to a continuing relationship with their siblings? If so, how far does the category extend? And perhaps most importantly, who decides how to answer these questions?

The thoughtful chapters that follow address these and many other difficult questions about siblings, foster care, and adoption. Even if we remain guided by the desire to act in the best interests of the child, conflicting realities often make it difficult to know what is in the child's best interest and experts will disagree. My own definition of sibling is grounded in the socioemotional bonds between people. Much like the proverbial definition of what is a duck, if it feels likes a sibling relationship to at least one of the children in the pair, complicated by all of the messiness of personal relationships—which will include ambivalence and even some negative emotions such as jealousy—then for all effective purposes, the two people are siblings.

From the Child's Point of View

The sibling relationship has a special meaning for children whose other family ties have been twisted, frayed, or severed in ways that do not occur in intact families. For most people, the relationships we have with our siblings are the longest ones in our lives. They outlast the relationships we have with our parents and last longer than most marriages. These relationships are complex in traditional intact families, and even more so for children whose lives may consist of multiple family arrangements and disruptions. Normal sibling conflict often does not appear peaceful; but for children in disrupted families, there may be sibling relationships that are not healthy—for example, ones that repeat abusive behaviors learned at home or other places. There are many types of unhealthy relationships that emerge among siblings in disrupted families. For example, siblings may form joint conspiracies to sabotage a placement in the hope of returning home. There are some scenarios where separating siblings—in some circumstances and for some period of time—may be more desirable than placing them together. The central question that decision-makers have to grapple with is how to make decisions about siblings. What are the criteria and considerations that might suggest that a separation is warranted, and if we can make these decisions wisely, where do we find the families and other resources to support the decisions? How do you balance the reality that most adoptive families are not willing to adopt large sibling groups with the sincere need to keep siblings together? Decisions about placing children into homes for the short or long term require the wisdom of Solomon, the openhearted trust and faith of Big Bird, and perhaps the cunning ability of Wily Coyote (to cut through bureaucratic red tape). These difficult decisions need to be made with incomplete and conflicting information, limited resources, and often involve angry, hostile people. This is not a job for the faint of heart.

One Story among Many

These are many stories about siblings. Here is a true story about a beautiful young woman who grew up in and out of foster care. Soon after leaving foster care at 18, with a GED diploma, she became pregnant. I knew her as a gentle and intelligent young woman, although later events proved either that I was wrong or that she was so impressionable that she could be seriously misled by anyone who cared for her. She had no real job skills (she still cannot drive a car), no money, and a baby on the way, and she moved in with the baby's father. This is not an unusual story for children in foster care, although the outcome was unusually tragic. The baby was born prematurely. Poor people do not have health insurance, and therefore they do not have prenatal doctor visits. She was a wonderful caring mother, but the stay with the father did not work out. When she had nowhere to go—alone with a two-year old who was developmentally delayed and with no way to earn a living—she retreated to her only attachment in the world: her foster sister now living 150 miles away. Who among us is to say that they are not sisters? This was the only "family bond," the only attachment that spanned a not very distant childhood and a very recent adulthood with a child in tow.

USING ATTACHMENT THEORY AS A GUIDE
TO DECISION-MAKING

What are the psychological theories that should be informing placement decisions about siblings? The basic reason we value families and arrange new families for children without them is a deep-seated belief that everyone benefits from feeling secure in their deep attachments to other people. The idea of adoption is implicitly rooted in Attachment Theory and the assumption that long-term well-being results from secure attachments. Attachment theory was originally articulated by John Bowlby (1969), who hypothesized that empathy develops as a by-product of normal mother-child bonds. According to Bowlby's Attachment Theory, the basis of emotional health comes from a secure attachment with one's mother that develops in early infancy. He omitted any mention of attachment to siblings, so if we use Attachment Theory as the theoretical basis for decisions about whether and when to place siblings in foster care together, it will be a loose extrapolation from a theory that was never designed for that purpose.

How can Attachment Theory help to guide decisions about siblings? If we begin with the essential notion of attachment, then we would need to find out about the nature of the sibling relationship, which are messy in intact families and can be complicated in multiple ways when family bonds dissolve. All normal sibling relationships are somewhat ambivalent. Even among the closest of siblings, there is always some jealousy, aggression, and some sense of connectedness. Under normal circumstances, the sibling relationship helps children develop their self-identity and their knowledge about the world (Tucker, McHale, & Crouter, 2001). Research has shown that sibling relationships can be both positive and negative, and, in general, siblings will get more support from same-sex siblings.

Some studies have found that older siblings transmit information about acceptable behaviors to younger siblings, and in this way, influence the attitudes and behaviors of the younger siblings. For example, in a study of the influence of older siblings on the developing sexual identity of younger siblings, researchers found that older siblings exert more influence on younger siblings than the reverse (Rodgers & Rowe, 1988). Researchers found that older siblings, in general, were less sexually active than younger siblings at the same age. The researchers hypothesized that when older siblings engaged in sexual activity, younger siblings used this knowledge as a guide to their own sexual activity and were more likely to become sexually active following the lead of their older sibling. Research of this sort has not been conducted with children in foster care, in part because there are many complicating factors, such as children often being placed into families with other foster children of mixed ages, so that even identifying the influences of various sibling relationships becomes very difficult.

Extrapolating to Different Family Types

We know that Attachment Theory cannot be applied automatically to families that do not conform to the traditional model of two biological parents with one or more children. For example, a longitudinal study of step-parents and a review of the relevant literature has shown that step-parents tend to favor their own biological children over the children of their spouse (Wallerstein & Lewis, 2007), so we should not expect that the bonds between stepmothers and stepchildren will be the same or have the same psychological effects as the bonds between mothers and their biological children. Given that step-parents treat the children in their families differently, we can conclude that siblings have different relationships with the same parents. These data, which suggest that Attachment Theory may not apply to step-families, are a reason to question whether Attachment Theory can be applied to siblings from disrupted families. It does not rule out the possibility, but given these data, it is less likely that we can use Attachment Theory as a guide for deciding on the placement of siblings from disrupted families.

On the other hand, there are data that show that siblings provide support to each other in high-conflict homes, so even if these data do not stem from Attachment Theory, they can be used to support decisions to place siblings together (Caija & Liem, 1998). In separated or divorced families, the children usually show lower self-esteem and reduced psychosocial competence relative to matched peers in intact homes. Sibling relationships are one protective factor that reduces the effect of family conflict on children's development. Researchers found that in highly conflictual families, siblings provided mutual support and confirmed reality for each other. When the sibling relationships were positive, they offered a buffer against the stress of disruptive homes.

Other researchers have found that when siblings had a positive image of each other, well-adjusted older siblings had a positive effect on the development of younger siblings (Widmer & Weiss, 2000). As in the earlier research, the positive benefits were only found for positive sibling relationships. It seems that whenever sibling relationships are positive and mutually supportive, the siblings should be kept together during foster care and, by extension, adoptive placements. Thus, I agree with the default assumption that it is in the best interest of children to keep sibling groups together, unless there is a good reason not to. The default assumptions about placing siblings together emerged from Washington's (2007) review of the relevant literature, although the data in support of this conclusion are not strong and much of the support for this idea comes from a sense that it seems like the right thing to do and not from empirically supported studies.

DECIDING WHAT IS IMPORTANT

There are countless different considerations that are important when making God-like decisions about children's lives. From the child's point of view, the sibling question is about maintaining, strengthening, or even creating meaningful quality attachments. Here are some questions to consider:

- Is there a biological tie to another child so that the child has someone he or she "belongs with" or might develop a "belonging with" or "attachment to" at some point in the future? Decisions about the placement of children are not just about the present but affect the children's futures, and so the possibility of developing a more positive relationship in the future is an essential part of the planning for foster children.
- Is the relationship between the siblings positive or could it be a positive relationship at some point in the future?

Slowly, states are recognizing that siblings in out-of-home care have rights. There is no rule-based system that can be followed for all decisions about the placement of children in care because sibling decisions will have to vary based on the nature of sibling relationships and the cold facts of reality—a family of 10 close siblings will probably not be placed 10 together, but they do have the right to visit regularly, a right to maintain family bonds, and a right to always know where the others are. All of these rights will need advocacy to remain protected, including education for judges and the general public and incentives for foster families to take sibling groups. There also needs to be the recognition that in rare circumstances it may be in the best interest of the child to place siblings apart, and when those decisions are well thought out and articulated they also need to be supported and planned.

In this age of evidence-based practice, it is reasonable to ask if there is evidence that children "do better" in any measurable way when they are placed together. At least one reference reported that adolescents who were placed alone after a history of joint placements were at greater risk for placement disruption (Leathers, 2005). This finding makes sense— the reference is to adolescents who presumably had multiple placements with the same set of siblings and are now separated—at each placement, they are older and not better, only this time they are alone. We do not know why the adolescents were placed alone, but it is not surprising that these are adolescents whose placements will not go well. Of course, we do not know if the placement did not go well because they were separated from their siblings. The solo placement might be a contributing factor, but it might also be an indicator that these are adolescents with multiple problems blooming. On the other hand, children placed with the same number of siblings consistently through their stay in foster care had a significantly greater chance of adoption (Leathers, 2005). Although data like these provide support for keeping siblings together, they also mean that sibling groups that are functioning well are probably more stable and for that reason both easier to place together and easier to place for adoption.

Even those siblings who are not living together need to be able to visit and maintain contacts, so the logistics of how they will visit is as important as how they will be placed. The decisions we make about children's lives are not just solutions for present problems; they are forward-looking strategies that will also need to turn negative sibling relationships to more positive ones and help strengthen positive ones. A second-best placement might place siblings in the same neighborhood or enroll them in the same schools. Sibling groups have shared histories that need to be respected, even when those histories have been chaotic.

What we are really talking about when we look at the reasons siblings should be placed together is a radical departure from traditional Attachment Theory. Bowlby's theory was limited to the attachment of an infant to her mother or primary caregiver and it was a secure attachment that was necessary for the development of coping skills, including the ability to regulate one's own emotional behavior. Other types of attachment were not given much consideration in the early child-development literature; yet we know that many children never have a chance to develop ties to a primary caregiver. This lack of attachment affects not just children who make it into foster care but also many other children who do not have stable primary caretakers—a fact that has been true throughout history. We need to consider attachment to siblings—siblings in the broadest sense—as the definition of family for children who have no other family. That raises another profound question of definition:

Who is family? There was a recent *Jumpstart* cartoon in which the grumpy old White cop, who is the partner of the protagonist Black cop, got a visit from a woman he had never met. She told him she was his long, lost sister—one he never knew about. Even this grumpy old cop jumped for joy at the news that he had a sister he never knew about. She immediately did a very sisterly thing and asked to borrow money. After all, she was family, even if only for a few minutes. And he loaned it to her—because we do things for family that we do not do for other people. We care for our children when they are infants and our family when they are ill and when they are old—or at least many of us do, even if we do not want to—just because they are family. In the true story that I told earlier in this chapter, one out-of-luck young woman traveled 150 miles with a seriously developmentally delayed two-year old and no money, and they were taken in by her foster sister because she was family. Of course, not all foster siblings become attached—that is become family—but then again, neither do all biological siblings. It is the nature of the attachment that makes these young women siblings. They became family by choice or perhaps by necessity. Whether it is a tie that binds us together or sometimes strangles or weaves a safety net, it is the attachment cord of family that we are really here to consider.

USING ATTACHMENT THEORY AS A GUIDE TO ADOPTION

The reason for adoption is the basic underlying premise that children need and deserve permanent families. This underlying assumption is based on a large body of theoretical and research literature showing that connectedness to a family is important for the adaptive functioning and individuation of children. If we believe in the power of attachment for children without families, then we need to be able to identify and quantify attachment when making decisions about children's lives. The staff at the Berger Institute for Work, Family, and Children at Claremont McKenna College worked with the staff at Kinship Center to develop a normed assessment of attachment for use with children between 18 months and six years old. One goal was to understand what typical attachment looks like. This collaboration led to the development of the Kinship Center Attachment Questionnaire (KCAQ)©. It is a caregiver-completed questionnaire developed for use with children under six years of age. It allows for the measurement of therapeutic change over time. The Questionnaire allows us to assess which factors predict treatment effectiveness and to identify treatment components that are most effective.

To establish a norm for child attachment, we randomly recruited early education centers, preschools, and elementary schools from the Los Angeles and Orange County, California, areas. The data gathered from parents of children in these schools represent "typical" child attachment and provide a comparison against which children at risk for attachment difficulties can be compared. One relationship that we are continuing to examine is that between work patterns and attachment. What influence does a parent's work status have on early attachment? The third goal of the project was to assess the factors that influence successful adoption. How do variables such as attachment, school readiness, and family work patterns influence adoption outcomes?

Performance outcome measures provide important feedback to therapists, caregivers, and the children themselves about what works with different children. It allows us to determine, for example, if certain serious behavior problems are improved, what is a realistic time for some kinds of changes, and what sorts of interventions work best for different sorts of problems. It is not a substitute for clinical judgment—it is an adjunct. These measures do not change behavior or make anyone less depressed or anxious; they are not a substitute for therapy, but they are a way of assessing progress made during therapy.

It is important to supplement clinical judgment with normed instruments. Looking at what is working is central to the process of therapy. As therapists push for mental-health parity, we need to be able to document our effectiveness, and we need to be able to provide realistic expectations for outcomes. None of this is quick or easy. We need multiple measures over time, along with information about the child and home situation and the kinds of services we are providing. The information that is collected should be used in planning for each child. But the measures need to be good measures—valid and reliable for all children. Scales that are standardized allow us to track changes over time as a function of time and frequency of therapy or other services, and therapists can compare scores to normed standards. Normed scales document the value of the work, which is important to funders, and they provide information that therapists should be using.

When the therapist's own assessment is in agreement with the KCAQ, the therapist can have more confidence in her judgment, and when they are not in agreement, then it should be a signal that the therapist should look again to see if there is something that is being overlooked. A score that signals a possible problem should be an early warning signal that changes need to be made in therapeutic approaches. In any case, normed scales provide additional information that should be incorporated in assessing and planning for any child and family. The original list of KCAQ items was derived from the following sources: (a) interviews with experts in the field of child attachment, (b) a literature review of the latest theories and empirical studies related to child attachment, and (c) the Randolph Attachment Disorder Questionnaire (Randolph, 1997), a caregiver-completed instrument that assesses child attachment difficulties in children five to 18 years of age.

Item wording and scale selection were guided by test theory. For example, all items asked about the presence/absence of a single behavior. Item content reflected behaviors associated with healthy attachment (e.g., "My child plays well with other children") and behaviors associated with attachment difficulty (e.g., "If things don't go his/her way, my child gets very upset").

Experts in the area of child attachment then were asked to review 37 items generated using the criteria described above. Expert feedback was obtained to examine the content validity of the KCAQ. Items were rated for their content validity (their relevance to attachment), age appropriateness, and wording. Details are explained in a recent publication by Kappenberg and Halpern (2006). The KCAQ was translated into Spanish following standard translation practices. First, a native Spanish speaker with high English language fluency translated the questionnaire into Spanish. A second native Spanish speaker with high English language fluency translated the Spanish version of the questionnaire into English. The two English versions, then, were compared to ensure that their item content was comparable. We hope readers will take the time to look at the KCAQ as they consider broader issues regarding attachment and children in care.

RECOGNIZING THE BASIC NEED TO BELONG

For children growing up in and out of care—children unsure of their family, or who have lost their family, or have no family at all—the question is "who is my group?" To whom am I attached? In every culture in the world there is an expectation that we behave differently and have more obligations for family than we do for others who are not family. We need to rethink belongingness for children who have no parents or aunts and uncles or other adults they can confidently claim as their own. These children have their attachments to family in their own generation—their siblings, who may be biologically related or live in the same foster or step-family. Who will be there for me? For those of us who can help them answer this question, there is an imperative to allow them to keep the family they know—the siblings who have traveled through life thus far with them. There are many barriers and challenges, but these are children that need us to help them find a way to stay attached. It is the least we can do for children who have lost so much.

CHAPTER 2

Siblings in Foster Care and Adoption: What We Know from Research

Susan Livingston Smith

As recognized earlier, siblings are not defined solely by biology. A British study investigated children's perceptions of closeness of family relationships across a range of family types. Children, ages four to seven, placed their family members and friends in a series of concentric circles representing their closeness to these individuals. Biological relatedness was associated with their perceptions of closeness to fathers but not to mothers or siblings. Being a full, half, or step-sibling did not influence children's perception of closeness (Sturgess, Dunn, & Davies, 2001).

Some cultures think more expansively about kinship; for example, African Americans often view persons with very close and enduring ties as part of one's family. The term "fictive kin" has been introduced in child welfare to recognize this type of adult in a child's life, and children also can have fictive-siblings. Child-centered practice should respect cultural values—and contemporary real life—by recognizing close, non-biological relationships as a source of support to those involved; for example, when foster parents stop providing their service, foster siblings with strong bonds would benefit from being placed together.

This chapter reviews research on sibling relationships and its implications for child-welfare practice. Although the primary focus is children in the child-welfare system, the same issues and needs apply to children entering adoption or out-of-home care through other avenues.

INTIMATE RELATIONSHIPS THAT CAN LAST A LIFETIME

Sibling relationships are a significant source of continuity and are typically the longest relationships any of us have. They are emotionally powerful and critically important for most individuals, not only in childhood but throughout our lives. A study of adults over 65 found that they were much more likely to have a living sibling (93 percent) than a child (61 percent) or spouse (38 percent) (Clark & Anderson, 1967). As children, siblings typically spend more time with each other than with anyone else, serving as playmates, protectors, models, and agents of socialization. Like other intimate relationships, those with siblings vary in intensity and quality; and they are complex, because rivalry, conflict, ambivalence, and hostility can coexist with affection and loyalty. Siblings form a child's first peer group, and children most often learn social skills, particularly rules of fair play such as self-control, sharing, and conflict resolution skills, from interacting with brothers and sisters. Research comparing children who have siblings with those who do not indicates that only children are more likely both to be victimized and to be aggressive with peers (Kitzmann, Cohen, & Lockwood, 2002). Sibling relationships also provide opportunities for development of empathy in young children. Their nature and importance varies with developmental stages—typically, there is intense rivalry in the preschool years; variability in closeness during middle childhood, depending on the level of warmth between siblings; and somewhat less closeness in adolescence, when teens are focused on peers.

Understanding sibling relationships in the field of psychology was shaped initially by psychoanalytic theorists, starting with Freud and Adler's emphasis on jealousy over sibling displacement in the mother-child relationship. Beginning in the 1930s, Levy focused on systematic observation of siblings, especially the aggressive response of a young child to a new baby in the family. It was Levy who coined the term "sibling rivalry." Later psychodynamic literature focused on factors affecting sibling relationships including parental availability, parental behavior toward individual children, gender, age difference, and others. Overall, however, psychodynamic theories have focused mainly on rivalry between siblings (Sanders, 2004).

The field of family therapy developed theory about sibling relationships and explored the question of how children in the same family can be so different. They ascribed important personality characteristics to specific family roles based on birth order and gender and described typical sibling roles in pathological family systems. In the 1990s, a leading theorist of this school of thought, Toman (1993), described 10 personality profiles based on sibling positions, which were thought to predict relationship patterns in future friendships and marriages.

The influence of gender, birth order, and other such factors in influencing personality characteristics and sibling relationships has been the subject of considerable research in the past two decades. Some report that firstborns score higher on dominance dimensions and later-born children score higher on sociability (Beck, Burnet, & Vosper, 2006). However, research generally has not found that family constellation variables explain significant variance in personality characteristics or experiences of siblings. For example, a study administering seven personality tests to college students found only one quality of all those examined (death obsession) that was consistently associated with variables of sibship size and birth order (Abdel-Khalek & Lester, 2005). Overall, sibling relationships are emotionally powerful and extremely complex relationships in their impact on individual siblings and in the forces that shape their dynamics.

FACTORS SHAPING SIBLING RELATIONSHIPS

A wide range of influences shapes sibling relationships; these range from culture to social class, from gender to family dynamics, and from innate personality traits to developed individual affinities. Sibling relationships are generally different in industrialized societies than in non-industrialized ones. Where families are larger and siblings closer in age, caretaking among them is commonplace. Many societies prescribe lifelong duties to siblings; however, these become more discretionary in industrialized nations where nuclear families and individual autonomy are the norm. Certain subcultures put more emphasis on communal values; in many African American families, a greater sense of sibling responsibility lays the foundation for lifelong reciprocal relationships. Gender also influences closeness, typically varying from closest to least close in the following order: sister-sister, brother-sister or sister-brother, and brother-brother (Sanders, 2004).

Sometimes professionals, who have a strong sense of the two-parent family with 2.3 children as the "normal" family form, can view caretaking of one child for another as harmful to children. In reality, such caretaking is quite normal in large families and others in which a parent(s) has difficulty meeting all children's needs. In reality caretaking has both benefits and stresses for the older sibling. For example, a study of Latino and African American youth providing care for an adolescent sister's child found that these youth were more stressed and had lower grades but reported greater life satisfaction, a stronger school orientation, and less likelihood of dropping out (East, Weisner, & Reyes, 2006).

The tradition in African American families of responsibility to siblings means that they are viewed not only as playmates but also as caretakers. While it is crucial to these children to be placed together, it also is important that they are placed in families who accept these traditions and allow opportunities for siblings to support each other (Goldstein, 1999).

Just as the closeness of biological relatedness does not determine closeness between siblings, adoption status is not associated with the level of closeness between siblings or their perceptions of closeness to parents. Joseph (2002) studied 30 pairs of young adult siblings in which one was adopted and the other a birth child, evaluating their feelings of trust, warmth, communication, conflict, and alienation with parents and with each other and found no significant differences between them. Sibling relationships vary somewhat by family structure; for example, there is evidence that sibling conflict is highest in single-mother families as compared with two-parent families (Deater-Deckard, Dunn, & Lussier, 2002). Throughout family types, sibling relationships vary greatly in all their qualities—and the presence of positive characteristics does not preclude negative ones. In evaluating the quality of sibling relationships, the most important factor is warmth/affection, followed by rivalry/hostility and relative power/status in the relationship. A social worker can evaluate the presence of positive behaviors (showing affection, protecting, teaching, and initiating or responding to play) as well as negative ones (hostility, aggression, blaming or getting siblings into trouble, dominating, quarreling, and jealousy). Primary factors shaping the quality of sibling relationships include the temperaments of children and the quality of the parent-child and marital relationships. Relationship patterns between siblings and dimensions of qualities such as conflict and warmth become established in early childhood and, according to research, are fairly stable from middle childhood into adolescence. Intense rivalry between siblings also persists into adult sibling relationships. Children with higher levels of activity and more negativity are likely to demonstrate higher levels of sibling conflict. In addition, dyads that are temperamentally dissimilar experience higher conflict. To some extent, parental attempts to promote pro-social behavior among siblings can mediate the development of conflictual patterns (Brody, 1998).

Marital disharmony and parental anger toward children cause negative emotional reactions in children that may be directed toward siblings. Psychologists have explored two lines of inquiry related to the impact of parental conflict on sibling relationships—the compensating sibling hypothesis where children turn toward each other to meet needs and the congruence hypothesis where parental conflict is modeled in sib relationships. Research evidence supports both hypotheses—adult-adult and adult-child conflict does predict greater conflict between children in the family; yet the presence of an older sibling can serve as a buffer to the impact of parental dysfunction on siblings. Research documents that in some families older siblings demonstrate a protective and pro-social response toward younger siblings when parents treat them harshly

(Cummings & Smith, 1993; Heatherington, 1989; Sanders, 2004; Gass, Jenkins, & Dunn, 2007). The last study found that sibling affection moderated the impact of stressful life events on children regardless of the quality of the mother-child relationship.

Adverse circumstances can magnify both positive and negative qualities of sibling relationships. There is research indicating that these ties grow closer as a result of helping each other through adversity. For example, an analysis of 53 studies comparing children with divorced and non-divorced parents found that siblings from divorced homes had more positive sibling relationships than those from intact homes (Kunz, 2001). Overall, siblings are a primary source of social support, and their dependency on each other increases with different life stages and circumstances.

One type of parent behavior that is consistently associated with compromised sibling relationships is differential treatment. A parent, particularly a mother, favoring one child over another is a primary cause of extreme conflict in sibling relationships (Dunn, 1988). Brody (1998) summarizes over 10 studies finding that unequal levels of control, responsiveness, and positive or negative emotion from parents to children are associated with more negative and less positive qualities in sibling relationships. This is particularly true when children interpret differential treatment to reflect less concern or love.

Extreme differential treatment, the experience of being singled out for rejection or maltreatment, is very harmful to children. Researchers in Britain have examined the impact of "preferential rejection" on children removed from their families while siblings remain. Their longitudinal study of factors influencing adoption adjustment have found that children who were singled out from siblings and rejected had an almost six times greater risk of disruption than others (Rushton & Dance, 2006). The authors perceived placing these children with parents who were high in sensitivity and responsiveness as critically important in facilitating their positive adjustment (Dancè, Rushton, & Quinton, 2002).

A CRITICALLY IMPORTANT ROLE FOR SIBLINGS IN MALTREATING FAMILIES

When families are dysfunctional to the point that children are maltreated, children may receive different treatment from their parents with varying effects on individual children. There is a body of research indicating that specific child characteristics are associated with higher risk of maltreatment, such as an irritable temperament, behavior problems, or medical or intellectual abnormalities. However, the similarities and differences in siblings' experiences of maltreatment have received very limited attention.

A number of studies have assessed the degree to which individuals perceive that parents treated them similarly, finding that the less genetically related the siblings are, the less similar they perceive their parents' treatment to be (Plomin, Reiss, Hetherington, & Howe, 1994). Only two studies with sizeable samples have investigated whether siblings have similar experiences of maltreatment. The first of these assessed 542 maltreating and normative families finding that parental treatment was very similar in sibling pairs in neglect cases but not in other types of maltreatment (Jean-Gilles & Crittenden, 1990). A recent study focusing only on neglect also found that most siblings report similar neglectful parenting behaviors. Differences were more common with opposite-sex siblings, and boys were more likely to be neglected than girls (Hines, Kantor, & Holt, 2006).

In many dysfunctional families, sibling relationships become even more salient and essential for survival, as brothers and sisters may provide support and nurture not consistently provided by parents. For children entering care, siblings can serve as a buffer against the worst effects of harsh circumstances. Research has demonstrated that warmth in sibling relationships is associated with less loneliness, fewer behavior problems, and higher self-worth (Stocker, 1994). Kosonen (1996) studied the emotional support and help that siblings provide and found that when they needed help, children would first seek out their mothers, but then turn to older siblings for support, even before they would go to their fathers. She also found that for isolated children (as many placed into foster care are) sibling support is especially crucial. For these children, an older sibling was often their only perceived source of help. While sibling relationships do not always compensate for deficits in families, research has validated that, for many children, they do promote resilience. For example, a young child's secure attachment to an older sibling can diminish the impact of adverse circumstances such as parental mental illness or loss (Werner, 1990; Sanders, 2004). A study of relationships in alcoholic families found that older siblings frequently served the role of surrogate parent, and the sibling relationship was as important as the mother-child relationship in predicting resilience (Kittmer, 2005). It is particularly important to protect these ties that offer support to children being removed from their families.

Foster children experience more losses of significant others, so siblings are often their only source for continuity of significant relationships. Kosonen's study (1999) of foster children ages eight to 12, compared to peers not in foster care, concluded that the former group's smaller networks of relationships with important persons made siblings proportionally more important to them. Nearly one-third of the related siblings named by foster children were not known to their social workers, particularly half- or step-siblings. This study also underscores the importance of obtaining children's perspectives as to which siblings they feel closest to.

When siblings could not all be placed together, workers often decided to keep those closest in age together and would sometimes inadvertently split siblings in configurations that did not fit their preferences or needs.

CONSIDERATIONS WHEN SIBLINGS HAVE SPECIAL NEEDS

A considerable body of research has examined the impact of having a sibling with special needs on other children in the family. Siblings of children with mental retardation, autism, and a range of health or other conditions have been studied with somewhat conflicting results. A meta-analysis of research on siblings of children with chronic disease concludes that they are at a slightly elevated risk of psychosocial distress, particularly for anxiety and depression (Barlow & Ellard, 2006). Some stresses that siblings reported include feeling ignored and unappreciated by parents, resenting the demands placed on the family by the disabled child, witnessing negative reactions from others to their sibling, and being given excessive caretaking responsibilities.

A study of siblings of autistic children reported that aggressive behavior was the most commonly reported interaction problem and anger was the usual response from the sibling. Forty percent of siblings scored in the borderline or clinical range on the Child Behavior Checklist summary scales, particularly the internalizing scale (Ross & Cuskelly, 2006). Some problems they described included aggression, destruction of property, invasion of privacy, lack of reciprocity and sharing, and worry about the sibling. Other research has found that children with disabled siblings are more sensitized to everyday family stresses and experience more emotional distress over family conflicts than children in other families (Nixon & Cummings, 1999).

To date, no quantitative studies have examined the impact of a special needs foster or adopted child on his or her siblings. A study of services to troubled adoptive families reports that sibling conflict is one of the primary presenting problems in these families—extreme anger and aggression in one child can create many stresses within the family that impact other siblings. In a situation described in one study, a young girl was afraid of her brother to the extent that she slept with a desk blocking her door at night (Smith, 2006). In a recent qualitative study of the impact of fostering on birth children, all parents and birth children interviewed reported a range of positive and negative consequences, but overall they indicated that fostering enriched their lives. Families reported experiencing shifts in family structure, roles, and expectations, and only 20 percent of parents discussed these changes with their children after foster children arrived. Recommendations included more involvement of children in the fostering decision, in preparation, and in communication about later adjustments (Younges & Harp, 2007).

Another qualitative study of the reactions of 17 biological children to the adoption of a sibling found that children's responses varied somewhat according to their own developmental stage. Latency-age children often experienced fears of abandonment by their parents, not understanding how the adopted child's mother did not keep her child. Teens were most resistant to the changes they envisioned an adoption bringing to their lives (Phillips, 1999).

Establishing conditions for successful integration of newly placed foster or adopted children involves assisting siblings to manage changes that occur with the addition of a new child. Research suggests that facilitating open communication within the family about the sibling's special needs and resulting changes, accepting and empathizing with children's feelings, and supporting the non-disabled siblings' self-esteem and interests through individualized attention are important. Social workers at a Midwest adoption agency developed a practice model for facilitating siblings' exploration of their thoughts and feelings about a new sibling both before and after placement and to proactively deal with stresses (Mullin & Johnson, 1999).

SIBLING PLACEMENTS IN FOSTER CARE AND ADOPTION

For children entering care, being with their brothers and sisters (in the broadest definition of those words) promotes a sense of safety and well-being, while being separated from them can trigger grief and anxiety. The impact of separating siblings is described poignantly in Folman's (1998) study of children's experiences of removal from their birth families. Children's responses to placement were typically a sense of being apprehended and of feeling unsupported and helpless; they experienced feelings of loss, abandonment, fear, and bewilderment, particularly because they were often given little explanation or preparation. They typically reported shock at being separated from siblings and were unaware of the separation until the first child was dropped off.

Continuity of sibling relationships through conjoint placements helps children to maintain a positive sense of identity and knowledge of their cultural, personal, and family histories. They provide natural support to each other and some sense of stability and belonging. Typically, these relationships also are permanent and unconditional, thus validating the child's fundamental sense of self-worth (Herrick & Piccus, 2005; Chapter. 3).

A foster youth advisory team described separation from siblings as being "like an extra punishment, a separate loss, and another pain that is not needed" (YLAT, 2002). These youth, along with many experts in the field, stress the support, solace, and continuity provided by siblings when placed together and the added trauma and negative developmental impact of losing siblings to whom a child is attached. Even for very young children, separation denies them the opportunity to develop relationships that can offer significant support over their lives.

While most professionals would attest to the value of siblings, the practicalities of managing their transitions when placement resources are scarce often bring them to question whether preserving these connections is of the utmost importance. Overall, research on siblings in child welfare is only beginning to examine siblings in a comprehensive way. Almost all existing studies demonstrate a range of positive benefits of keeping siblings together and negative outcomes of separating them, although there has been more thorough examination of sibling placements in foster care than in adoption. There are only a few studies that have examined a large population of children and used multivariate methods to control for the effects of multiple variables.

OUTCOMES AMONG SIBLINGS PLACED TOGETHER AND APART

Placement Stability

Both in foster care and adoption, professionals have used placement stability as a basis for evaluating the outcomes of sibling placements, finding that joint placements are likely to be more stable. One of the first studies to assess foster disruptions by sibling status was a British study of 88 children in long-term care (Berridge & Cleaver, 1987). They found that 50 percent of children placed in care alone experienced a placement disruption, as compared to 26 percent of children placed with some siblings and 33 percent of those placed with all siblings. Staff and Fein (1992) assessed the stability of foster placements made within a 14-year period in a network of private agencies. For 108 sibling pairs, siblings placed together were more likely to remain in their placement (56 percent) than those placed apart (38 percent). Another study of fostered adolescents found that those placed alone after a history of joint sibling placements were at greater risk for disruption than those consistently placed with their siblings (Leathers, 2005). In addition, adolescents placed alone who had been with their siblings demonstrated a weaker sense of integration and belonging in the foster home.

A Canadian study assessing intact and split sibling groups in foster care and divorced families found that foster siblings placed together had fewer placement changes than those separated in care (Drapeau, Simard, Beaudry, & Charbonneau, 2000).

Placement Stability in Adoption

A widespread belief in the child-welfare field has been that sibling groups are harder to place with adoptive families than single children; however, a study of over 10,000 children photo-listed for adoption in

New York found that members of sibling groups were more likely to be adopted and were placed more quickly than single children. In fact, the time to adoption was decreased by 3.2 months for each additional child in the sibling group (Avery & Butler, 2001).

The research examining the stability of sibling placements in adoption is not as consistent in its findings as studies examining foster placements. Some early studies of disruption in child-welfare adoptions found that sibling placements had higher rates of disruption than single-child placements (Boneh, 1979; Urban Systems Research and Engineering, 1985). However, Festinger (1986) found that children placed separately had a higher disruption rate than those placed with siblings, and a study examining samples of children in two states found a reduced risk of disruption for sibling placements in one state, but in the other, there was an interaction of age and sibling status—that is, children over eight years placed with siblings were at less risk of disruption, but not children eight and under (Rosenthal, Schmidt, & Conner, 1988). A recent Illinois study of approximately 16,000 adoptive placements found that while the actual rate of disruption declined with each additional sibling from single placements to groups of five or more, this association was due to other factors. In the multivariate analysis, sibling placements of two to four children were at higher risk of disruption than single child placements but very large sibling groups of five or more children were at less risk (Smith, Howard, Garnier, & Ryan, 2006).

Finally, most studies on adoption disruption showed no significant differences in risk for either group (Barth, Berry, Yoshikami, Goodfield, & Carson, 1988; Berry & Barth, 1990; Smith & Howard, 1991; Wedge & Mantle, 1991; Holloway, 1997; Rushton, Dance, Quinton, & Mayes, 2001). Taken as a group, these studies are more likely to show reduced disruption risk or no differences in risk for sibling adoptive placements than an increased risk.

Disruption in international adoptions has received less examination. A study in the Netherlands found that siblings placed together did not have a higher risk of disruption than children adopted singly (Boer, Versluis-den Bieman, & Verhulst, 1994).

OUTCOMES AMONG SIBLINGS PLACED TOGETHER AND APART: ADJUSTMENT AND PERMANENCY

On a range of measures, children with siblings who are placed together have a more positive adjustment than those separated from siblings in placement. Significant findings include the following:

- Siblings who perceive a high level of emotional support from a favorite sibling experience the most impact from separation and the most benefit from joint placement. A study of 47 children, ages seven to ten, who were entering foster care found that children perceiving high emotional support from a favorite sibling with whom they were placed had the lowest maladjustment scores. In contrast, those separated from a favorite sibling perceived as supportive had the highest maladjustment (Kim, 2002).

- A study of 38 preschool foster children found that those placed with siblings had more pre-placement problems but fewer emotional and behavioral problems at the time of the study (Smith, 1998).

- Youth in care who are placed with siblings are less likely to run away than those placed singly (Courtney, Skyles, Zinn, Howard, & Goerge, 2005).

- Girls separated from all of their siblings are at the greatest risk for poorer mental health and socialization. An Australian study assessing the mental health of 347 foster children found no significant difference for boys according to placement status, but girls living with siblings had lower prevalence of mental disorders than those separated (Tarren-Sweeney & Hazell, 2005).

Only a few studies have looked at the achievement of permanency by placement status of siblings. A study by Leathers (2005) of 197 adolescents in care reported that youth placed alone were less likely to exit the system to adoption or subsidized guardianship. According to other studies, siblings who come into care together or are placed together later are more likely to be reunited with their parents than those entering care alone (Farmer, 1996; Kosonen, 1996).

The most sophisticated analysis of the impact of sibling-specific factors on reunification is a study examining a California statewide sample of 15,517 siblings, who entered care for the first time in 2000, and following them for 12 months. A number of sibling factors predicted increased likelihood of reunification—being placed initially with all siblings who are in care (almost twice as likely to reunify); being placed with at least one sibling (one-third greater odds of reunification); and entering care within 1 month of siblings (Webster, Shlonsky, Shaw, & Brookhart, 2005).

SIBLINGS IN INTERNATIONAL ADOPTION

Less is known about sibling placements in international adoptions. The decisions about sibling groups are made by the sending country, and many try to keep them together if they think they can be adopted. In large orphanages, children are typically segregated by age, so that biological siblings may have very little attachment to each other at the time of adoption—while they may be attached as "siblings" to children not biologically related to them. Often, when a birth sibling becomes available for adoption later, the country contacts the adoptive parents of the first sibling, through their agency, to explore their interest in bringing home the second child. Some parents also seek to simultaneously adopt two children who have developed a common bond in the same orphanage as a means of providing natural support to them and of maintaining their sibling relationship.

One study has evaluated international adoptive placements according to sibling placement status—researchers in the Netherlands assessed the outcomes of 399 sibling groups adopted internationally compared with 1,749 children placed singly. They found that those placed with siblings had fewer behavior problems (a small but significant difference) than children placed singly (Boer et al., 1994).

THE PLACEMENT OF SIBLINGS IN PRACTICE

An estimated 70 percent of boys and girls in the U.S. child-welfare system have at least one sibling also in care (Shlonsky, Elkins, Bellamy, & Ashare, 2005). We do not know conclusively how many are separated from siblings, but the best research available indicates a substantial number are not placed with siblings. The most reliable research on this subject, examining large populations of children, includes two recent studies. (It should be noted that these were conducted in two states that have strong emphasis in law and policy on keeping siblings together, so they may not represent practice throughout the country). The first, a study of California foster children with brothers and/or sisters in care, found that about 46 percent were placed with all their siblings, and 66 percent were placed with at least one of them (Shlonsky, Webster, & Needell, 2003). In this study, entering care at the same time (within 30 days of each other) was the most powerful predictor of all siblings being placed together, increasing the odds by almost four times. The second study, a longitudinal analysis of placement patterns of over 168,000 foster youth with siblings in care in New York City over a 15-year period, found that 43 percent of siblings entered care on the same day, with another 10 percent entering within 30 days. Most of the remaining children entered care longer than six months apart. The 47 percent of siblings who entered care more than a month apart were at the highest risk of being separated; in fact, two-thirds were not placed together initially. However, if siblings entered care together, 78 percent were all placed together. Initial placement status is a strong determinant of sibling placement over time, although some placed together are later separated and some separated initially come together over time (Wulczyn & Zimmerman, 2005).

Other factors associated with the likelihood of placing siblings together include size of sibling group, age gap, gender, type of placement (kin, foster, group home), ethnicity, and behavioral issues. Being in kinship care is a powerful predictor of intact sibling placements. In the California study, children placed with kin had almost three times the odds of being placed with all of their siblings. Generally, larger sibling groups with a wide age span who are not placed with kin are less likely to be together.

In addition, Caucasian children, boys, opposite gendered pairs, adolescents, and children who have behavior problems or reside in group homes are more likely to be placed singly. Organizational policies and procedures, personal beliefs of workers and foster parents, and adequacy of placement resources and supports are also critical factors influencing sibling placement patterns (Hegar, 2005; Shlonsky, et al., 2003).

REASONS FOR SEPARATE PLACEMENT OF SIBLINGS

Experts in the field generally agree that there is only one valid child-centered reason for separating siblings early in foster placement—that one child poses a significant threat to the safety or well-being of another sibling(s). In most cases, however, it is the system that is unable to accommodate the best interests of children by finding a placement arrangement that meets the needs of sibling groups.

In her study of adolescents in care, Leathers (2005) interviewed caseworkers, asking for all the reasons and the most important reason that siblings had been placed separately. While 19 percent did not know the reason, almost all others fell into four categories: couldn't find a placement for all (33 percent); different behavioral or mental health needs or too many behavior problems for one foster family (19 percent); foster parent requested removal of one child because of behavior problems (11 percent); and sexual risk posed by one sibling to others (6 percent).

Siblings also are often separated as a result of the beliefs and attitudes of workers, foster parents, and therapists. In a study of foster parents' and workers' views on placing siblings, over half of the foster mothers (55 percent) did not believe it was easier for a foster child to fit into the foster family if placed with siblings. One foster parent reported that siblings depend on one another too much and shut other people out (Smith, 1996). About 45 percent of foster parents believed children placed with siblings were easier to foster because they felt more secure having their brothers or sisters with them. When siblings were separated, the most common reasons given by caseworkers (each in over one-quarter of cases) were a lack of available space, the child would fit in better if separated, and too wide an age span between children. Another barrier to keeping siblings together is a relative placement in which one or more children are not biologically related to the relative caregiver, who does not want to keep all siblings.

A recent study based on interviews with caregivers of 14 foster and adopted children with significant behavior problems found that caregivers play a pivotal role in influencing the course of sibling placements. Their willingness and ability to handle multiple children and the extent of sibling conflict were key factors. Caregivers were primary gatekeepers in maintaining contact for siblings not placed together, with caseworkers having minimal involvement (James, Monn, Palinkas, & Leslie, 2008). Clinical judgments also serve to justify separating siblings: there is too much conflict between siblings to keep them together; the special needs of one child require separate placements; an older child is too involved in taking care of a younger one; or the siblings act out sexually with each other. Researchers in Britain used a phenomenological approach to scrutinize the decision-making process of workers throughout five specific cases of large sibling groups, and identified the values of equity (moral justice is central) and pragmatism (dominated by practicalities) as key influences in worker judgments. Also, the concept of the "least detrimental alternative" became dominant at times in decision-making. Often the eventual outcome of a case was never planned for but resulted from the long-term impact of a series of "holding judgments" based on the needs of the immediate situation. In only one case did a strong ideological commitment to maintaining sibling relationships lead the worker to advocate successfully to keep them together. While early judgments to separate siblings sometimes may be unavoidable, careful planning needs to focus on sibling group preservation, or short-term solutions become long-term realities (Hollows & Nelson, 2006).

There are many constraints in the realities of child welfare that make finding homes for large sibling groups and siblings who enter care sequentially very difficult. Concerted and exceptional efforts are needed to promote the well-being of siblings through keeping them together in foster care and adoption. Chapter 10 presents practice strategies that facilitate preserving sibling connections in foster care and adoption.

CHAPTER 3

Sibling Connections: The Importance of Nurturing Sibling Bonds in the Foster Care System[1]

Mary Anne Herrick and Wendy Piccus

INTRODUCTION

Over half a million children in the United States resided in foster care on September 30, 2001 (U.S. Department of Health and Human Services, 2004), but we can only estimate the number of these children who are part of a sibling group because the federal government does not systematically collect sibling data. States report that over two-thirds of children in their care have siblings in substitute care, and 47 to 59 percent of them are separated from at least one of their brothers or sisters (Kentucky Cabinet for Families and Children, 2003; Needell, Webster, Cuccaro-Alamin, Armijo, Lee, & Lery, 2004; New York City Administration for Children's Services, 2000).

State policies on siblings in out-of-home care vary considerably. At least 26 states address siblings to some degree in their legislation. The most common policies compel child-welfare agencies to consider siblings in placement and permanency planning practices and to make provisions for maintaining sibling contact when children are placed separately. Additionally, some states require post-placement visits with siblings, formal descriptions of efforts to keep siblings together, and consideration of sibling relationships in determining a child's best interest (Casey Family Programs, 2002). Furthermore, prevailing professional opinion also endorses the idea that keeping sibling groups intact is generally in their best interest unless it would compromise the safety or well-being of one or more of the children (Kosonen, 1996; Staff & Fein, 1992;

Timberlake & Hamlin, 1982; Ward, 1984). However, because best interest is subject to interpretation, many social workers face the challenge of determining exactly how much influence to assign sibling connections when balancing competing priorities such as each child's permanency, safety, and well-being. Understanding the nature of sibling relationships for children in out-of-home care can help social workers in this endeavor.

Studies on siblings in substitute care generally demonstrate positive outcomes when siblings are placed together, although findings should be viewed cautiously because some studies do not control for baseline group differences. In 1995, Smith found that children placed with their siblings had more positive behavior toward their peers (Smith, 1995). In a later study, Smith (1998) also found that siblings placed together had fewer emotional and behavioral problems, although they scored lower on receptive vocabulary testing.

Additionally, research has demonstrated that siblings placed together performed better at school (Thorpe & Swart, 1992) and had fewer overall placement disruptions than siblings placed separately (Staff & Fein, 1992). Furthermore, studies on siblings who are not in out-of-home care have found that brothers and sisters can function as confidants and companions (Buhrmester, 1992) and provide an attachment figure for infants in the absence of parents (Stewart, 1983; Teti & Ablard, 1989). Studies have also shown that siblings placed together in divorced families exhibit fewer externalizing behavior problems (Kempton, Armistead, Wierson, & Forehand, 1991), and aspects of pro-social and cooperative behavior, pretend play, and conflict management in the preschool period have all been reported to be associated with positive sibling interaction (Dale, 1989; Dunn, 1992). On the other hand, these findings may also indicate that negative sibling interaction is associated with negative effects on social behavior and play.

Qualitative interviews with foster youth and alumni of foster care have revealed that they generally prefer to be placed with their siblings (Festinger, 1983; Herrick, 2002; Knipe & Warren, 1999; Herrick & Piccus, 2005; Washington State Department of Social and Health Services [WS DSHS], 2002). When placement together is not feasible, they request frequent visits (Bernstein, 2000; Festinger, 1983; Gardner, 1996; Harrison, 1999a; Knipe & Warren, 1999; Triseliotis & Russell, 1984; WS DSHS, 2002), and information about their brothers and sisters (Festinger, 1983; Knipe & Warren, 1999; Triseliotis & Russell, 1984; WS DSHS, 2002).

However, what a sibling relationship means or can potentially mean to any child in foster care is as diverse as the children who have experienced life in care. As such, some authors have emphasized that child-welfare workers should elicit and consider the wishes of the children in their care (Casey Family Programs, 2003; Timberlake & Hamlin, 1982; Ward, 1984). In reference to sibling placements, Ward stated that the final decision should be based on the needs and wishes of the children rather than on administrative expediency or difficulty in finding homes (Ward, 1984). Furthermore, one of the most prevalent themes from interviews with foster youth and alumni is their desire for professionals to support more of their independent decisions (Festinger, 1983; Johnson, Yoken, & Voss, 1995; Knipe & Warren, 1999; Sanchez, 2003; WS DSHS, 2002). For example, in one study, a former foster youth stated, "Some kids are forced to see their parents when they don't want to and others aren't able to see their parents when they [do] want to" (WS DSHS, 2002, p. 8). Clearly, their choices need more support. Moreover, because social work impacts the lives of foster youth personally, workers in the field should involve foster youth in the decisions they make whenever possible and ensure that social work practice, policy, and research reflect the needs and concerns voiced by foster youth themselves.

It is the authors' stance that sibling connections are extremely important to children in foster care, and except in situations where there are safety concerns such as sibling abuse or extreme trauma that is triggered by sibling contact, professionals should make every effort to maintain sibling relationships. This paper will elaborate on the issue of sibling connections in substitute care by adding a unique perspective to the discussion. Both of the authors are child-welfare researchers who also spent a significant amount of time in foster care, together and separated from siblings. Below, we describe the events surrounding our time in foster care to allow the reader insight into our experiences and to personalize the value of sibling connections. This paper presents literature on central themes, followed by sections of our stories to highlight those themes. The paper concludes with a discussion of the implications for child-welfare practice and policy. We realize this paper does not represent an unbiased sample and only presents two viewpoints on the many issues faced by siblings in foster care.

Wendy

I was 16 when I entered foster care after calling the police to pick up my mother. I remember the day very well because I waited outside my neighbor's house for my sisters to come back from school so that I could keep them from going in the house where my mother waited for us all to return. After waiting and hoping for years that our family would become normal, my mother's most recent drunken binge and abusive behavior had proven to me that it wasn't possible and that the only course of action was complete escape and separation.

Unfortunately, I had not fully realized what kind of separation was in store for my five sisters and myself. I understood that I would probably never see my mother again and that it was very unlikely that I would go back to my high school, but it never occurred to me that I would be separated from what I considered my sole purpose in life. That I would not be able to live with and care for my sisters was unbelievable—and devastating. If anything, I would move into an apartment and mother them by myself. Surely, my social worker would understand how important being a big sister was to me and that my sisters kept me moving forward, giving meaning and joy to my life.

Mary

At 10 years old, I was placed in foster care permanently after being removed numerous times due to abuse by my mother's partners and lack of supervision by my mother. At that point, I found myself being swept away from my family, friends, and the life I knew. Since it wasn't my first time in foster care, I understood what was in store. I would have to move in with people I didn't know, start another school with new teachers and no friends, and attempt to fit into an unfamiliar place that didn't make sense to me. What I felt strongest was sadness over having to leave the people I loved.

I am the youngest of five siblings, all one year apart in age. We were placed in foster care around the same time. Probably because of our close age span, we played together, watched out for each other and spent most of our time together before we entered foster care. Despite the circumstances that led to my placement in foster care, and my journey through the system, I was ultimately fortunate. My sister Lissa and I were together for almost our entire stay in care. However, our other three siblings were all placed in separate homes. Our contact with them was infrequent because our foster homes were spread across the western side of the state—hundreds of miles of distance. Lissa and I began to rely on each other more when the other people in our lives were gone. Because we were placed in foster care, we had to cope with profound loss and at the same time try to build new ties to new people and new places. Social workers and foster families placed the nearly impossible expectation on me to build a new life when all I wanted was my old life. Besides, I had no idea how long I would actually stay in each home. Settling in and investing in any foster home was a major risk of additional loss. I had to explain to my foster mother on more than one occasion, "No, I can't call you mom because I already have a mom." For years, I couldn't relinquish the desire and expectation that one day I would be reunited with my family.

INTRAPSYCHIC FACTORS

For children entering foster care, the pain that they experience goes far beyond the anxiety and trauma that results from separation from the life and people that they knew before they entered care. Because of the significant attachment relationships that children have with their parents and siblings before they enter care, many foster youth recall their entry into care as marked by grief, worry, guilt, and lost identity (Harrison, 1999a, 1999b; Triseliotis & Russell, 1984; Wedge & Mantle, 1991). For example, in a series of interviews with youth entering foster care, Harrison (1999a) found that youth with siblings mentioned their worries about brothers or sisters and, on many occasions, their accounts of their own lives included detailed stories about their siblings. Whiting and Lee (2003) also documented that many children told life stories that revolved around their siblings, and felt that they had suffered with and relied on their siblings to the extent that they were dismayed at being separated. Furthermore, studies have shown that many children believe they have lost a part of themselves when they are separated from their brothers and sisters, and their grief at this loss is aggravated by the worry and guilt they feel when they enter care (Harrison, 1999a; Timberlake & Hamlin, 1982).

Young people who experience abuse before their entry into foster care and leave siblings behind with their biological family frequently feel a considerable amount of guilt and distress. In these situations, many foster youth feel that they have moved on to an undeserved safer life while their siblings are left behind to take all the abuse (Harrison, 1999a). On other occasions, children may think of placement away from siblings as a deserved punishment and feel that they are responsible for the separation or at least could have prevented it (Timberlake & Hamlin, 1982). These feelings may be exacerbated by the loneliness that some children feel when they are placed with new families. If there is no one in these families to contradict the blame and responsibility that children can place on themselves, these children can become convinced that they are mean or uncaring because they have escaped their abusive homes.

Interviews with young people in care have also shown that many of them are involved in day-to-day struggles to establish and maintain a positive sense of identity in the face of considerable disadvantage (Harrison, 1999a). Studies have documented how the separation of children from their families left them without any knowledge of their cultural, ethnic, linguistic, personal, and family histories (Harrison, 1999b; Triseliotis & Russell, 1984). As some children have attested, this emptiness can have a profound impact on their personal development and cause them considerable pain and worry (Harrison, 1999b; Triseliotis & Russell, 1984). Children have expressed that when they entered care, they were left with many unanswered questions about their individual histories, which made it hard for them to cultivate a sense of self and maintain their self-esteem (Harrison, 1999b; Triseliotis & Russell, 1984).

Entry into foster care can also have a stigmatizing effect on many children, making them doubt their worth and acceptability to other people. If children develop self-images that are influenced by the way others see them (Goffman, 1963; Triseliotis & Russell, 1984), being considered by other children as different or as having no home can have serious consequences (Triseliotis & Russell, 1984; WS DSHS, 2002). Without background information to fight these negative projections, children in care may begin to internalize the negative images (real or imagined) that others have of them. Children can sometimes feel as though they are worthless, unwanted, or unlovable (Littner, 1956; Triseliotis & Russell, 1984).

Some children who are separated from their siblings may also grieve the loss of a caregiving role they had assumed with their siblings before separation (Harrison, 1999b; Ward, 1984). According to Kaplan, Hennon, and Ade-Ridder (1993), a child's self-identity is in part determined by what he or she sees as his or her role in the world. When a child has a role where another person relies on him or her, this relationship can provide the child with a sense of responsibility, a clear self-concept, and enhanced self-esteem and serve as a source of social support. This idea has important implications for child-welfare workers who feel they should separate siblings when a particular child develops a caregiving role toward other siblings and seemingly takes on too much responsibility. On the other hand, literature also supports the concern that maintaining a child's caregiving role can be harmful to his or her development, interfering with his or her ability to adapt to a new foster family (Aldridge & Cautley, 1976; Bank & Kahn, 1982; Hegar, 1988a; Smith, 1996). This can create difficulties in adjustment between foster parents and the parentified child, particularly when the child disputes disciplinary decisions or creates situations of mixed loyalties with his or her siblings (Aldridge & Cautley, 1976). However, professionals should exercise special caution in determining whether the caregiving role is truly negatively affecting the child's well-being since it may actually be a natural and healthy role for a sibling to adopt, and is considered normal and common in many families and cultures (Elgar & Head, 1999).

Wendy

As it was, my social worker couldn't place me with my sisters. There were just too many of us and no one would take six children in their home all at once. Luckily for me, I was able to live with my stepsister and her grandparents during my stay in foster care. Having known me for 10 years, they felt it only a small burden to take me into their home and care for me until I went to college. I never had to walk into a strange home and introduce myself to my new family, and I never had a stranger ask me to call her mother.

Nevertheless, there were many problems in my new life, the first of which was the lack of meaning that I felt. Who was I and what was I doing? Why did I continue to excel in school and for whom? Why was

I moving forward when I only wanted to go back to the time when I could brush my sisters' hair and make their breakfasts? Furthermore, what gave me the right to succeed and be happy when my little sisters were scattered all over? How could I ever consider myself a success when I had failed at the only truly important responsibility charged to me?

While in care these questions burned in me, making me doubt my worth and acceptability to decent people. I felt as though nothing I ever did would make me worthy of the kindness and generosity that people afforded me. Over time, I worked harder and harder at school to prove to my foster parents that I appreciated what they did for me and the care that they gave me was well placed. I wanted to prove to them and to myself that I wasn't selfish and mean and that I didn't scatter my sisters to the wind to benefit myself. I wanted not only love but to be worthy of love.

NATURAL SUPPORT AND PERMANENT RELATIONSHIPS

Emotional support is especially critical for foster children as they attempt to cope with feelings of grief and loss when separated from loved ones. Brothers and sisters who grew up in the same family, built relationships with similar people, or were separated from common loved ones can understand their siblings in a unique way because of their mutual experiences. These children may have learned to relate to people and cope with stress in comparable ways and, in the end, they may face grieving shared losses. Thus, siblings can potentially offer emotional support to one another in the face of adversity (Bank & Kahn, 1982; Hegar, 1988a; Kosonen, 1994a; Kosonen, 1994b; Lamb, 1982; Mullender, 1999; Timberlake & Hamlin, 1982; Ward, 1984).

During adverse circumstances, siblings can function as a buffer (Kempton et al., 1991) and provide each other with comfort (Stewart, 1983; Teti & Ablard, 1989). Festinger (1983) reported in her study on alumni of foster care that siblings viewed each other as allies, and natural supports. Buhrmester's (1992) study on the developmental course of siblings found that throughout childhood siblings confided in and provided companionship for one another. Bernstein (2000) recounted the sentiments of one such former foster youth who was placed in care with her sisters. It attests to the support and companionship they were able to offer each other:

My sisters and I lived in a group home specifically for siblings. People would ask us why we were so emotionally stable. We always had each other's backs. The Sisters—that's what they'd call us. People who didn't have their sisters or brothers with them always had more problems than the rest of us. They really didn't have anybody that they could talk to about what was going on with them. (p. 19)

Some authors have also observed that maintaining sibling relationships can help nurture a sense of stability (Aldgate, Stein, & Carey, 1989;

Kaplan et al., 1993) and continuity in the lives of foster youth (Kaplan et al., 1993; Kosonen, 1994a; Kosonen, 1994b; Timberlake & Hamlin, 1982; Triseliotis & Russell, 1984). In 1984, Ward stated, the presence of a sibling provides at least one predictable element in a frightening situation, since placement with a sibling retains an important link with the past. Furthermore, some authors have noted that sibling relationships can be sources of love (Buhrmester, 1992; Jenkins, 1992; Triseliotis & Russell, 1984; Whelan, 2003) and long-term relationship stability (Elgar & Head, 1999; Kaplan et al., 1993; Timberlake & Hamlin, 1982; Triseliotis & Russell, 1984; WS DSHS, 2002), even in the midst of unpredictable and temporary placement situations.

Permanent, unconditional relationships are essential components of a child's growth and development because they afford a child the opportunity to make mistakes and still be loved. In 1982, Cicirelli observed, "To be a sibling is an ascribed rather than an earned role, so that an individual remains a brother or a sister regardless of achievements or circumstances." These relationships validate the child's fundamental worth as a human being because the love he or she receives does not have to be earned. Permanent, unconditional relationships can also produce hope and motivation in an individual. Foster children do not always have these permanent, unconditional relationships because of abusive family circumstances and the unstable nature of foster care itself. However, one natural means of fostering long-term relationships for children in substitute care is through maintaining their sibling connections. In 1994a, 1994b, Kosonen noted, "Sibling bonds formed during childhood are likely to be an investment for the future, ensuring opportunities for the development of life-long relationships."

Triseliotis and Russell (1984) reported that children who were fortunate enough to be placed into care with their siblings relied on these relationships for information and meaning about themselves. Children and young people interviewed by Harrison (1999a) who had maintained or renewed contact with brothers, sisters, or other family members often commented that these experiences had given them an important sense of belonging and made a positive contribution to their sense of personal identity because they could get feedback on their personalities from people close to them.

Not all sibling relationships are supportive and nurturing, however, and in some situations, the trauma that siblings can cause each other is more significant than the overall benefit that sibling contact can offer them. In some cases, siblings develop unhealthy, rivalrous, or abusive relationships with each other (Bank, 1992; Bank & Kahn, 1982; Drapeau, Simard, Beaudry, & Chardonneau, 2000; Ward, 1984). Other children may have behavior problems that predispose them to conflictual sibling relationships (Aldridge & Cautley, 1976), or the children may reinforce behavioral problems in each other (Howe, Dooley, & Hinings, 2000). For some children, traumatic memories of past parental abuse can be surfaced by contact with siblings, causing the child additional trauma while in care (Bank, 1992). Often in these situations, psychological counseling can help to heal the relationship between siblings. If this option has been tried but failed to reduce the negative effects of sibling contact, then it might be better to place such siblings separately.

Apart from situations involving sibling abuse or extreme trauma triggered by contact with siblings, maintenance of sibling relationships can be extremely beneficial to children entering foster care. Brothers and sisters are unique in that they are able to offer each other a shared history (Cicirelli, 1995; Elgar & Head, 1999). Because of this history and the natural connection that they have with each other, often established and nurtured through very difficult circumstances, siblings can provide a source of love and support during the traumatic experiences of foster care. Siblings can also provide a way of ensuring that children remain in touch with their past, enhance their sense of belonging, provide them with the framework for developing an identity, and increase their sense of self-esteem (Elgar & Head, 1999).

Wendy

Even over many years, the feeling that I needed to prove that I was worthy of love never went away. The more that I worked for love, the more convinced I felt that it wasn't real when I received it. The harder I tried to be accepted, the more I felt that it wasn't really me that people were accepting; it was only the person that I created for their benefit. I longed for a natural relationship where I could be imperfect and loved unconditionally. I longed for my family.

Mary

For years I lived with families who told me how much they loved me. I came to realize that their love for me was tied to the way they wanted me to behave and believe. I was ceaselessly conscious of the fact that I could be told to leave my home if I didn't do what my foster parents expected of me. My experience in foster care was permeated with feelings of inadequacy as I constantly struggled to earn my family's approval. Like all children, I needed to be loved unconditionally for who I was.

There were times when my sister and I were lied to, manipulated, and treated as if we were inherently bad. Some of our foster parents told us we wouldn't amount to anything. Sorting out what was true and what was someone else's emotional abuse was confusing and difficult. Because Lissa and I shared the same past, we truly knew and trusted each other.

Lissa and I were able to be each other's truth when the world around us and the adults around us were not healthy.

I never questioned the permanency or unconditional nature of my relationship with my sister. I knew that my sister would be in my life forever, unlike so many other people who certainly left their mark, but were now gone. Lissa was my family. My sister and I each believed in the other's potential to be amazing and so we were able to encourage the other's hopes and dreams. My relationship with my sister is irreplaceable.

DISCUSSION AND IMPLICATIONS

Barriers to Maintaining Sibling Connections

Child-welfare workers face serious practical limitations when attempting to keep sibling groups intact. The most challenging of these limitations is that it can be difficult to find foster homes that will take in large sibling groups and finding one home for the entire sibling group may delay or disrupt permanency for each child. Another significant barrier to maintaining sibling connections is that the preservation of sibling ties takes a considerable amount of time and effort, which is limited by lack of funding and resources. Without additional funding for staff to do the legwork of preserving sibling connections, this very important task can be left behind in order to address more immediate or pressing concerns. Other issues also complicate maintaining sibling connections. For example, should social workers disrupt established placements in order to place brothers and sisters in the same home if siblings enter care at different times? Also, at what point do children, especially young children, suffer more harm from a move than benefit from reunification with siblings? What should be done if siblings have never met? What should be done if siblings fight or have inappropriate or abusive relationships? For a more detailed discussion of barriers to placing siblings together, see Kosonen (1996) or California Department of Social Services (1997).

Nevertheless, the practical difficulties of maintaining sibling connections must not discourage child-welfare workers from this essential assignment. As a result of practical difficulties, many children have been separated from their brothers and sisters for reasons that were not in their best interests. It was simply too hard for social workers to maintain linkages. Consequently, many children's attempts to visit their siblings have been met with so many difficulties that they have given up and attempted to move on with their lives without their brothers and sisters. Some studies have shown that foster youth believe social workers discourage sibling contact or make sibling visitation unnecessarily difficult (Grigsby, 1994; Harrison, 1999a; Millham, Bullock, Hosie, & Haak, 1986; Wedge & Mantle, 1991). If the maintenance of sibling relationships is important to child-welfare professionals, greater effort needs to be focused on determining the nature of children's relationships with their siblings, the benefit or harm in maintaining these relationships, and, where it is in the children's best interests, maintaining the links between brothers and sisters. We offer two methods for determining the nature of children's relationships with their siblings. The first approach is developing a system of unbiased assessment of the relationship utilizing published literature in order to evaluate and weigh different aspects of sibling relationships. The second and more important approach is consulting the children themselves when their age and intellectual capacity allow this option. Systemic barriers to maintaining the linkages between brothers and sisters can only be seriously resolved when child-welfare professionals place precedence on the importance of sibling relationships and apportion money and resources toward this goal.

Assessment

The process of determining a child's best interest and whether a sibling relationship will have a negative effect on a child's well-being is difficult. In the absence of policy and practice protocols related to these issues, social workers must rely on their intuition when they weigh the various complexities of families, sibling relationships, and child-welfare situations, as well as the possibility that their decisions may negatively effect the rest of a child's life (Wedge & Mantle, 1991). This is particularly true when siblings share a traumatic, abusive, or rivalrous past relationship. However, the fear of harm should not automatically preclude the joint placement of siblings, because in so doing children are denied essential relationships that could be their only support while in care and afterward. In these cases, efforts should be made to mitigate difficult sibling relationships with counseling or services. If child-welfare workers are to consider themselves good providers, then they must meet the challenges that sibling issues present and handle them to the best of their ability. To address these problems by automatically separating siblings avoids the difficult task that is their responsibility, and denies children the support that sibling relationships can provide them while in care.

Fortunately, there has been a lot of progress in developing techniques to assess and measure the quality of sibling relationships (Department of Health, 1991; Dunn, Stocker, & Plomin, 1990; Furman & Buhrmester, 1985; Kramer & Baron, 1995; Riggio, 2000; Schaefer & Edgerton, 1981; Stocker, Lanthier, & Furman, 1997). Additionally, various authors have discussed important aspects of family and sibling relationships and the assessment thereof to help inform placement decisions. These topics include clarifying various definitions of siblings (Elgar & Head, 1999; Kosonen, 1999; Lord & Borthwick, 2001), assessing children's individual needs (Fahlberg, 1991; Jewett, 1978; Lord & Borthwick, 2001; Palmer,

1976; Parker, 1966; Ward, 1984; Wedge & Mantle, 1991), investigating children's understanding of what has happened to their family and their wishes for the future (Lord & Borthwick, 2001), determining the dynamics of the sibling group based on the context in which the sibling relationships developed (Bank & Kahn, 1982; Harrison, 1999b; Lord & Borthwick, 2001; Triseliotis & Russell, 1984; Ward, 1984), assessing sibling attachment (Hegar, 1993; Howe et al., 2000; Ryan, 2002; Ward, 1984; Whelan, 2003), and determining any exceptional circumstances that may indicate that siblings should be placed separately, such as intense sibling rivalry or possible sexual involvement (Bank & Kahn, 1982; Bentovim, Elton, Hildebrand, Tranter, & Vizard, 1988; Head & Elgar, 1999; Lord & Borthwick, 2001; Ward, 1984). These resources can help social workers balance the familial needs of children in care against the stresses that sibling placements can put on a child and his or her foster family.

Caution should be taken in assessing children's sibling relationships, however, due to the difficulties inherent in measuring complex human emotions with scientific tools. It is important to bear in mind that, in an effort to boil relationships down to something measurable, the more subtle aspects of the relationships are often overlooked (Mullender, 1999). One should also consider the additional complexities in assessing from the child's perspective the value and meaning of their sibling relationships (Wedge & Mantle, 1991). It is important to remember that children do not always understand relationships the same way that adults do and that adult measurements of warmth and closeness may not reflect childhood realities. Considering these limitations, we believe that assessments should be used primarily to gather background information during interviews and discussions with the children themselves.

The Child's Wishes

Perhaps the best way to determine the possible effects of joint sibling placement on brothers and sisters is talking to the children themselves whenever age and developmental capacity allow for it. Speaking with children can shed light on whether placing siblings together will contribute to a secure caregiving environment (Whelan, 2003). Given that many children who enter care have had their most essential attachment relationships severed and may be struggling to recreate a feeling of security, the potential for sibling relationships to support these attempts should be explored with each child.

Not all children can effectively convey their thoughts and feelings regarding their brothers and sisters. They may not have the language or developmental capacity to do so, or they may be accustomed to having their siblings around them and have no concept of what life without their siblings might entail. Additionally, some children may not have previously had a relationship with their siblings, or they may simply be unsure of what they want. If any of these situations is a relevant concern in a case, it should be taken into consideration when attempting to assess how the child feels about his or her brothers and sisters. In addition, because some children will answer questions with what they presume the adult wants to hear, questions should be phrased in an objective manner and answers should be probed further. Some questions a social worker could ask the child might include the following:

Would you like to receive pictures of [sibling], hear about things happening in [sibling]'s life or be able to send them letters or birthday cards?

Do you like seeing or hearing from [sibling]?

Would you like to be able to visit with or talk to [sibling] on the phone?

Would you like to live in the same home as [sibling]?

Do you feel safe with [sibling]?

Do you ever feel scared around [sibling]?

These questions should be asked by the social worker when the child enters foster care, and reviewed with the child on a regular basis, as his or her feelings may change. If it is not possible to place the siblings together, then the social worker should leave that question out to avoid confusion and disappointment for the child. If a child does not wish to live with or visit a sibling, his or her choice should be respected. Once the child has identified what he or she wants, social workers should make every effort to follow through on his or her wishes, or clearly communicate to the child why it is not possible. Otherwise, the child might become disempowered and feel as though his or her desires do not matter to professionals. The social worker should also consider what the sibling relationship would provide to the child when he or she is an adolescent during holidays, birthdays, major life events, and emancipation from care, and later in life.

Sibling Policy

Approximately half of the states in the United States have enacted policy on siblings in out-of-home care, though most of these only address the issue minimally. Some states have ratified exemplary pieces of legislation, but no state has a body of legislation that holistically addresses sibling relationships. For example, California's sibling legislation is extensive but lacks some key elements, such as provisions for consideration of sibling relationships in determining a child's best interest, or a statement regarding the right to sibling contact when brothers and sisters are placed separately in foster care. New York State has also passed some significant legislation on siblings, but does not require child-welfare agencies to consider siblings in permanency planning, nor do they require post-adoption contact between siblings (Casey Family Programs, 2002). Ideal policy on siblings in out-of-home care would be comprehensive and comparable in all states. The authors recommend that such a policy would include the following:

1. A broad definition of siblings that includes the child's own perception of who his or her brothers and sisters are. This definition may include relationships with siblings that have not yet been established.

2. The presumption that it is generally in the child's best interest to be placed with siblings and, when this is not possible, to maintain contact between siblings.

3. Consideration of sibling relationships in determining a child's best interest, noting that the child's best interest should take into account their long-term emotional well-being.

4. Consideration of the sibling relationship in case planning especially regarding placement, permanency planning, termination of parental rights and adoption.

5. A requirement that social workers conduct a comprehensive assessment of the sibling relationships at intake, including the wishes of the children, best interest determinations regarding sibling placement and visitation, and a plan to place siblings together or maintain contact when it is determined to be in their best interest.

6. Documentation of efforts made to place siblings together when in their best interest. If placement together is not possible, frequent meaningful visitation would be required, including documentation of such efforts. This documentation should include any siblings the child identifies, such as siblings who were adopted into another family or siblings who do not already have an established relationship.

7. Systematic review at hearings of sibling relationships, placement, visitation, contact and the authority of the court to direct these actions.

8. The opportunity for family members, friends and professionals involved with the family to petition to assert a sibling relationship, placement of siblings together and visitation between siblings or sibling information sharing.

9. Documentation of sibling contact information in the child's case file.

10. Whenever possible, siblings placed separately are referred to the same counseling agency when seeking therapy.

RECONCILIATION AND LIFE AFTER FOSTER CARE

Wendy

Some time ago, I was able to restart a relationship with my younger sisters when they came to stay with me over their Spring break. Almost immediately, it struck me how self-confident and assured the girls felt about themselves and their relationships to each other. Whether they were being kind or unkind, one thing remained true and that was that they accepted each other. I believe that this had a lot to do with the fact that they had been placed together during most of their stay in foster care.

Following that visit, two of my sisters moved in with me. At the time, it came as a shock how easy the transition was for all of us. Despite the many logistical problems surrounding their move, their addition to my home brought an instant sense of peace and well-being to my life that I had forgotten existed. I felt content and happy with myself in a way that was never possible before. I attribute this feeling to my family and the sense of belonging that they brought back to my life.

Mary

Lissa and I have remained as close as we were when we were younger and continue to be vital in each other's lives. My sister was physically present and emotionally available to me when I transitioned out of foster care; we shared our first apartment together when I was 18 and she was 19. I was the maid of honor in her wedding and she will be mine. Today, we both work in human services and continue to fuel each other's passion for social justice for children and families.

Now my siblings and I are all adults, and because we are all so important to each other, we have rebuilt the relationships that were withered by our separation. At first, my physical and emotional resemblance to my siblings surprised me, perhaps because for so long I was unable to see myself reflected in each one of them. But it was comforting to finally realize that I fit in well somewhere. After years of getting to know each other again, we are finally able to be a family and can give each other the love and encouragement that we did not all have as children in foster care.

In summary, out-of-home care can result in trauma, grief, guilt, and loss. Siblings are an extremely important part of children's families, and may provide their brothers and sisters with stability, support, love, and permanent relationships. Although maintaining sibling relationships can have an ameliorating effect on the trauma and loss that foster youth experience, not all youth should maintain contact with their siblings due to safety concerns. Sibling relationships can be best understood by speaking directly with the youth themselves whenever age and developmental capacity allow for it. Because a child's best interest is subject to interpretation, a structured method of assessing the sibling relationship should also be used. Currently, sibling practice and policy vary drastically across states because state policies are inconsistent and incomplete. Given that sibling relationships can be tremendously beneficial, efforts toward systematically supporting the maintenance of sibling relationships in foster care practice and policy are essential. Research investigating the role that siblings play in foster care outcomes is also necessary to guide future policies, reforms, and funding aimed at reducing the concrete systemic obstacles many social workers face in placing siblings together.

We felt it important to incorporate our personal experiences into a discussion on sibling placement in foster care in order to emphasize the significance and feasibility of listening to the voices of foster children and former foster youth. Our unique perspectives as people who have lived within the child-welfare system can offer other professionals alternative ways to look at the issues, and new ideas for resolving challenges within the system. In the same spirit, we hope to inspire others to value this unique perspective, and work toward empowering former and current foster youth to be their own advocates. Finally, our stories should serve as a reminder that behind child-welfare research and policies are children whose lives are significantly impacted everyday.

NOTE

1. Reprinted from *Children and Youth Services Review,* Vol. 27, Issue 7, Herrick, M. A. and Piccus, W., Sibling connections: The importance of nurturing sibling bonds in the foster care system, pp. 845–61, Copyright © 2005 with permission from Elsevier.

CHAPTER 4

The Experience of Sibling Loss in the Adjustment of Foster and Adopted Children

David Brodzinsky

Siblings are an extremely important part of children's experience; for most, they constitute the longest lived of all their social and emotional connections. Yet for children who enter foster care and those who are adopted, separation from siblings—sometimes permanently—is a relatively common experience (Shlonsky, Elkins, Bellamy, & Ashare, 2005; Wulczyn & Zimmerman, 2005). What are the reasons for sibling separation in foster care and adoption? How does this experience impact these youngsters? And what are the implications of sibling loss for child-welfare policy and practice? These questions, and others, represent the focus of the current chapter.

Before addressing these questions, let me begin by describing two cases I consulted on several years ago—the first, a forensic one, and the second, a clinical one:

Case 1: John (age 12), William (11) and Sara (8) were removed from their unmarried parents because of physical abuse by their father. The children, who are African American, were placed in separate foster homes, with visitation scheduled with one another and their mother twice a month at a local office. After six months, the children returned to their mother, with the provision that she not allow contact with their father. However, she repeatedly violated this provision and, within two months, the children were returned to care when the father had physically abused her and John on several occasions. The children were again in separate homes, with monthly supervised contact with their mother, which she sporadically adhered to. After more than two years, the service plan changed from family reunification to adoption for all children. Unfortunately, no single family was identified, and the plan was to place them separately [for Sara, this involved a transracial placement], despite the fact that a psychological evaluation found the two youngest children had a very strong attachment to each other and wanted to live together; in contrast, the oldest boy was found to have serious psychological and behavioral problems and a conflict-ridden relationship with his siblings. In addition, the mother was assessed as clinically depressed and unable to protect the children. When the mother was informed of this plan, she challenged it, whereupon her legal aid attorney asked me to consult on various issues, including: (a) the likelihood that adoption would not result in reunification of the children, nor guarantee them ongoing contact; (b) the fact that the two younger children had a strong and secure attachment and desired to live together; (c) the potential impact on the children of being permanently separated; (d) the potential impact of a transracial placement for Sara, who had expressed a desire to live with her brother in an African American family; and (e) the agency's failure to provide therapeutic services to ameliorate problems between the oldest child and his siblings.

Case 2: Lia (age 5) was placed for adoption with her parents soon after birth. At the hospital, the adoptive parents met Lia's birth parents, as well as her two older birth siblings, who were ages four and five, and agreed to ongoing contact between the two families. Although regular email and telephone contact was maintained over the first two years, the birth parents subsequently separated; and contact with the birth father ceased. A year later, the adoptive family, including Lia, who had just turned three, visited the birth mother and birth siblings. According to her adoptive parents, Lia was very much taken with the other children, although she appeared somewhat indifferent to her birth mother. Following this visit, the birth mother stopped responding to the adoptive parents' emails and calls and disappeared. Nearly two years went by before she recontacted the adoptive parents. At that time, she acknowledged that the previous visit had shaken her emotionally. She stated that saying goodbye after the visit was like relinquishing her daughter once again, and she had needed time to recover. She apologized for abruptly withdrawing and expressed a desire to resume email and phone contact, with the possibility of another visit in the coming summer. When the adoptive parents consulted with me, they expressed support for maintaining an open adoption, but were concerned that the birth mother's withdrawing again might create distress for Lia. They noted that Lia had expressed considerable curiosity about her siblings during the two-year hiatus, referring to them as her brother and sister, and frequently asked why she was unable to visit or talk with them. The question of interest at the time of the initial contact was the importance of sibling relationships for their daughter and how to protect her from possible feelings of rejection or loss should the birth mother fail to follow through with contact.

Although each of these cases has unique characteristics, the one common feature is the issue of sibling separation and its impact on the children. Whether separated through foster care or adoption, the children in both of these cases experienced disruption in relationships with birth siblings—an experience with the potential for creating both short- and long-term adjustment difficulties, as well as the risk for placement instability (Leathers, 2005; Tarren-Sweeney & Hazell, 2005). As the issue of sibling separation and loss is analyzed and discussed in this chapter, the reader should keep these cases in mind.

ROLE OF SIBLINGS IN THE LIVES OF CHILDREN

Despite their obvious salience as agents for socialization, it is only in the past 10–15 years that the role of siblings in the development and adjustment of children and adolescents (Dunn, 2007), as well as adults (van Volkom, 2006), has received much empirical attention. The ensuing research has yielded valuable insights into the positive and negative influences that siblings have on one another over the course of development.

For most children, sibling relationships constitute the earliest opportunity to interact on a regular basis with other youngsters. Siblings serve as companions and playmates and as important attachment figures. Their interactions can support the development of social and emotional skills such as empathy, perspective taking, sharing, emotion regulation, and conflict resolution. Children also learn to balance competitive and cooperative tendencies in their interactions with brothers and sisters. Furthermore, cognitive and language development are facilitated through sibling exchanges, especially those promoting fantasy, problem solving, and negotiation. Brothers and sisters serve as role models for appropriate behavior and are an important source of advice about age-related cultural issues. In addition, siblings can serve as confidants, providing care and emotional comfort during times of stress or loss (such as when they are placed in foster care). And, as children approach adolescence, they often look to their brothers and sisters as a way of defining who they are and establishing a more secure identity. Overall, positive sibling relationships have been shown to be a strong predictor of healthier adjustment in children and teenagers (Dunn, 2007).

Yet siblings also can play a negative role in the lives of children. For example, boys and girls sometimes are victimized verbally, emotionally, physically, and even sexually by their older or more powerful siblings. Moreover, siblings can model inappropriate and/or risky behavior such as smoking and substance use, early sexual activity, and delinquent behavior, as well as defiance of parents and other authorities. Finally, children often learn inappropriate conflict resolution strategies, such as the use of aggression, during their ongoing struggles with siblings. In short, when exposed to negative interactions with siblings, children and adolescents often display adverse patterns of psychological, behavioral, and school adjustment (Dunn, 2007).

SEPARATION OF SIBLINGS IN CARE

When children are removed from their biological family and placed into foster care or in adoptive homes, they often are separated from siblings (Shlonsky et al., 2005). This is done despite child-welfare policy and experience, as well as research, suggesting both that children often do better psychologically and that the placement usually is more stable when they are placed together, especially when children have a preestablished positive relationship (Linares, Li, Shrout, Brody, & Pettit, 2007). Nevertheless, it is widely recognized that a substantial percentage of foster children have siblings who are in care but not living with them. Moreover, it is not uncommon for children placed for adoption as infants to have half or full brothers and sisters, either living with birth family or in other adoptive homes. In analyzing this issue, Groza, Maschmeier, Jamison, and Piccola (2003) identified a number of systemic, organizational, demographic, behavioral, and attitudinal barriers to maintaining siblings together when they are placed for foster care or adoption. They emphasized that before barriers can be removed, they must be recognized, understood, and challenged by child-welfare policy-makers, agency directors, supervisors, and frontline caseworkers who are directly involved in assessing and developing placement plans for children. These individuals also must understand the legacy of sibling separation on children.

IMPACT OF SIBLING SEPARATION ON CHILDREN

Given the widespread acceptance of the importance of sibling relationships, it is surprising that relatively little research has been conducted on the impact of sibling separation on foster and adopted children. Part of the problem stems from a lack of clarity as to what constitutes a "sibling relationship." Typically, researchers define siblings as those who share one or more biological or adoptive parents, but this definition doesn't account for the full range of close connections that children form with one another when they live together. For example, biologically unrelated children who live together in a foster home often develop close and secure emotional bonds. When these relationships are severed because one or both of these youngsters are returned to their biological families or are placed in separate adoptive homes, the impact on them can be devastating.

Vagueness regarding the definition of "sibling separation" also complicates this field of research. Some children initially enter foster care separately but are reunited in the same home thereafter; others live in different homes but visit one another periodically; still other children experience multiple residential moves, occasionally living with brothers and sisters, only to be separated during subsequent placements; and, finally, there are children who have little, if any, contact with siblings once they enter care. The variability in separation experiences makes it difficult for researchers to understand the nature and impact of sibling separation on these youngsters.

Despite these conceptual and methodological issues, research tends to support the long-standing belief of child-welfare professionals that foster children who are placed together show fewer placement changes

(Drapeau, Simarad, Beaudry, & Charbonneau, 2000), less placement disruption (Leathers, 2005; Staff & Fein, 1992), a higher probability of being reunited with birth family (Leathers, 2005; Staff & Fein, 1992), and better emotional adjustment than those who are separated at placement (Courtney, Skyles, Miranda, Zinn, Howard, & Goerge, 2005; Tarren-Sweeney & Hazell, 2005), especially when there is a preexisting positive relationship between these youngsters (Linares et al., 2007). On the other hand, research on placement stability of siblings in adoptive homes is more mixed, with some finding less disruption for sibling groups compared to individual children (Festinger, 1986) and other studies showing the reverse pattern (Boneh, 1979) or no differences between the groups (Barth & Berry, 1988).

Finally, an interesting qualitative study by Folman (1998) focused on 8–14-year-old children's perceptions of being removed from birth family, including siblings, when first placed in foster care. Themes of being apprehended and feeling confused, bewildered, helpless, unsupported, and fearful were common among these youngsters. So too were the experiences of loss and abandonment, which frequently have been noted as a common dynamic in the psychology of foster and adopted children (Brodzinsky, 1990; Brodzinsky & Pinderhughes, 2002; Leon, 2002; Nickman, 1985).

EXPERIENCE OF LOSS IN FOSTER AND ADOPTED CHILDREN

To appreciate the impact of sibling separation on foster and adopted children, one must understand it in the broader context of the role of loss in the lives of these youngsters. It is commonly recognized that when children enter foster care or are adopted, they often experience a profound sense of loss in being separated from birth parents (Brodzinsky, 1990; Nickman, 1985). Often forgotten, however, is that this is just a small part of the disruption they experience. Children not only have to cope with the *loss of birth parents* but also *birth siblings and the entire extended birth family* (e.g., uncles, aunts, cousins, grandparents). For older-placed children, these are meaningful relationships that have become integrated into the fabric of their lives, including their sense of themselves. For younger-placed children, there may be little, if any, memory of these individuals. Yet, as children develop cognitively, the capacity for understanding the link to unknown birth-family members grows, as does the likelihood of feeling distress at being separated from them (Brodzinsky & Pinderhughes, 2002). This experience is exemplified by Lia, in Case 2 described previously. Although only having met her birth siblings once, when she was three years old, her ability to understand the nature of their relationship grew over the two years she was separated from them. In turn, her curiosity about them increased, and she frequently asked her parents questions about them, including why she couldn't see or talk to them. Her parents described this period as a time of confusion and sadness for Lia. When she was eventually reunited with them, just prior to turning six, she experienced a deep sense of joy and emotional connection. According to her parents, being a member of a sibling group became an extremely important part of Lia's sense of herself. They noted that she spoke proudly to others of having an older brother and sister. As a result, they have made a concerted effort to ensure that she maintains frequent contact with her siblings through visits as well as weekly phone and email communication.

Another aspect of loss experienced by foster and adopted children that is often overlooked or minimized is their separation from *previous non-biological caregivers and siblings/peers.* Children often form very positive relationships with former foster parents, foster siblings, and orphanage staff, as well as previous therapists, teachers, and friends, only to have these relationships severed when they enter a new foster or adoptive home. Moreover, too little attention is given by professionals to maintaining these relationships once children enter their new placement.

To be a foster or adopted child is also to experience *status loss.* This aspect of loss is tied to the societal stigma associated with foster care and adoption (Miall, 1987; Leon, 2002). Ask any foster or adopted child, and she will confirm that despite all the positive things her friends and classmates may say about her family status, they do not envy her nor do they wish to be fostered or adopted themselves. "Even when they say good things about me [sic] being adopted, I know they don't want to be me" (Indira [age 9], adopted from India at 14 months of age).

Loss of family stability also is experienced by foster and adopted children. For foster children, the reality of moving from one home to another, often abruptly, only reinforces the fragility of their home life and undermines any sense of stability and relationship permanence in their world. Furthermore, because children do not understand the legal basis of adoption until adolescence (Brodzinsky, Singer, & Braff, 1984), they sometimes worry that their birth parents can reclaim them, thereby creating additional emotional distress.

As children enter adolescence, other aspects of loss associated with foster care and adoption emerge. As they begin to contemplate their place within a family, teenagers sometimes begin to express what Sants (1964) referred to as "genealogical bewilderment," or, more simply put, a *loss of connection to a family line.* Adolescents are often curious about where their traits come from and begin to look to their parents, grandparents, and other relatives for answers. For those who are cut off from biological family, their ability to see their place in a family line is thwarted. This can be very frustrating and compromise their emerging sense of themselves.

Transracial placements also can lead to another aspect of loss—the *loss of racial, ethnic, and/or cultural origins.* Although even transracially placed preschool age children are aware of the physical differences, it is not until the adolescent years that most youngsters explore the meaning of those differences and their place within their racial, ethnic, and cultural origins (Baden & Steward, 2007). In the absence of appropriate role models and opportunities to explore and understand these origins, transracially placed individuals sometimes feel alienated from themselves and from their biological roots. "I don't know many Black kids...only a few others go to my school or live in town...the other [Black] kids make me feel as if I'm not Black...I'm just not like them and I sometimes wish I was... I don't know what it's supposed to feel like [to be Black]...no one taught me" (Jason [age 15], African American; transracially adopted at birth).

Another adoption-related loss primarily found in transracially placed individuals is the *loss of privacy* regarding their adoption. "Whenever I'm out with my family, I feel as if I'm in a spotlight. It feels like everyone is looking at us...at me...and they just know I'm not really a part of this family...I mean born to my parents...they know I'm adopted and I just hate it that people know something so private about me without having control over it...there's no privacy when you look so different from your parents" (Amy [age 16], adopted from China at 9 months).

Adolescence also is a time for exploring identity, both in its broadest sense and in terms of adoption (Grotevant, 1997). Integrating adoption into an emerging sense of self can be a complex process and is influenced by a myriad of individual, familial, and societal factors (Grotevant, Dunbar, Kohler, & Esau, 2000). For some individuals, adoption plays a very limited role in their self-perception and identity, whereas for others it is an extremely important part of themselves. Establishing a secure and positive adoption identity can be compromised, however, when there is limited information about one's origins or one is prevented from accessing the information. In such circumstances, adopted adolescents and young adults sometimes experience a *loss of self or identity*, expressed as "feeling cut off from one's origins," "having experienced a psychic amputation," "feeling alienated from oneself," and "feeling as if part of the self is missing."

In short, understanding the unique impact of sibling separation on foster and adopted children is complicated because it typically is part of a broader pattern of losses that are common to children in care. Moreover, these losses often emerge at different times over the course of development and have unique characteristics that make them difficult to resolve.

UNIQUE ASPECTS OF LOSS RELATED TO FOSTER CARE AND ADOPTION

The natural reaction to loss is grief and bereavement (Bowlby, 1980), which involves a complicated set of emotions and behavior—e.g., confusion, bewilderment, sadness, crying, depression, anxiety, frustration, anger. Grief is a process that takes time to unfold and varies from person to person in its form and outcome. Resolving loss, however, does not mean an end to the feelings associated with it. Rather, it means understanding the loss and finding ways of adaptively integrating it into the fabric of one's life.

Loss is an inherent part of life, something that everyone experiences on multiple levels. However, some types of loss are more difficult to understand and resolve than others. Loss associated with foster care and adoption falls into this category for many reasons (Brodzinsky, 1990).

First of all, compared to the millions and millions of children who live with their biological families, relatively few children are in foster care or in adoptive homes. Consequently, there are few peers who truly understand what it means to be fostered or adopted. In turn, this reality often accentuates a sense of being different among foster and adopted children.

In addition, some forms of loss, as in death, are permanent; however, others are not, which can complicate grieving because of the ambiguity represented by the loss (Boss, 2004; Lee & Whiting, 2007). For foster and adopted children, knowing that birth-family members usually are alive, even if they do not know where they live, means that their loss potentially is reversible. Fantasies of searching for and reuniting with birth family, which is extremely common among adopted individuals (Schechter & Bertocci, 1990), as well as those in foster care (Lee & Whiting, 2007), can make it difficult to find a comfortable way of living with their loss.

People who lose loved ones through death usually have a relationship history with the deceased which is remembered and can be used to facilitate grieving. Stories of the deceased are told again and again; memories of having experiences with them are shared repeatedly with others. However, for foster and adopted children, the situation is more complicated. For example, children who are placed at an early age generally have few, if any, memories of their lost relatives. Consequently, their grieving is based on fantasies of their birth kin as opposed to actual memories—a situation that can create confusion for the bereaved, especially if the fantasies change over time, something that is quite common. Furthermore, older-placed children often are removed from the care of their parents due to maltreatment. These children are likely to have many well-developed memories of family experiences, filled with a mixture of positive and negative images. The latter, which may be tied to their history of maltreatment, can create considerable conflict for children as they struggle to resolve their loss and can undermine self-esteem.

The knowledge that birth parents sometimes voluntarily made a decision to place their child for adoption also can affect children's self-esteem, especially when they believe that this decision was somehow related to their behavior or other personal characteristics. As Seth, age

14, who was adopted at two months, said, "I've tried to understand how she could have given up her own child...lots of people are poor or unmarried but they don't just give away their babies...at times I feel that maybe it was because of something about me...maybe she didn't like boys or I did things she didn't like...maybe she just didn't like me...it gets me mad."

As noted previously, loss associated with foster care and adoption is pervasive, although often subtle, ambiguous, and not fully recognized by others. As a result, some foster and adopted individuals feel misunderstood and unsupported in grieving their losses—an experience similar to what Doka (1989) refers to as *disenfranchised grief*. According to Doka, grief and mourning are compromised when people experience a loss that cannot be openly acknowledged or is trivialized or simply not recognized by others. In these circumstances, emotions associated with grieving are suppressed, leaving the individual feeling isolated and unsupported by others. Too often, this is the experience of children in foster care or adoptive homes. "Everyone used to say how lucky I was to be adopted... how grateful I should be to have been given such a good home...they never recognized how sad I felt about not knowing who my real parents were and why they gave me up...I couldn't share my feelings with my parents and other relatives...they didn't want to hear them...it made me feel really separate from them...really alone" (Alan [age 25], adopted at birth).

SIBLING LOSS IN LATER-PLACED VERSUS EARLY-PLACED CHILDREN

There are clear differences in the experience of being separated from a sibling with whom one has an established relationship (later-placed children) compared to the experiences of those who are placed as infants and do not know the siblings left behind or those born after them. In older-child placements, the loss of a sibling typically is more acute and potentially traumatic. The abrupt separation, not only from one's parents, but also from brothers and sisters, can be extremely destabilizing for children, leading to heightened anxiety, depression, acting out, and other behavioral and psychological problems, especially for those for whom preexisting sibling relationships were a source of companionship, comfort, and emotional security (Linares et al., 2007). Furthermore, even when there has been significant conflict between siblings, separation from them can undermine feelings of family connection and identity. In addition, separating siblings who have had ongoing problems with one another prevents these youngsters from resolving their difficulties and may reinforce avoidance and withdrawal as a means of solving relationship difficulties.

Returning to Case 1, it is important to note that the judge cited the failure to adequately support sibling relationships and to help John and
his siblings resolve their difficulties as factors in his decision to deny the
state's adoption plan (at least temporarily) and to support the birth
mother's motion to continue family reunification services. Parenthetically,
these children were eventually adopted by two different families,
with John in one home and William and Sara in another. Moreover,
additional services were successful in improving sibling relationships
and in supporting ongoing sibling contact through the two adoptive
families.

Compared with children who experience sibling separation when
they are older, those who go through this process as infants or young
children generally display a more subtle, ambiguous, and less traumatic
reaction, at least initially. Their more subdued response is based on a
lack of involvement with their brothers and sisters. In these cases, attachments are limited or nonexistent, as are separation reactions. However,
it would be a mistake to underestimate the importance of siblings for the
early-placed child, as seen in the case of Lia. Her experience is not uncommon in children who have some knowledge about but limited (or no)
contact with birth siblings living elsewhere. Research and clinical experience suggest that as children move into middle childhood, their understanding of out-of-home placement and adoption grows considerably
(Brodzinsky et al., 1984; Brodzinsky, Schecter, & Henig, 1992). For
preschool-age children, family is defined primarily in terms of the people
they live with and who care for them; biological relatedness plays a
limited role at this age. However, as children get older, they begin to
understand the importance of biological relations as a defining feature of
a family. When this happens, it is common for them to begin to question
their foster and/or adoptive parents about the birth family, including
possible siblings.

To the best of my knowledge, there is no empirical research on foster or
adopted children's understanding of sibling relationships, or on the
extent to which these youngsters experience a sense of loss or disconnec-
tion from their brothers and sisters. However, most clinicians who work
in the area can attest to the fact that there certainly is curiosity about the
possibility of siblings among early-placed adopted children. Moreover,
when these children learn that they have brothers and/or sisters, they
often desire contact with them (Brodzinsky et al., 1992).

In many cases, adoptive parents are reluctant to share information with
their children about biological siblings, especially when siblings continue
to reside with birth parents or other birth relatives. They are afraid their
children will question why they were placed when their siblings were
kept in the family, a situation which is not uncommon. Adoptive parents
often fear that their children will internalize responsibility for the birth

parents' adoption decision. In other words, they will assume that there was something wrong with them that led to the adoption—i.e., they were too difficult to care for, not pretty enough, the wrong gender.

Because of their anxiety, adoptive parents often choose to withhold information about the reality of their child's siblings. But this decision doesn't prevent children from speculating, fantasizing, and asking questions about the possibility of having brothers or sisters. In fact, clinical experience suggests that such speculation and questions are extremely common during the childhood and teenage years. After evading the child's questions for a while, adoptive parents either have to lie about the reality of the birth siblings or share what they know about them. Unfortunately, too many parents choose to continue to withhold the truth. This decision, however, often comes back to haunt them because it eventually undermines the child's trust.

Talking about sibling relationships with their children is an area in which many foster and adoptive parents, as well as birth parents, need help to become more open and forthcoming in family discussions. They need to recognize the normality of children's curiosity about their origins, including the possibility of siblings. Moreover, they need to understand the normality of experiencing grief associated with foster-care and adoption-related loss and, in particular, grief associated with being separated from brothers and sisters. Foster and adoptive parents need to understand the normality of the youth's desire to connect or reconnect with members of the birth family, including siblings, even when there has been some conflict in their relationships. To date, too little attention has been paid to these issues by professionals, although at least one children's book, *Sam's Sister* (Bond, 2004), is available to assist parents in helping youngsters to understand and adjust to sibling separation and loss.

Finally, it is important to recognize that for early-placed children, curiosity about birth siblings does not diminish with time; in fact, it often grows. As adopted individuals move from adolescence to young adulthood and begin to think more about searching for their origins, many show a marked interest in finding their siblings (Brodzinsky et al., 1992; Schechter & Bertocci, 1990). For some, this is part of a broader desire to understand their heritage and themselves—to connect with as many different birth-family members as possible; for others, however, the search is tied more specifically to siblings. In my clinical experience, many adopted individuals who have begun an active search find it safer to look for siblings than birth parents because it was not the siblings who made the decision to place them for adoption; hence, they worry less about the possibility of a second rejection.

In summary, although children placed early in life and those placed later in life both experience a sense of loss (including the possibility of sibling loss), their experiences can be quite different, with the later-placed child much more likely to have acute feelings of loss and trauma-related symptoms (e.g., heightened anxiety, depression, acting out behavior); whereas the early-placed child is more likely to manifest subtle expressions of grief as his/her understanding of the loss grows slowly over time.

IMPLICATIONS FOR CASEWORK PRACTICE

Having briefly reviewed and analyzed the issues in sibling separation in foster care and adoption, what implications can be drawn for this knowledge base for policy and practice?

First, agencies need to have a well-developed and articulated policy regarding the priority of placing siblings together. Unless there is a compelling reason, siblings should not be separated from one another when they enter foster care or are adopted. This recommendation is consistent with that put forth by the Child Welfare League of America (2000) and generally is supported by empirical research (Groza et al., 2003; Hegar, 2005).

Second, agencies should foster improved staff training so as to translate policy into routine practice. Without adequate training, individual staff biases, inconsistent assessment techniques, and/or inadequate family recruitment and support is likely to unduly influence decision-making regarding sibling placements. The likely outcome is that too many children will be placed in foster or adoptive homes without adequate consideration of maintaining existing sibling relationships.

Third, agencies need to develop more refined, theory-based assessment procedures for determining the nature and meaningfulness of sibling relationships for children who need out-of-home placement. Unfortunately, there has been little application of developmental and/or family-based theory to decision-making involving sibling placements. However, recent efforts focusing on the meaning of the sibling relationship from the perspectives of the children involved (Hindle, 2007), and the utilization of Attachment Theory as an organizing framework guiding decision-making for children in care (Whelan, 2003), appear to be promising additions to this practice area.

Fourth, at the time of placement, agencies also need to collect more information about sibling relationships, as well as the children's relationships to significant others beyond the family, including previous foster parents, foster siblings, peers, teachers, therapists, and coaches. Unfortunately, even when efforts are made to support children's relationships with important individuals from the past, the identification of those relationships to be maintained is often much too narrow. Children can benefit from the preservation of any past relationships in which they have been loved, nurtured, supported, stimulated, and/or respected. Although it is unlikely that all such relationships can be sustained when children enter foster care or are adopted, caseworkers and others involved in the process must be more attuned to the powerful role that positive familial and non-familial relationships can have for children's development and do everything possible to help maintain them.

Fifth, agencies need to do a better job recruiting foster and adoptive families who would be motivated to take on the challenge of parenting sibling groups. Of course, recruitment must be coupled with appropriate training to support these placements. Training should help parents develop appropriate expectations of the children and themselves, foster improved skills to manage family conflict (e.g., behavior management and communication strategies), and connect parents to appropriate support systems. The provision of additional financial subsidies and referral of families for therapeutic services also may be critical in preventing placement disruption when siblings are placed together (Barth & Berry, 1988).

Sixth, agencies also need to do a better job in finding temporary care for children within the extended biological family. Kinship placements typically lead to less sibling separation or, at the very least, greater access of siblings to one another (Hegar, 2005) and typically are more stable than non-kinship placements.

Seventh, when siblings must be placed in separate homes, agencies should make it a priority to ensure consistent and frequent access among sibling group members. Placement of children within the same geographical region can help facilitate this process. So too can training of foster and adoptive parents in the importance of maintaining sibling relationships, as well as providing families with different types of support to ensure contact can be maintained in a healthy manner (i.e., sharing of information on children's background experiences, transportation aid, therapeutic services to manage sibling conflict).

Finally, when a history of sibling conflict, or serious psychopathology in one of the children, is the basis for placing siblings in separate homes, agencies need to ensure that appropriate mental health services are put into place that focus on reducing the identified problems and supporting sibling contact and/or reunification, whenever possible. Generally, individual therapy for the children, by itself, is not the answer. Rather, conjoint therapy for the siblings, family therapy, and/or clinically guided visitation has the best chance of reducing the problems and normalizing the sibling relationships (Pavao, St. John, Cannole, Fischer, Maluccio, & Peining, 2007). In fact, when a history of conflict is used as the basis for separating children and there is no effort made to overcome the problems, a primary message sent to the children is that conflict is best handled through avoidance and withdrawal. This is hardly a constructive message for children whose lives often have been filled with adversity.

CONCLUSION

Family reunification and preservation are central tenets of child-welfare policy and practice. Too often, however, the focus of family preservation services is only on parent-child relationships. Equally important are sibling relationships. When children are placed in foster care, every effort must be made to ensure they live together in the same home, or if in different homes, at least in the same community with ready access to one another. When children are separated because of a history of conflict, a priority must be given to sustaining the relationships and reducing the conflict through therapeutic interventions. And when children are placed for adoption, more attention must be given to helping children maintain (or develop) relationships with siblings left behind or with those born after them. These efforts will require greater attention and creativity on the part of child-welfare and mental-health professionals. However, they are efforts that undoubtedly will prove to be in most children's best interests.

CHAPTER 5

The Rights of Siblings in Foster Care and Adoption: A Legal Perspective

William Wesley Patton

Even though social workers and other mental-health professionals may conclude that it is in the best interest of siblings to continue association during and after foster care, in order for their relationships to be sustained law and policy must protect their rights of association including being placed together, maintaining contact when placed apart, and continuing their relationship after adoption. In addition, court decisions and legislative regulations must reinforce these protections. This chapter will address protections for siblings who enter foster care, both from a historical view of efforts to establish constitutional protections for sibling relationships and based on states' efforts to protect the relationships that foster children have with their siblings.

Historically "[u]ncodified by law, uncelebrated by religious ritual, and unacknowledged by rights of passage" (Patton & Latz, 1994, p. 760), siblings' rights to association were largely ignored by mental-health literature until the 1970s; as late as 1987 one court noted that it was "unable to find any cases which recognize the right of siblings whose custody has been granted to the state to reside together" (*Crim. v. Harrison*). However, in the mid-1990s courts and legislatures began to regulate a number of sibling issues, including "sibling visitation, siblings' desire to find one another after court separation...and expedited termination of parental rights and statutory presumptions based upon sibling relationships" (Patton, 2001, p. 3). By 2005, 32 states had codified sibling visitation statutes and 28 states promulgated sibling placement policies (National

Resource Center for Family-Centered Practice and Permanency Planning [NRCFCPPP], 2005). But the evolution of siblings' association rights has been hampered by constitutional, policy, and economic impediments. First, siblings' rights were not included in the Supreme Court's elucidation and framing of First Amendment familial association rights in its landmark decisions from 1920 to the 1980s: *Meyer v. Nebraska* and *Pierce v. Society of Sisters* [parents' rights to care and custody of children]; *Moore v. City of E. Cleveland* [family unit is protected by the due process clause]; *Lassiter v. Dept. of Social Services* and *Santosky v. Kramer* [parents' due process rights in termination of parental rights hearings] (Marrus, 2004). Therefore, siblings' rights analysis has been more of a patchwork of analogies to the comparative rights of other family members, including: (1) biological versus putative parents; (2) step-parents; (3) custodial versus non-custodial parents; (4) grandparents; and, (5) custodial parents versus adult siblings seeking visitation with their younger siblings still under the care and supervision of parents. Second, the psychological literature regarding the importance of the sibling relationship did not sufficiently filter into legislative and judicial determinations until the late 1980s and early 1990s. Therefore, siblings' emotional interests were neither properly considered nor balanced in policy decisions regarding biological and third-party association rights. And finally, the economics of requiring significant social worker, attorney, and court involvement in the investigation, planning, and implementation of sibling placement and visitation militated against an expanded recognition of states' responsibilities to foster and prospective adoptive siblings. For instance, one of the nation's first sibling visitation bills, *California Assembly Bill 3332*, was almost defeated until a compromise amendment excluded the requirement of social worker or probation officer supervision of sibling visits because of the fiscal impact of this requirement (Patton & Latz, 1994). However, other states such as New Jersey have placed the burden of arranging transportation for separated siblings on the government (*N.J. Stat. Ann.* § 9:6B-4(f)). Because the Supreme Court has not defined the constitutional nature and extent of siblings' association rights, it is not surprising that so much variation exists among different states' judicial opinions and statutory schemes.

AN OVERVIEW OF THE PATCHWORK OF SIBLING ASSOCIATION STATUTES

It should not be surprising that there is little uniformity among states' sibling rights statutes. Homogeneity in foster-care statutes rarely exists unless the federal government mandates specific reforms pursuant to *Adoption and Safe Families Act* (*ASFA*) funding. The federal government has shown little interest in sibling issues, and as late as 1994 it did not even track the number or types of sibling foster placements (Patton & Latz, 1994). The federal government's interest in sibling placements increased marginally with its mandates for concurrent planning (Williams, 1998), and it was not until 2004 that federal inspections of state's foster care programs in the Child and Family Service Reviews considered efforts to place siblings together (Shlonsky, Bellamy, Elkins, & Ashare, 2005). The following discussion of sibling statutes first surveys the breadth and types of sibling issues promulgated in different states, and the second half of the analysis focuses on California, the first state to pass a comprehensive sibling association scheme that includes a statutory right to sibling association, and if in the siblings' best interests, a right to either placement together, contact if separated into different placements, or post-adoption sibling visitation.

THE VARIETY OF STATE SIBLING STATUTES AND THE SCOPE OF REGULATED ACTIVITIES

The first issue in determining siblings' statutory rights is to determine whether or not the children meet the state's definition of "siblings." In Chapter 1, the potential catalogue of different children's contacts that might constitute a sibling relationship was explored. However, few states have adopted a comprehensive definition of "sibling" sufficient to trigger all potential siblings' rights. The definitional issue relates to whether or not a sibling statute will be simply limited to biologically connected brothers and sisters, or whether step-siblings, adoptive siblings, and coplacement emotionally bonded non-biological children will be covered by statutory protection (Shlonsky et al., 2005). Perhaps the broadest statutory definition of "sibling" is contained in *California Welfare & Institutions Code* [*W. & I.*] §362.1: "a child related to another person by blood, adoption, or affinity through a common legal or biological parent" (Schwartz, 2001, p. 709).

Another initial question is whether or not a child has statutory standing to raise a sibling association issue. Prior to 1991 statutes simply did not address the sibling standing issue. A majority of state courts have held that siblings have no standing absent a specific legislative enactment (Williams, 1995). Some states, such as Maryland, specifically grant siblings standing: "[a]ny siblings who are separated due to a foster care or adoptive placement may petition the court...." (*Md. Code Ann. Fam. Law* § 5-525.2(a)). Another variation is to tie standing to a particular age of maturity determined to assure that the child has the capacity to make a knowing choice among alternatives regarding sibling contact. For instance, Massachusetts ties standing to age: "[a]ny child who has attained the age of 12 years, may request visitation rights with siblings who have been separated and placed in care or have been adopted in a foster or adoptive home other than where the child resides" (Mass. Gen. Laws ch. 119 §26(5)). However, even if sibling statutes provide children with standing, two impediments remain. First, the statute must trigger a right to notice regarding what sibling rights exist. Unless children realize that they have a right to association they may not exercise that right. Additionally, unless a young foster child or prospective adoptive child still has legal representation after termination of parental rights, the child will not have a zealous advocate to marshal the relevant facts necessary for establishing sibling contact and the details of that association.

State statutes differ regarding "when" sibling issues are relevant. For instance, must the Department of Child and Family Services address sibling association at initial custody, jurisdiction, disposition, periodic review, termination of parental rights, and/or post-adoption proceedings? Since passage of the federal mandate for concurrent planning, some states are beginning to consider sibling issues much earlier in dependency court processes. For instance, in 2000, Mississippi provided that "concurrent planning... [shall include] placement of siblings." (*Miss. Code Ann.* § 43-15-13(8)(h)). Because the initial out-of-home placements may be determinative of the quality and duration of sibling association, states should address sibling issues at the initial custody hearing.

Prior to 1991 almost all state courts denied post-adoption sibling visitation. However, many states have provided post-adoption sibling association by statute. For example, by 1999 Florida not only recognized siblings' rights and interests to post-adoption contact, the legislature mandated that courts determine the "nature and frequency of the communication and contact" between siblings. (*Fla. Stat. Ann.* § 39.001(k);*Fla. Stat. Ann.* § 63.022(1)). Other states, such as Illinois, have gone further in requiring the court to consider sibling association in the court's selection of which set of prospective adoptive parents to choose as the children's adoptive parents. (*Ill. Adoption Code* § 15.1(b)(7)). Of course, these post-adoption sibling visitation statutes raise concern regarding their constitutionality after *Troxel v. Granville, supra.* But *Troxel* is distinguishable because it was not a child-dependency foster-care case in which the biological parents had been proven to have abused and/or neglected their children; it was not a case of state action against the family; and the number of third parties who could seek visitation with the children were numerous. In addition, prospective adoptive parents, unlike biological or adoptive parents, do not have a vested constitutional right in the permanent custody of the foster children. We will have to wait for courts to decide the legality of post-adoption sibling visitation agreements signed by prospective adoptive parents that are attacked after those parents become adoptive parents. The California legislature has made it abundantly clear that violations of post-adoption sibling visitation agreements are not grounds for setting aside an adoption: "The court may not set aside a decree of adoption, rescind a relinquishment, or modify an order to terminate parental rights...because of failure...to comply with...the postadoption contact agreement...." (*Cal. Fam. L.* §8616.5; *Cal. W & I* § 366.26(a)).

CALIFORNIA'S SIBLING VISITATION SCHEME

In 1993 California was one of the first states to recognize the importance of sibling association by mandating the court to consider state-assisted sibling visitation for foster children placed into different custodial homes (Patton, 2003). The California Legislature defined the state's general sibling policy "to maintain the continuity of the family unit, and ensure the preservation and strengthening of the minor's family ties by ensuring that when siblings have been removed from their home...siblings will be placed in foster care together, unless it has been determined that placement is not in the best interest of one or more siblings." (*Cal. W & I* §16002). Since 1993, California's commitment to siblings has dramatically expanded. The legislature provided siblings two methods of demonstrating standing: (1) "[e]ach minor who is the subject of a dependency proceeding is a party to that proceeding" (*Cal. W & I* §317.5(b)); and (2) non-dependent children "may petition the court to assert a relationship as a sibling related by blood, adoption, or affinity" (*Cal. W & I* § 388(b)). Further, in a series of statutes and statutory amendments from 2000 to 2003, the California Legislature promulgated post-adoption sibling visitation (*Cal. W & I* § 366.26(a)), increased the burden of demonstrating that sibling association is not in a child's best interest from a preponderance of evidence to clear and convincing evidence, increased social workers' responsibility from merely "maintaining" sibling contacts to "developing" those bonds, and required the social workers' reports to justify at every hearing why the siblings have not been placed together. (*Cal. W & I*§ 16002). Finally, the legislature provided that the state may not terminate parental rights if such termination will result in substantial emotional damage to siblings who will be placed into separate post-termination placements:

There would be substantial interference with a child's sibling relationship, taking into consideration the nature and extent of the relationship, including, but not limited to, whether the child was raised with a sibling in the same home, whether the child shared significant common experiences or has existing close and strong bonds with a sibling, and whether ongoing contact is in the child's best interest, including the child's long-term emotional interest, as compared to the benefit of legal permanence through adoption. (*Cal. W & I* § 366.26(B)(v))

Of course, by providing siblings party status and standing, and by creating a sibling presumption that focuses on the emotional harm of each sibling rather than on the sibling unit in determining whether and to what extent sibling association will be realized, California experienced one unintended consequence. What happens when one attorney is appointed to represent multiple siblings and those siblings' wishes regarding sibling association differ? Does such a conflict of interest require the appointment of separate attorneys for the siblings? The California Supreme Court held that one attorney may represent multiple siblings unless an actual conflict of interest exists among them or it appears that it is reasonably likely that an actual conflict will arise (*In re Celine R.*). In order to avoid conflicts of interest among multiple siblings, children's dependency attorneys should consider the following variables: (1) siblings' ages; (2) siblings' special needs; (3) siblings' varying capacities to verbally express their association preference; (4) strength of the sibling bond; (5) adoptability of each sibling; (6) siblings' varying status as a percipient witness to abuse and/ or neglect; and (7) the siblings' varying placement desires (Patton, 2003). The further apart the siblings' ages, the more disparate their special needs, the greater difference in verbal capacity, the greater the relative degree of bonding of each child, and the wider the range of adoptability, the greater the likelihood that conflicts of interest will develop. In those cases counsel should decline multiple representation (Patton, 2006).

IS THERE A CONSTITUTIONAL BASIS FOR SIBLING ASSOCIATION RIGHTS?

The Supreme Court in 1999 declined to decide an important siblings' rights case and in so doing has failed to establish a firm constitutional basis for the rights of foster siblings to be together. In *Adoption of Hugo* the Massachusetts courts, after terminating the parents' rights, decided not to place a four-year-old sibling with special needs into the same adoptive home of his six-year-old sister. The court determined that sibling association was just one variable, not a constitutional right, in determining the placements that were in each siblings' best interest. Because a paternal aunt, but not the sister's adoptive parents, had special needs training, the court found that splitting the siblings was necessary to protect the younger child's best interest. In *Adoption of Hugo* the Massachusetts Supreme Court specifically rejected sibling association as a fundamental liberty interest.

No state supreme court has determined that siblings possess either a federal or independent state constitutional right to association. However, a few lower court opinions seemed to auger recognition of siblings' fundamental rights to have meaningful contact. For instance, in 1989 an Illinois federal district court in *Aristotle P. v. Johnson* refused to dismiss foster children's actions against the Illinois Department of Child and Family Services for denying the siblings a right to visitation while placed in different foster homes. The *Aristotle P.* court found that siblings had both a First Amendment and a federal due process right to association that required courts to exercise a heightened scrutiny analysis to determine whether or not the government had exercised the least restrictive means of denying their association rights (Ferraris, 2005). However, no other courts have accepted *Aristotle*'s constitutional rights analysis. A lower New Jersey court in *L. v. G.* (p. 222) in 1985 found that "siblings possess the natural, inherent and inalienable right to visit with each other". But other courts have declined to follow *L. v. G.*, especially as applied to foster children's associational rights because that cause of action was brought by emancipated siblings who were attempting to visit with their minor siblings who still remained in their parents' custody.

NON-CONSTITUTIONAL JUDICIAL DETERMINATIONS OF SIBLINGS' RIGHTS

Foster sibling case law can be grouped according to the factual scenarios in which siblings assert their rights to communicate with one another. These cases vary according to the procedural context within which the right is asserted (dependency adjudication, disposition, permanency planning, or adoption), the status of the individual seeking contact (minor sibling versus emancipated sibling, foster child, child freed for adoption, adopted child), and the nature of the request (locating a sibling, visiting with a sibling, or joint placement with siblings).

CASES WHERE ONE SIBLING LIVES AT HOME AND ANOTHER SIBLING RESIDES OUTSIDE THE PARENTS' HOME

This group of cases involves the issue of whether state courts have the power to order custodial parents to permit sibling association between siblings still living at home and either siblings placed in other foster care or emancipated siblings. Courts are split on whether they have the ability to order such sibling contact without the approval of the state legislature.

For instance, in *In re Interest of D.W.*, the state declared a 13-year-old boy a ward of the state and placed him outside his parents' home. The boy sought visitation rights with his three-year-old sister who still resided at home with her parents. The Nebraska trial court ordered sibling visitation against the parents' wishes. The Nebraska Supreme Court reversed, holding that although the trial court had jurisdiction over the parents and the older son, the court did not have personal jurisdiction over the younger sister and therefore lacked the authority to order sibling visitation over the parents' objections. The *D. W.* case is problematic for several reasons. First, because the court never defined the nature of siblings' rights, it is difficult to discern the reach of this opinion. For instance, did it hold that the son as a ward of the state did not have any right to sibling visitation, or merely that even if such a right exists, the court lacked jurisdiction to order visitation with his sister; or did the court *sub silentio* find that even if the brother had a right of association it was not in his sister's best interest to visit with the boy whom his parents described as a juvenile delinquent? Or did the *D. W.* court presage the U.S. Supreme Court's opinion in *Troxel v. Granville* that determined that state statutes that permit third parties' visitation [grandparents] with children over the objections of the child's parents must be narrowly tailored and provide some degree of presumptive value to the parents' objections? Of course, one must be careful not to overgeneralize from *Troxel* because that case did not involve state action or foster children, but rather was a private action by paternal grandparents, whose son had committed suicide, to visit their grandchildren over the objections of the children's mother. *Troxel* does not prevent juvenile courts from permitting sibling visitation between minor siblings who are wards of the dependency court and their emancipated siblings if the court finds such association in the minor child's best interest. Therefore, *Troxel* should have little impact on foster-care visitation.

Some courts have held that they lack inherent jurisdiction to order sibling visitation. In *Scruggs v. Saterfiel*, after a girl's mother died, she went to live with her aunt while her half-brother remained with his father. The aunt and girl sought visitation with the half-brother, but the trial court denied contact in the absence of a statute. The court of appeal noted that the legislature had addressed grandparent visitation, but in the absence of a sibling visitation statute, the court held that the legislature is the appropriate public policy-making branch of government to provide siblings with a right to associate.

SIBLING BONDS AS A VARIABLE IN DEPENDENCY DISPOSITIONS AFTER TERMINATION OF PARENTAL RIGHTS

Because many of the Supreme Court's concerns about third-party visitation involve questions regarding parents' fundamental right to rear their children, one might expect that courts, after terminating parents' rights, would feel free to perfect the placements and visitation schedules that would promote sibling association. However, courts have taken a number of different positions even after termination of parental rights: (1) siblings have a presumptive right to associate; (2) sibling bonds are just one variable in placement decisions; and (3) the new custodial or prospective adoptive parents' desires receive presumptive weight over siblings' wishes.

In *In the Interests of David A.*, two young siblings were separated in two post-termination homes, and they were permitted some visitation during which they developed a close bond. However, one of the boys also had a close bond with his foster mother. The court did not provide any presumptive weight to the sibling bond, but instead, used a straight best-interest-of-the-child analysis to compare the psychological effects of separating the siblings versus the harm caused by separating the sibling from the foster mother. However, the problem with the *David A.* approach is that it devalues the siblings' rights to associate by providing equal weight to foster parents who merely have temporary custodial rights that may never ripen into a permanent custodial arrangement. A better approach would be, after termination of parental rights, to treat sibling rights as either a vested constitutional right or as a right with presumptive value. If evidence rebuts the presumption of sibling placement and association, then the court can, of course, provide for the best interests of each sibling by applying a less drastic alternative analysis that selects among the options of joint placement, separate placement with unsupervised or supervised visitation, telephone communication, or no sibling contact.

In *In re Christina L.* the court terminated parental rights but did not consider the sibling bond in post-termination placement. The court of appeal determined that sibling bonding is a relevant and necessary variable in determining the proper post-termination placement, even absent a sibling statute. *Christina L.* serves as a transition case to the next section that discusses the sibling bond as a variable in determining adoptive placement.

THE RELEVANCE OF SIBLING BONDS TO DETERMINING ADOPTIVE PLACEMENTS

Because many states for decades operated under the assumption that adoptions were closed and confidential, the concept of post-adoptive sibling visitation was rarely considered. However, as adoptions have become more open, courts are now struggling with post-adoption sibling visitation in the absence of statutory authority. Some courts have held that post-termination visitation and post-adoptive sibling visitation are not issues to be resolved at the termination of parental rights hearing. For instance, in *Adoption of Vito* the trial court required the mother's consent to a post-adoption visitation plan among the three siblings. The court of appeal held that the trial court erred because the issue of post-termination sibling visitation is not relevant to the question of whether the mother's parental rights should be terminated. A decision like that in *Vito* clearly weakens siblings' association rights because the dependency trial judge cannot tie the decision regarding whether or not to sever parental rights to the question regarding the outcome for the children; i.e., will siblings have post-termination visitation? Some courts, as in the case of *Vito*, are concerned with setting up preconditions for adoption that might reduce the pool of prospective adoptive parents because parents may not want to permit visitation between the children they adopt and other siblings. Seifert (2004, p. 1486) recognizes "a fear that the biological family will come back to claim the child, or the biological family's actual, ongoing involvement in the child's life may hinder" the bonding process between the adopted child and the adoptive parents. Of course, that concern can be allayed by an educational program that informs prospective adoptive parents of the distinct advantages of permitting closely bonded children to have post-adoptive sibling visitation. For instance, California requires the State Department of Social Services to "[i]nclude in training provided to prospective adoptive parents information about the importance of sibling relationships to the adopted child and counseling on methods for maintaining sibling relationships." (*California Welfare & Institutions Code* § 16002(e)(1)).

Other jurisdictions have determined that courts possess inherent authority to order post-termination sibling visitation over the objections of prospective adoptive parents. For instance, in *Adoption of Lars* the court determined that even though adoption is a statutory creation, courts have inherent equitable authority to determine post-termination visitation. The court noted that prospective adoptive parents' willingness to provide post-adoptive sibling visitation is relevant in determining which adoptive parents to select for the siblings.

As the preceding discussion of sibling association case law has demonstrated, state courts vary considerably regarding whether issues of sibling association are relevant, whether or not they receive any presumptive weight, and whether courts can impose post-termination and post-adoptive sibling visitation. However, state legislatures have provided many proscriptions that have advanced siblings' association rights well beyond their judicially defined realm.

THE UNEXPECTED CONSEQUENCES OF CONCURRENT PLANNING AND RAPID PERMANENCY ON SIBLING ASSOCIATION

The child-dependency policy pendulum has swung from an overriding emphasis on family preservation until the mid-1980s to the current emphasis on "permanency" of placements sometimes at the sacrifice of children's close bonds with third parties (Patton & Pellman, 2005; Binn, 2004; Ross, 2004). The requirement for expedited termination of parental rights and earlier focus on permanency planning in the 1997 *Adoption and Safe Families Act* has increased the use of concurrent planning, which involves simultaneous efforts to work toward family reunification and alternative permanency for foster children. In fact, almost half of the federally mandated outcome measurements for permanency planning involve timed permanency issues that look at abuses in foster care, multiple foster care placements, reentry into foster care, the time to achieve

family reunification, and the time to achieve adoption (Grimm &
Hurtusbise, 2003).

This shift in priorities from family reunification to rapid permanency
and concurrent planning may have the unintended consequence of *decreas-
ing* the number of siblings placed together outside the home, as appears to
be the case in California. Table 5.1 illustrates the type of placement of California children placed outside the home from 1999 to 2002 under concurrent planning (*California Children's Services Archive*, 2003, p. 1):

Table 5.1

Type of Out-of-Home Placement, California, 1999–2002

	1999	2000	2001	2002
Pre-Adopt	1.3%	2.8%	3.7%	4.1%
Kinship Foster	46.8%	44.6%	41.7%	38.9%
Non-Relative Foster	18.9%	16.8%	15.9%	15.6%
Private Foster Agency	16.3%	17.6%	18.3%	20.3%

As one might expect, the new emphasis on rapid permanency helped to
increase the number of foster child placements in pre-adoptive homes from
1.3% to 4.1%, but it is the drop from 46.8% to 38.9% in kinship foster placements that is of most concern to siblings' rights to associate because the percentage and number of siblings placed together outside their home is
greatest in kinship care arrangements (Patton & Pellman, 2005; Center for
Social Services Research, 1998–2002). For instance, in California in 2003 the
percentage of siblings placed together varied by type of placement, as
reported in Table 5.2 (*California Children's Services Archive*, 2003, p. 1):

Table 5.2

Siblings in Foster Placement, California, 2003

	All Siblings Placed Together	No Siblings Placed Together
Kinship	56%	21%
Non-Relative Foster	33%	42%
Private Foster Agency	32%	35%
Group Home	7%	84%

These data from California demonstrate that under a concurrent plan-
ning/rapid permanency model in a span of just three years, kinship placements decreased by approximately 8 percent even though kinship
placements result in the highest percentage of entire sibling units being
placed together and in the lowest percentage of cases in which no foster siblings are placed together. Thus, a policy of rapid permanency through adoption may result in a significant loss of sibling association; and states are left
with a dilemma of balancing the public policies of sibling association and

rapid permanency through adoption. The California Supreme Court found that adoption permanency trumps sibling association unless compelling reasons for joint sibling placement are demonstrated (*In re Celine R.*, 2003). Most other states have not yet made that determination.

CONCLUSION

Siblings' associational rights currently lack constitutional validation. For now, siblings must rely on state legislatures to define the nature and extent of their right to communicate with one another. As with the birth of any new set of rights, it is important to educate the public regarding the importance of those rights. We already have a National Grandparents' Day; the time is ripe for a National Siblings' Day. Perhaps public opinion can help reshape the balance between adoption permanency and the critical psychological necessity for abused and/or neglected children to have continuing contact with their brothers and sisters.

CHAPTER 6

Sibling Issues in Open Adoption Arrangements: Non-biologically Related Adopted Siblings' Experiences with Birth-Family Contact

Jerica M. Berge, Kevin M. Green, Harold Grotevant, and Ruth McRoy

INTRODUCTION

This chapter addresses a unique aspect of adopted sibling relationships: non-biologically related adopted siblings' experiences with varying levels of birth-mother/birth-family contact. This topic is significant for adoptive families because it is common for families to have more than one adopted child who is not biologically related to the other children in the family. These siblings not only face the same types of issues that biologically related siblings do, connected to family functioning, but they also have additional issues related to birth-family contact. Differences such as one adopted child having birth-family contact while the other does not can add complexity to the family dynamics and have the potential to create difficult interpersonal interactions including sibling rivalry, jealousy, or anger.

We first review the extant literature regarding adopted sibling research in general and non-biologically related adopted siblings in specific. Next, we address the most common questions we are asked when presenting our research on adopted siblings, with an emphasis on our research findings related to non-biologically related adopted siblings (Berge, Green,

Grotevant, & McRoy, 2006). In conclusion, we discuss implications for families, adoption workers, and adoption agencies.

REVIEW OF ADOPTED SIBLING RESEARCH

Importance of Sibling Relationships

Sibling relationships tend to be the longest-lasting relationships among family members—even longer than parent-child or husband-wife relationships. Most children grow up with at least one sibling in the household. As siblings grow older, their physical proximity may change, but the majority still maintain contact by sharing visits and recreational activities (Noller, 2005).

Sibling relationships are important to study because they have the potential to affect one's health and well-being. There is ample empirical evidence that siblings have a beneficial influence on one another's cognitive, social, and emotional development (Noller, 2005). Positive sibling dynamics have been shown to serve as a buffer from the negative effects of family strife (Brody, 2004). Conversely, negative sibling interactions can also have an adverse effect on the quality of the sibling relationship (Brody, 1998).

Adopted Sibling Research

Research on adoptive siblings has focused to a great extent on such areas as the dynamics of biologically related sibling group placements (Ward, 1987), foster placement and sibling separations (Cicirelli, 1995; Drapeau, Simard, Beaudry, & Charbonneau, 2000), and the factors associated with keeping sib groups intact or separating them (Shlonsky, Webster, & Needell, 2003; Wulczyn & Zimmerman, 2005). This research has supported the importance of keeping biologically related siblings together in foster care and adoption. However, there are many more changes to be made in order to safeguard sibling bonds. The research on adopted siblings to date has not focused specifically on sibling relationships of non-biologically related adopted siblings in the same family. Rather, research has focused on topics such as the biological child's reaction to having an adopted sibling (Phillips, 1999), behavioral problems in adopted siblings (Simmel, Barth, & Brooks, 2007), intellectual functioning in adopted siblings (IJzendoorn, Marinus, Juffer, Poelhuis, & Klein, 2005; Devlin, Daniels, & Roeder, 1997), or shared and non-shared environmental effects on psychological development (Buchanan, McGue, Keyes, Elkins, & Iacono, 2006). Thus, it is important to begin researching non-biologically related adopted siblings due to the frequency of these types of arrangements in adoptive families.

Non-biologically Related Adopted Siblings Research

Non-biologically related adopted siblings, although not connected through biological bonds, are connected through emotional bonds—relationships that are equally as important as genetic bonds. Although it is very common for adoptive families to have more than one non-biologically related adopted child, there is a paucity of research studying the sibling relationship of these non-biologically related siblings (Berge et al., 2006; Groza, Maschmeier, Jamison, & Piccola, 2003). Thus, there is a need to research this unique type of sibling relationship. A review of the literature found only one other specific study on non-biologically related adopted siblings (van der Valk Verhulst, Neale, & Boomsma, 1998) besides our own (Berge et al., 2006). Van der Valk et al.'s (1998) study looked at problem behaviors in biologically related and non-biologically related adoptees. They found that the stability of externalizing problem behaviors (acting out, aggression, conduct disorder, oppositional defiant disorder, and attention problems) was explained by genetic factors, whereas the stability of internalizing problem behaviors (depression, anxiety, thought problems) was explained by non-shared environment. This study indicates that overall problem behavior for adoptees was more related to genetics and individual characteristics than environmental causes. Although this study provides insight to individual functioning, it does not speak specifically to the relationships between siblings, nor what to do when birth-mother/birth-family contact is part of the family system dynamics. Berge et al. (2006) attempted to answer these specific unanswered questions, and we report on that study throughout this chapter.

ADOPTIVE KINSHIP NETWORK (AKN)

Adoptive siblings, biologically and non-biologically related, often have contact with members of one another's birth families and develop relationships with each other's birth-family members. This relationship between adoptive-family members and birth-family members has been termed the adoptive kinship network (AKN) in the adoption literature. The AKN has not yet received much attention in the area of openness, or contact, in adoption. The AKN is defined as the connections among the birth-family members, adoptive-family members, and the adopted child (Grotevant & McRoy, 1998). Recent studies have begun to examine the family dynamics of openness (i.e., contact with birth family) in AKNs (Grotevant, McRoy, Elde, & Fravel, 1994), as well as adopted adolescents' views of their contact in their AKNs (Mendenhall, Berge, Wrobel, Grotevant, & McRoy, 2004). Grotevant et al. (1994) were among the first to study openness in AKNs. Using a national sample they explored the family dynamics of openness by looking at adoptive families with varying levels of openness in their AKN. Similarly, Mendenhall et al. (2004) and Berge, Mendenhall, Grotevant, & McRoy (2007) studied adolescents' satisfaction with varying levels of openness in their AKN. These studies have focused primarily on the individual experiences of adolescent adoptees around openness in adoption.

Studying sibling dynamics in adoptive families where there are non-biologically related adopted siblings provides yet another context for examining the complexity and interaction of openness in adoption, as well as another area for examining the potential for sibling conflict, the negotiation of contact, and siblings' perceptions of these issues within the AKN. We address these uncharted topics in this chapter.

FREQUENTLY ASKED QUESTIONS REGARDING NON-BIOLOGICALLY RELATED ADOPTED SIBLING RELATIONSHIPS

When presenting our research results at research conferences and to adoption agencies and families with adopted siblings, we are commonly asked questions such as, "Is there sibling rivalry between adopted children when one sibling has contact with her birth mother/birth family and the other does not?" and "How do families manage boundaries in families when there are differing levels of openness/contact between the siblings?" In this section we address the commonly asked questions we receive regarding openness/contact in adoption in relation to our research with non-biologically related adopted siblings (Berge et al., 2006). We will use the voices (all names have been changed) of the non-biologically related adopted siblings themselves and their birth mothers when appropriate.

Our research on adopted non-biologically related siblings is part of a larger research project called the Minnesota Texas Adoption Research Project (MTARP) (Grotevant & McRoy, 1998; Grotevant, Perry, & McRoy, 2005). MTARP is a longitudinal project that includes a nationwide sample of adoptive families and birth mothers who were recruited through 35 adoption agencies located in 23 different states, from all regions of the United States. Wave I data were collected between 1987 and 1992, and Wave II data were collected between 1996 and 2000; interviews were spaced approximately eight years apart. The larger Wave II MTARP sample includes 173 adoptive mothers, 162 adoptive fathers, 127 birth mothers, 152 "target child" adopted adolescents (74 boys and 78 girls), and 88 adopted siblings.

This analysis is based on a subsample from the MTARP project and included 29 adopted non-biologically related sibling sets (total $n = 58$), with 32 females and 26 males. The age range of the siblings was 13–18 (mean = 15.8 years). Twenty-one of the adopted sibling sets were in adoptions in which both siblings had contact with his or her respective birth mother/birth family. These sets of adopted siblings were called the "dual contact" (DC) group. Eight sets of adopted siblings were in mixed arrangements, where one sibling had contact with her or his birth mother/birth family and one sibling did not have contact. These sets of adopted siblings were called the "mixed contact" (MC) group. Birth-mother/birth-family contact was occurring in all 29 sibling sets. For ease of reading, from this point on we will refer to the contact the adopted adolescents were having with their birth mothers and birth families as "birth-family" contact, unless the results are specific to birth-mother contact only. Our study used deductive thematic qualitative analysis (Huberman & Miles, 1994) to analyze adolescents' interview transcripts in order to understand their experience as adopted non-biologically related siblings in the same family with varying levels of birth-family contact, or openness. When the identified themes from the adolescents included relationship viewpoints about birth mothers, their transcripts were also checked for corroborating themes in order to enrich the analysis. This established the systemic nature of the themes.

Sibling Rivalry

One of the most common questions we are asked at our research presentations is, "Is there sibling rivalry when one sibling has contact with his birth family and the other does not?" According to our study, half (four of the eight) of the mixed contact (MC) group directly indicated no sibling rivalry or jealousy related to differing contact status with their respective birth families. The following quotes suggest that having contact with birth-family members may be a positive experience for the entire adoptive family:

- ...it's [birth-mother contact] never been a big issue at our house. It's never been used as like leverage in a fight or anything like that. It's kind-of, out of sight, out of mind, I guess. That, you know, I was adopted and don't see my birthparents but Jack does. It's like these people [Jack's birth family] are our family so...it's been like that since the day we can remember so, it's never been a big deal" (male adolescent).
- I used to be mad that Sara got to see her birth mom...then I started visiting her [adopted sibling's birth mother] too...it didn't bother me anymore because she was so nice...it [visiting sibling's birth mother] brought us [adopted siblings] closer I think (female adolescent).

The other half of the MC siblings had different responses to the issue of feeling jealous of their sibling who had birth-family contact. Three of the sets didn't mention the issue of jealousy at all, and one stated that it was a problem and she wished she had contact with her birth mother, like her sister did, and that it caused significant conflict or jealousy between them.

We postulated that one of the reasons that jealousy or sibling rivalry between non-biologically related adopted siblings was minimal, or not mentioned, was because the sibling in the confidential arrangement had contact with the other sibling's birth family (see below) and this contact met some of the needs of the sibling in a confidential arrangement.

Managing Boundaries

Another common question we are asked when we present our research is: "How do families manage boundaries with differing levels of openness/contact with each of the adopted siblings' birth families?" Our research indicated that for both the MC and DC sibling sets there was some type of contact with birth families and that the boundaries were flexible.

Dual Contact Sibling Sets

In the dual contact (DC) group, 17 of the 21 sibling sets described enjoying contact with their own birth families, as well as their non-biologically related siblings' birth families. Furthermore, the majority indicated that they looked forward to both types of contact. The following quotes suggest that flexible boundaries exist within adoptive kinship networks (AKNs) (e.g. adopted child, adopted siblings, adoptive parents, and birth family) when both non-biologically related siblings have contact with their birth families:

- *I like seeing them [adopted sibling's birth family] (female adolescent).*
- *We all go to each other's birth families and have a blast. We like to see both birth families, not just mine (female adolescent).*
- *He [adopted sibling] sees them the same times as I do...so all the siblings know everybody else's birth mothers. It's fun because we go on tons of trips to visit all of them and we have a lot of visitors when they come and visit us (male adolescent).*

Our birth-mother data from the DC group corroborated this idea. Seven of the eight birth mothers identified in the DC group stated that they had contact with several members of their biological child's adoptive family. The following quotes support the idea that flexible boundaries exist among the AKN:

- *I've sent things to him [biological child] and things to his sister and brother. I've sent things to his mom and dad...I've sent his mom Mother's Day cards. I've sent his dad Father's Day cards. And different times, I've sent them all gifts (birth mother).*
- *They [adoptive parents] always bring their other kids besides Nathan [adopted child], two of them, or all seven of them. There's never a dull moment. We don't know whether to expect one kid or all of them. It's pretty fun, though, and I know they [the kids] enjoy it (birth mother).*

- *They [birth mother's family] have met all his [biological child's] entire family and they've [adopted child's family] met all my [birth mother's] family (birth mother).*

- *Another birth mother stated, My parents, my daughter, my boyfriend, my sisters—all three of them—and my grandma, when she was alive, met Dan's [biological child's] adoptive family (birth mother).*

Mixed Contact Sibling Sets

In the MC non-biologically related sibling sets seven of the eight sibling sets had contact with the other sibling's birth family. We further found that the sibling who did not have contact with his or her own birth family compared the contact they were having with his or her sibling's birth family to what it would be like to have contact with his or her own birth family. This was true for five of the seven MC adolescent sibling sets. The following quotes represent this point:

- *She [sibling's birth mother] doesn't write to me, she writes to Pam [adopted sibling with contact], but she like wants to know what I'm doing and I talk to her and stuff, she'll talk to me and stuff. I'm friends with her and it kinda makes me think of her like how my birth mother would be (female adolescent).*

- *Well, it was exciting to meet her [brother's birth mother]…it's like I'm meeting my birth mom, and I'm so excited for Garner [adopted sibling with contact]…you know, 'cause he got to meet his birth mother so it's real nice and stuff (female adolescent).*

- *They're [adopted siblings without contact] involved in and…want to…be a part of it, so they can experience it themselves…you know, because they have this desire to meet theirs [birth mothers]…at some point…but they can kind of see what it's going to be like or experience it through me (adolescent male).*

We also found that several of the non-biologically related adopted MC sibling sets described situations where the birth mother of the sibling who had contact would send things to the sibling who had no contact with his birth family. This was the case for four of the seven adolescents with sibling birth-mother contact. The following quotes imply that the birth mothers of the adopted sibling with contact were actively reaching out to the adopted child without birth-family contact:

- *My birth mom will like send her [adopted sibling with no contact] presents and stuff when it's her birthday and she'll send her cards every once in a while (female adolescent).*

- *On my birthday is pretty much when I get presents or birthday cards, and sometimes on holidays, she'll [sibling's birth mother] send me a card. I just feel like it's from my mom like it would be from anybody else (male adolescent).*

Our birth-mother data supported this point. Three of the four birth mothers in the MC group identified that they actively had contact with their biological child's adoptive family, or inquired about them. The following quotes suggest that at least some birth mothers may have viewed their role as extending beyond the relationship with their biological child to having relationships with their biological child's family members:

- *I ask him [biological child], 'how's your mother, your brothers, sisters, everybody' when we talk on the phone (birth mother).*
- *I really care about how they [adoptive family] are doing and enjoy seeing them when I see Kimmy [biological child] (birth mother).*
- *I think it's important to have a relationship with David's [biological child's] adopted family, I really like them (birth mother).*

Communication

At research presentations we also are commonly asked: "How do families talk about adoption with adopted siblings?" In our research we found that the DC and MC groups had different needs regarding the intensity level of the conversation related to adoption.

Dual Contact Sibling Sets

In the DC group of non-biologically related adopted siblings we found a low need for discussion about their adoption status. Thirteen of the 21 sibling sets in the DC group viewed adoption as a "normal process" in the family. The following quotes exemplify this idea:

- *It's just not anything uncomfortable. It's [adoption] normal—it's like a normal word in my vocabulary…so we don't need to talk about it much (female adolescent).*
- *I never really need to talk about it, for me. And it's, it's not like a great emotional experience for me. Because, like I said, it was how, just how I grew-up, it was never like a secret, or it was never hidden or there's no like, conspiracy about it or anything (male adolescent).*
- *being adopted doesn't change anything like it doesn't change how you are, I don't think (male adolescent).*

These quotes suggest that when adopted children had contact with their birth families they may have fewer unanswered questions about their adoption and thus experience a decreased need to discuss adoption issues.

Mixed Contact Sibling Sets

In the MC group we found that the sibling in a confidential adoption reported frequent conversations about their adoption. Five of the eight MC adolescents in a confidential arrangement identified this need.

The following quotes suggest that non-biologically related adopted adolescents who did not have contact with their birth families had a desire to talk about their adoption and specifically about contact in adoption:

- *Well, I always talk to her [adopted sibling with contact] about, like, who my father was, and what life would be like if I—if I weren't adopted, and how life would be with my own birth mother (adolescent male).*
- *We've been talking about it a lot lately since Geoff...knows his birth parents and we talk about what my birth parents might be like (i.e., looks, medical, etc.) (adolescent female).*
- *I ask how it is for him to have...contact with his birth mom and his family. I ask him what it's like sometimes 'cause I don't have that and he does...and I think it's kind of cool...I feel thoughtful after conversations about adoption (female adolescent).*

Relationships

A final common question we are asked at our research presentations is: "What do families say about the relationship between the adopted sibling's birth family and the adoptive family?" In our research we found that in both the MC and DC groups, families referred to the birth-family members using relational or familial terms. We further found that birth-family contact increased the desire for relationships with the adopted sibling's biological siblings.

Dual Contact Sibling Sets

The DC non-biologically related sibling sets indicated that they used relational terms when talking about either sibling's birth mother. This was the case for 12 of the 21 DC sibling sets. The following quotes imply that birth mothers had the status of "friend" or "relative" regardless of whether they were the adopted child's birth mother or their sibling's birth mother:

- *It's just like..., she's [adopted sibling's birth mother] a friend,...like any other friend or something (male adolescent).*
- *Both mine and my sister's birth mothers are like relatives, actually. Just kind of like, they're part of our family...we have a Christmas party every year for my dad's family... we only invite family and one close friend of the family and they're [both birth mothers] not counted as a close friend of the family, we just count them as family. Not...any different, so...they're just my family (female adolescent).*

Data from our DC birth mothers supported this idea. Six of the eight DC birth mothers indicated that they felt a familial connection with their biological child's adoptive family. The following quotes corroborate this finding:

- *I feel pretty close to them [adoptive family]. I feel like they could be relatives of mine. I mean, his [adopted child] mom could be my aunt, or like a sister-in-law. His [adopted child] siblings could be nephew/nieces of mine...I feel like we're related (birth mother).*

- *My mom, my dad, my sisters... I mean everybody thinks they're [adoptive family] family. It's like he's [biological child] my little brother and his family [adoptive family] are my cousins or something (birth mother).*

Mixed Contact Sibling Sets

In the MC non-biologically related sibling sets the birth mother of the sibling who had contact was viewed as a friend by both adopted siblings. This was the case for five of the eight MC sibling sets. The following quotes identify, just as the DC quotes did, that birth mothers were viewed as someone with whom the non-biologically related sibling has a relationship:

- *We both think of my birth mother as a friend...we both like seeing her and she talks to us like a friend would, and...we hang out with her" [when asked how his adopted sibling was involved in their contact with their birth mother]. [The adopted sibling of this adolescent said], "my brother's birth mother is just like a friend to me" (male adolescent).*

- *Well, there's Sam's [adopted sibling with contact] birth mother that I see often......and I like her...she's like a friend (male adolescent).*

Our research further found that the adopted sibling with no birth-family contact, and the birth family of the adopted sibling with contact, both actively treated each other like birth-family members. This occurred for five of the seven adolescents with birth-family contact. The following quotes highlight the idea that the term "family" became flexible in adoptions in which there was contact with the birth family:

- *My birth grandparents treat her [adopted sibling with no contact] like their grandkid too. They treat her about the same way...kind of like step-grandparents or something (male adolescent).*

- *Elisa [adopted sibling with no contact] sees my biological sisters...and Elisa thinks of them as her sisters, too (female adolescent).*

- *Lars's [adopted sibling with no contact], since he's my brother, he's all of their brother, too, Chris, Lucus and Cindy [birth siblings].*

Our birth-mother data confirm this finding. Three of the four MC birth mothers identified flexibility in boundaries regarding contact. The following quotes suggest that boundaries were permeable in order for both the adoptive-family members and birth families to include other members that were neither biologically nor legally related to them in familial interactions:

- *He [biological son] spends the night over at my mom's [birth grandmother] all the time on the weekends. My little brother, him [adopted child] and his brother [adopted child's sibling], who is also adopted, are all like 2 years apart. So they hang out (birth mother).*

- *We have very flexible relationships around here because they [biological child and adoptive family] think of us [birth mother and spouse] as godparents. And you know, our family is not necessarily our blood line. Our "family" are people who we treat as family (birth mother).*

Our research also found a connection between birth-family contact and a desire to meet birth-family members for the adopted adolescent with no contact. The MC siblings in confidential adoptions desired to have contact with their own birth-family members, especially siblings, as a result of having contact with their non-biologically related adopted sibling's birth family. Seven of the eight MC adolescents in a confidential arrangement identified this need. The following quotes identify the desire of siblings to know their other siblings in establishing their identity:

- *Because I met Mike's [adopted sibling with contact] birth mother and family I really want to meet mine. You know, like especially my siblings…they would probably be similar to me and I want to know them……hang out with them (male adolescent).*

- *Oh, I'd really like to know if I have any sisters or any brothers…and if we are alike (female adolescent).*

IMPLICATIONS

This study is the first to examine the dynamics of sibling relationships and birth-family relationships at varying levels of openness, based on the voices of the adolescents, rather than parents, and both siblings, rather than one. The voices of the birth mothers add a unique contribution allowing for a more global understanding of the contact dynamics. At the same time, the study's limitations must be taken into consideration when interpreting these results. It is important to note that the results apply to domestic adoptions of healthy children, with the majority of them having two parents who are middle class and highly educated. Thus, the following implications need to be interpreted within the context of the sample. This study's findings may not generalize to adoptions that are international or those involving the placement of children from foster care, because such adoptions can involve additional complexities. Also, the small size of the MC group ($n = 8$ sibling sets) suggests that generalizations be made with caution. Within the limits described, several implications from our research are relevant for parents of non-biologically related adopted siblings, adoption workers, and adoption agencies.

Parents and Families

Our research indicated several important take-home messages for parents and families with non-biologically related adopted siblings: (1) contact with the birth family was viewed as positive regardless of whether one or both siblings had contact; (2) families with mixed contact status reported that sibling rivalry and jealousy was not an issue. In fact, siblings without contact portrayed a sense of excitement and anticipation in seeing the other sibling's birth family; (3) flexible, or permeable, boundaries within the AKN worked well for both sibling sets; (4) communication about adoption varied by intensity depending on dual or mixed contact status. Mixed contact status siblings had a greater need to discuss adoption issues compared to dual contact status siblings; and (5) the desire to know other biological siblings was strong. Because it is increasingly common for multiple adoptions to occur within the same family these findings would be helpful for families considering adopting more than one child.

Adoption Workers and Agencies

Adoption workers and agencies can share findings from this research in order to help families anticipate issues that may arise with multiple adoptions with non-biologically related adopted siblings. For example, this information could help alleviate concerns that an adoptive parent may have regarding the potential of sibling rivalry between siblings if their first adopted child is in a confidential adoption and their second adopted child would have contact with birth-family members. This information could also give birth-family members and adoptive-family members concrete examples of positive outcomes that exist for all members involved in the adoption when there are dual or mixed levels of contact in the same family.

Our research results also suggest that understanding the adoptive kinship network is essential for the non-biologically related adopted siblings in our research. For instance, both groups of siblings reported flexibility in defining who their family was. Boundaries were permeable for both the adoptive-family members and birth-family members to include other members who were neither biologically nor legally related to them in familial interactions. There is support for the idea that the AKN is influential in providing added support and identity information for the adopted child, as well as potential support for the birth parents and adoptive parents (Grotevant & McRoy, 1998; Grotevant et al. 2005). Our research supported this idea. The AKN provided another level of support for the adopted child and in the majority of cases their siblings and adoptive parents too. Support from the adopted child's families also allowed them to have contact with their birth families and in some cases helped drive the contact. Birth mothers also indicated desire for ongoing contact with their biological child and the adoptive-family members. Adoption workers and agencies should consider educating birth-family members, adoptive-family members and the adopted child about the AKN and assist them in establishing connections when desired, in order to increase the likelihood of positive outcomes for the entire system. This type of knowledge serves to normalize these relationships and to reduce the sense of threat that adoptive parents may feel related to their child's contact with birth family.

Communication about adoption status was also a finding of importance from our study. Non-biologically related adoptive siblings with mixed contact desired to talk more about their adoption status than did siblings with dual contact. This may be an outcome related to "not knowing." The sibling in a confidential arrangement, within the mixed contact sibling sets, may have had unanswered questions about identity and what their biological parents/family were like that naturally led to more conversations about adoption. Adoption workers and agencies could normalize these conversations and help parents understand the need for this type of discussion.

Our research also found that the adopted sibling sets in mixed contact had a strong desire to know if they had additional birth siblings and to meet them. Because sibling relationships are one of the longest-lasting relationships, it is not surprising that adopted siblings wanted to know biological siblings and have a relationship with them. This finding is essential for adoption workers and agencies. Agencies and adoption workers should consider placing more emphasis on educating about sibling relationships in adoption. This finding also suggests that birth-sibling contact may be paramount in the AKN. Because adopted siblings—regardless of mixed contact or dual contact groups—voiced a desire to know other siblings, it is essential that more emphasis be placed on birth-sibling contact. This finding coincides with the other chapters in this book that highlight the need for strengthening biological sibling relationships among adopted children. Incorporating this information into adoption agencies' policies would seem to benefit all siblings, whether non-biologically related or biologically related.

CHAPTER 7

Keeping Sibling Connection Alive

Sharon Roszia and Cynthia Roe

Professionals involved in the placement of children into permanent homes have the opportunity to make decisions that can either enhance or hinder the development of healthy sibling relationships. How we approach this work influences children's identity formation, self-esteem, and mental health. An unwavering commitment to keeping siblings firmly connected as they move through the foster care system and into permanency is required.

The authors have chosen to illustrate their commitment to keeping sibling connections alive through the telling of three stories of siblings who never fully lost contact with their siblings and those who were joined or rejoined later in life. The authors have each known these families for many years. They reconvened the families prior to writing this chapter, in order to gain current insights into how the siblings' connections have unfolded over time, and how the kept and lost connections have helped shape each family member's life story. *The authors thank the families for sharing their hearts and wisdom.*

OUT OF CONFLICT, CONNECTION

The first story is the one that brought the two authors together; Cynthia Roe provides the public and Sharon Roszia, the private, agency perspective. The story conveys the complex challenges confronting adoptive families who choose to address the needs of all the siblings in a system.

Four sisters, ranging from two to eight years of age, were placed into foster care due to parental substance abuse, neglect, and sexual abuse, as reported by the oldest sister. The disclosure of the abuse subsequently became an issue between her and her three younger sisters, who were angry for her disclosure of the abuse. At the time these authors became involved with the children, the oldest and youngest of this sibling set were living alone in separate foster homes, and the two middle children had been placed together. The placement of the two living together was on the verge of disruption because of intense physical aggression between them. In addition, the oldest girl's placement was jeopardized by her oppositional behaviors. The youngest sister's foster parents wanted to adopt her, but not any of her sisters.

As is often the case, the social workers faced the challenge of minimizing loss while simultaneously securing permanency for all four girls. Concern about the two siblings placed together who were exhibiting aggressive behaviors forced a decision that they be placed in separate homes. The reasons justifying separation of all of these children included the large number of siblings that needed to be placed and the children's aggressive behaviors toward each other. The authors' commitment to sibling connections was factored into the final decision. If the children were to be separated, the families would have to be committed to forming a larger kinship circle on behalf of their shared children.

A single mother, who had a prior relationship with the oldest sibling, was chosen for placement of the two older sisters. The two younger sisters would be placed together into a two-parent family. Rearranging the sibling placements so that the two oldest were together and the two youngest were together preserved the girls' birth order and addressed the issue of physical violence between the two middle girls. In addition, when the girls were living with their birth mother, the second oldest was injured in an accident and had some neurological deficits. The oldest sibling had been left "in charge" of her younger siblings when her sister had wandered off and was hit by a car. The oldest felt responsible for the accident and was hyper-protective of her younger sibling. The placement with the single mother was viewed as an opportunity for the oldest child to "forgive" herself and experience an environment where children were not held responsible for their own safety or that of their sisters. At the outset of these placements, all of the parents were educated and guided in the building of the two families' connections. To their credit, they have been true to their commitment over these past 10 years. The girls see each other frequently; more than just "visits," these meetings are true family gatherings, including weekend overnights, camping trips, regular phone calls, and emails. The relationship mirrors that of close cousins, even though the girls are aware that they are biological sisters.

Author Roe met with the all four siblings and their parents to discuss the past 10 years of their adoption experience. The gathering was as healing as it was illuminating. The parents shared lessons learned over the years, as a new, expanded definition of family emerged. Neither family had originally considered such open adoptions, but trusted the workers' guidance as to the importance of this extended family relationship.

As all the parents looked back, they shared that they could not imagine things turning out better.

Meeting the Challenges and Gleaning the Rewards

The oldest sister felt she was the outsider since she had a different father, making her a Caucasian-Latina mix, while the other sisters are Latina and African American. She was also the one who disclosed the abuse. Now, in her late teens, she feels very attached to her sisters and grateful to the adults who supported these connections. Upon reflection, had the girls been separated, the oldest sister might have been emotionally "stuck" at the moment she disclosed and "destroyed" her family. Time has given her sisters the opportunity to understand, forgive, and even thank her for that decision. Keeping the siblings connected allowed for deeper healing to occur, as the pieces of the puzzle surfaced and were gently and slowly fit together.

The oldest child came into her new family with an identity as her sisters' "mom." She did not want to surrender that role to their new single parent. However, over time, the adoptive mother was able to redefine roles. Had the sisters been separated, this older child may have felt guilt and worry about her younger, more vulnerable sisters, unable to enjoy the benefits of being someone's daughter. Had the girls not stayed connected, this sister may have believed that she was the only one who had been molested, that she was not only responsible for the abuse, but for the disintegration of her family "caused" by her disclosure.

The "baby" of the family was two years old at the time of placement. She did not initially understand that the two older siblings placed with their single mother were her sisters. She thought they were only the sisters of the girl with whom she was placed. At age five, she began to understand that these were her sisters also. She experienced the separation from her siblings in a different way, perhaps without as much sadness because she takes the current relationships for granted and has never fully been without her sisters.

The children arrived with both emotional trauma and behavioral challenges. The three adoptive parents indicated that they felt less alone and less judged, as they learned together how to manage the children's behaviors by sharing, supporting, and providing much-needed respite. Routinely, the "re-breaking" of the connection between the girls when a visit is ending can trigger deep feelings of sadness at having to say goodbye. This preoccupation is not typical of siblings who grow up together. The girls share a hope that all their close relationships will last; that someday they will "live together in a big house"; and that they can go to the same college.

Bridging two adoptive families from differing educational, financial, social, and familial backgrounds has been an ongoing challenge. The two sets of parents disagreed over whether or not to have contact with the girls' birth mother. The two-parent family was supportive and encouraging of contact via letters and phone calls, while the single mom was opposed to any contact at all. The parents agreed to disagree about this particular issue and decided that each could pursue the relationship with the birth mother as they felt best for their children. Had they not been able to work this out, the parents would have chosen to prioritize the siblings' relationships over communication with the birth mother. At times, these differences have given rise to envy, jealousy, and verbal expressions of wanting to live with the other family. The parents responded to most differences by simply acknowledging them; keeping activities simple, fun, and inexpensive, and giving gifts that could be made or done for one another. Extended family on all sides of the equation is inclusive of all the siblings at family gatherings and in gift giving.

There are additional siblings who do not yet participate in this extended family constellation. The question of the "missing" siblings comes up for all of the children. The sisters hope to search to retrieve those relationships. A question for the girls remains as to why some siblings were parented by the birth mother or remained connected to the birth family when they were not. Some of their siblings were also adopted into other families. The sisters wonder why those families are unwilling to participate in their open adoption system. The two oldest girls wonder what happened to the foster siblings they had been placed with before adoption. With the support of their parents and each other, they will be in a healthier position to accept whatever they find.

The conclusions shared by these sisters follow:

- *Don't get stuck in the past; there's nothing you can do to change it.*
- *Emphasize the good things you do have.*
- *Don't blame yourself; you didn't do anything wrong.*

The authors believe that in the absence of the opportunity to grow up knowing their sisters, these girls might have blamed themselves for the tragic events in their lives and therefore might have experienced compromised self-esteem, less gratifying interpersonal relationships, and a lack of trust in themselves and others. Their sustained relationships have created four healthy individual adolescents.

HOW MANY BROTHERS AND SISTERS? MORE THAN I CAN COUNT ON MY FINGERS

The second story exemplifies the importance of the acceptance of difference; the clarity that maturity brings about the circumstances of adoption, and the roles that adults play in preserving these connections long before children have any true understanding of their importance. It also points to the deep and abiding feelings of siblings who remain with the birth parents as they observe the decision to place their siblings into adoption.

This extended family clan built through adoption includes six biological siblings, two siblings by adoption, and seven nieces and nephews, as well as two close cousins. Ages overlap throughout the generations.

In 1993, prospective adoptive parents had learned of a child who would be born to a family dealing with many life challenges, including addictions and incarceration of the father. The prospective adoptive parents' own life experiences allowed them to avoid judgments that could have affected the relationship with the birth family. The birth parents were already raising four children, and they feared that the birth of this son might push them beyond their already stretched resources. The birth mother chose these adoptive parents. It was quickly evident that the children being raised by the birth family were being deeply affected by this adoption plan. They expressed both anger and sadness, with the oldest daughter expressing her belief that she could raise their brother, if given the chance.

A year after this son was placed into an adoptive family, another child was conceived by the birth parents. This child, another boy, was placed with a second adoptive family, as the first adoptive couple felt that they could not adequately parent another young child. Placing that sibling with yet another family expanded the "kinship" circle even further.

When the first-placed boy was still a toddler, he had not yet fully comprehended the roles of all the people in his life. Following a visit with his birth family where he played with an older brother, he told his adoptive father: "I really like that boy; he is a funny guy." This early awareness of something special between these two brothers offered a glimpse into an important relationship that continues to this day. At such an early age, they recognized in each other something familiar and comfortable.

Four years after this boy's adoption, his parents adopted a three year-old girl who had been born in China and had no available connections to birth family. Watching this little girl with her brother's siblings leaves one wondering what she thinks about all these children who look so much like her brother. The siblings, however, welcomed her and have treated her as a "sibling" from the beginning. She plays and interacts with her brother's siblings, but as an adolescent, she is aware of standing out physically, as the one who does not look like anybody present.

The boy placed with the first adoptive family has had a very difficult time socially; he has been treated for mental illnesses with genetic links that are evident in the behaviors of his birth father and one sister. He states that he feels most "normal" when he is with his birth siblings and feels accepted by them, as opposed to the difficulties he experiences in other peer settings.

He has been raised in a Jewish family. At his recent Bar Mitzvah, he spoke of both his adoptive family and his birth family—how they are different and what he has gained from each. His birth siblings, along with the birth and adoptive fathers, hoisted him over their heads on a chair for the traditional dance out of the synagogue. It really did take *all of them* to move him into manhood. A year later, his sister was Bat Mitzvah, and her brother's birth family was there again to carry her forth.

In a recent gathering of this extensive clan, attendance includes the now 14-year-old, first son placed for adoption and his 13-year-old sister; the oldest birth sibling in her thirties and her five children; the next oldest sibling in her mid-twenties and her two toddlers; the 17-year-old birth brother of the adopted son, and an older female cousin from the birth family. This cousin and her family are active participants in this expanded family. The second boy placed for adoption and his family were present but did not participate as the second adoptive family is more private and has been more tentative around their full participation in this extended clan. The limited participation of this young man in the discussion triggered some very strong emotions among the siblings regarding the importance of these connections and the "unfairness" of his parents' decision. They didn't blame his exclusion on their brother; they were angry with his adoptive parents and each took this "affront" personally.

Meeting the Challenges and Gleaning the Benefits

Setting boundaries between the adoptive parents and the birth parents was challenging at first due to poverty, life planning, and homelessness. The birth family moved several times during the pregnancy, each requiring the physical and financial support of the prospective adoptive family. Crisis seemed to surround the birth family. The prospective adoptive family needed assistance in defining their role during these early hard times.

One sister, who was 11 at the time of her brother's placement, struggled to find ways to identify her feelings about the adoption. She once asked, "If that is my brother's father, who is that man to me?" She was angry and devastated by the adoption. She needed to place herself in her brother's adoptive family. At the recent gathering, she shared "If I couldn't find my place in their family, then, it wouldn't work for me." She also worried about what this meant for her future. "I was a kid; I had to know they had ownership of me in some way also, in case my family placed me for adoption."

Many of the children shared that they like explaining their family system to others and like being part of an atypical family. When the question arises: "How many brothers and sisters do you have?" the adoptee answers, "More than I can count on my fingers."

The siblings' relationships have evolved over the years. The older brother closest to the first-placed boy shared that initially he did not really like his brother's adoptive family, but has felt more comfortable with them recently. The oldest daughter was bereft and angry at the thought of having her sibling placed outside of the family: "That is my brother;

I will take that baby." Over time, she has seen the wisdom of the decision, *because* all the siblings have had the opportunity to stay connected. "That has made all the difference."

The birth of an additional child who could not be placed with the first adoptive family, created a more complex family system, particularly since the two families have different beliefs and practices around openness in adoption. The adoptive child placed first shared that he "doesn't have a little brother to beat up. It isn't fair." The adoptee in the second adoptive home would have been that little brother. This was a reflection on how adoption disrupts sibling birth order. These three intertwined families differ in religious beliefs, lifestyles, economic opportunities, and cultures. These differences could have easily overwhelmed the participants. From the siblings' perspectives, what has allowed them to create such a healthy extended family includes the following:

- *Don't sweat the small stuff.*
- *Be open to the good and the bad.*
- *You lead different lives; be open and honest about feelings and needs.*
- *If you can't share stuff with family, who [sic] can you share it with?*
- *It is what it is; enjoy the ride; things keep changing.*
- *One of the hardest issues is the difference in lifestyle; watch judgments on all sides of the family; practice accepting difference.*
- *You learn a lot when you have a diverse family.*
- *We totally prefer it this way.*

The children all agreed that they could not imagine life without knowing each other. The oldest birth sister stated that her brother's adoptive father is a mentor to her; she seeks him out for advice; that the entire adoptive family is important to her whole family. Both older sisters add that the adoptive families have brought some "functionality" to their often chaotic family. The son placed for adoption first shared that he did not think it would have worked out well for anyone if he had not been placed for adoption. He is now able to understand the vulnerability of his birth family at the time he was born. "It is good that they split us up. Having different families, and, then, coming together as one worked out."

TWO BROTHERS

Separation, Loss, Reunion, and Breaks that May Never Heal

The final story illustrates the challenges for siblings whose connections are first severed. It becomes clear that the long-term costs of separating siblings can have a life-altering impact. Even with later reunion, the damage may indeed be so deep as to prevent complete healing for the sibling relationship. This is the personal story of author Ciynthia Roe. Coauthor Sharon Roszia joined Roe's family for an afternoon session of reflection, tears, and expressions of hope and love.

Child Protective Services detained two brothers when they were ages two and four. Their birth mother, struggling with alcoholism and drug addiction, had left them in the care of a companion who, in turn, left them unattended outside a bar. They were then placed with their maternal grandfather and great-grandmother. Two years later, they were re-detained. The older of the two boys was placed in the adoptive home of his therapist and her husband. (They did not include the younger brother due to his hyperactivity and developmental delays.) The younger was placed in a residential treatment center. The child being adopted recalls this as the day he was placed in a car with his possessions in a garbage bag and told he was going to his new parents, whom he was expected to now call "mom and dad." He does not remember being told what was happening to his little brother or why they were not moving together. The younger boy remembers it simply as "the day I lost my brother."

The older sibling explained that he decided from the beginning that these new parents were "never really going to be my mom and dad because I couldn't trust them," since they had "cost" him his brother. The younger boy recalled that during his time in the group home, he imagined his older brother as a super hero who would come to rescue him or "beat up any kids who picked on me." The younger brother's journey went from placement in the group home, to a subsequent placement in a foster home, and the eventual return to the group home. There were infrequent supervised visits between the boys with social workers carefully monitoring the visits. They observed a close bond between the brothers. One of the social workers facilitating and monitoring these meetings was the author, who would eventually become his adoptive parent. Initially, the boys seemed able to resume their relationship where it had left off; playing with one another with an ease and comfort that was not evident in any of the younger boy's other social interactions. Over time, this effortless reconnection diminished, and the time between the meetings was greater. The older boy's adoptive parents were uncomfortable with much contact between the two families, declining invitations to attend activities, either for the family together or just the boys.

As it became clear that the younger sibling was to be adopted, the older boy's family became less available for any sort of contact. The younger boy would talk about his big brother frequently, expressing intense sadness at the separation and requesting visitation. He would frequently cry himself to sleep, longing for his brother. When the boys were 13 and 15, a visit was finally arranged. However, the older boy's adoptive parents placed so many limitations around the meeting that the brothers' time together was prematurely ended. The younger boy expressed such deep sadness and intense anger following this truncated visit that he asked to have a picture of the two brothers removed from his dresser. Over the next three years, the siblings had no contact.

The winter holiday months had always been difficult for the younger boy, since the original separation occurred during that time period. Therapy helped somewhat, but the recurring themes of loss and of grief were annual challenges. November 2000 was no different. The older brother had turned 18 the previous May, and the family had heard nothing from him or his parents in three years. As the younger boy's seasonal depression emerged, his family decided that the time had come to find his lost brother and, if possible, bring him into the family. The older boy's adoptive mother did return the phone call this time, leaving a message that she was no longer her son's "keeper," and that he was living in another state. A computer search generated a rapid reply from the young man. He was homeless, and "just happened" to check his email on the same day that his brother sent his "searching for my brother" message. The young man hitched a ride to join his brother's family for Thanksgiving. The experience of being with these two brothers, was "like being in a bubble, filled with joy and sadness." The brothers were initially tentative with one another. When they had last met, they were little boys; now they were young men who had difficulty even recognizing each other. There was awkwardness between them that continues to manifest itself. The older brother has difficulty trusting and attaching to other people, due to the early break from all the people who had meaning to him, most importantly his younger brother. He reflects on the abrupt severing of his day-to-day relationship with his younger brother as a major contributing factor to his reluctance to get close to others.

Since the reunion weekend, and with many struggles and challenges, the older boy came to live with the brother's family, "divorced" his first adoptive family and was legally adopted into his brother's family at age 23. The young men were once again brothers, both legally and emotionally. Additionally, the boys have been reunited with their birth mother and have gotten to know two younger siblings. The boys had known about these younger siblings through information supplied by social services. This younger brother and sister, raised by the birth mother, grew up not knowing that they had two older siblings, until the grandmother told them in anger following their mother's relapse into addiction. The oldest brother had remembered seeing his baby brother during a visit with his birth mother at the Social Services office when he was six years old. That son, raised by the birth mother, has stated that somehow he always felt that he had older brothers, even though every time he asked his mother about it, she denied their existence. He doesn't understand how he "just knew."

The lack of genuine, ongoing connection over time among these siblings has created an emotional fragmentation that may never fully heal. The losses for each sibling become clearer over time. Had these relationships been available to all four siblings when they were children, they might have had the opportunity to grow their connections through various developmental phases and could be enjoying the gifts that siblings bring to adult life. The lack of opportunities to practice their relationships seems to have left them unable to reach out to one another. Without the opportunity to grow up together and experience normal sibling rivalry and the working out of their relationships at a deeper level, as adults they seem unable to risk conflict for fear of losing each other again. Relational authenticity appears to have been sacrificed to a fear of loss. Having said that, when the parents facilitate meetings among the siblings, they are like "peas in a pod," talking, playing, and socializing, as if no time has passed.

In the "truth is stranger than fiction" department, during this same time frame, author Roe and her sister, who grew up in foster care and were sometimes separated, were contacted by a brother they did not know existed. The dynamics that have played out between their sons and their siblings are manifesting themselves as the author and her sister try to integrate this "new" sibling into their lives. The author's sister's response has been characterized by polite but disconnected interactions with the newly found sibling. Although they can talk on a superficial level, the author's sister continues to be hesitant to welcome this sibling into the already established relationship with the author, while the author struggles with ambivalence about the difficult work of building a relationship between adult siblings who did not share a childhood connection, but are physical mirror images of one another and their shared mother.

CONCLUSIONS

It has been our professional experience that adoptive parents may offer the following reasons for avoiding ongoing contact:

- *I'm not comfortable with that other family.*
- *It's too difficult to maintain the relationship at a distance.*
- *I have so little time between my own family and my work.*
- *We have nothing in common.*
- *The children don't want to see their siblings.*

Professionals have the skills, knowledge and opportunity to educate, support, and confront the fears and beliefs of adoptive parents. The authors' experiences emphasize the fact that children deeply respect their parents for preserving their linkages in spite of the challenges or maybe because of them. As social workers confront the difficult and complex needs surrounding the placement of siblings, the preference must be to keep them together whenever feasible. If the siblings must be separated, consideration of placement with families that will commit to ongoing contact can dramatically minimize losses for children. These newly created clans often need professional support while they define their roles and obligations to each other and to each other's children.

It is important to explore with children whom *they* consider to be their brothers and sisters, as important connections can be overlooked if we hold to a narrow definition of "sibling." Concrete plans for maintaining connections are helpful and reduce anxiety and fear. As professionals, we play a crucial role in keeping children informed as to what is happening to them and their siblings. They also need to know why those decisions are being made and by whom. This strategy can decrease anxiety for all the children being affected by the placement. Consideration of the developmental level and cognitive skills of the children must be factored into the explanations. Documentation about the decisions made must be given to the families and preserved in the case record. Information that cannot be digested by a seven-year old may be more palatable and relevant to a 20-year old. Birth and adoptive parents may need help in explaining the circumstances of the separation to the children. Families also need assistance in expressing and confronting differences in discipline techniques and safety issues. Professionals can help the adults create boundaries, not walls, that separate the siblings from each other.

The authors suggest that there is a need to alter the language used to describe contact among siblings. The word "visit" connotes a court- or case-plan-ordered requirement to which there is some natural resistance. The authors suggest the word "meeting" or "gathering" because it allows for a more natural and healthy relationship to blossom. Each of the three stories reflects on overnights, holiday gatherings, sharing of birthdays and even vacations. The contact among the families has become as normal as any other family get-together. Families who have different life styles, religious beliefs, and economic opportunities need support to find ways to play together, share rituals, and explain one anothers' beliefs without judgment or efforts to change the other family. Homemade gift items, shared picnics, free museums, camping, and BBQs all build the memories that allow children to "feel at home" in one anothers' lives. Professionals may also find themselves helping families address crises and inequities in life. When a child's siblings are in need of food, shelter, clothing, or medical care, the adopted child may worry and feel guilt that she has resources that her siblings do not. If the birth and adoptive families have built connections surrounding the siblings, the siblings become like nieces and nephews. Consideration needs to be given as to handling these needs as they would with any other relatives.

Many professionals are approached by adopted adults for help in reconnecting with their separated siblings. Adoptees, regardless of their age or developmental stage at placement, have a deep need to know their siblings. The connection to siblings who entered the world after the adoptive placement may be as important in this expanded family experience as those with the ones who are present at the beginning of the adoption.

Adopting children from different birth families can create differences in extended-family contact, due to proximity, birth-family availability, and, occasionally, safety concerns. Families must understand that adoption can be inherently unfair for children who come from entirely different beginnings. Parents may feel uncomfortable dealing with the pain of one sibling who may not have what another sibling has, but avoidance of this inequity does not change that truth. The birth family of one child belongs to the *whole* adoptive family and plays an important role for the child whose birth family may not presently be available.

People and secrets do not stay buried. Siblings will seek each other out with or without their parents' help. The outcome is more likely to be positive when the children have the support and guidance of adults who love them and of professionals who understand the importance of these connections.

SUMMARY

These three stories illustrate the widely different long-term outcomes that occur when siblings either have the opportunity to grow up knowing each other or must deal with the mystery of broken connections and the hard work of reconnection. Whether siblings always like each other or not, those of us who have not been impacted by adoption have had the opportunity to know them and to make decisions as adults as to how we choose to relate to them. Adoption is complex and has the potential to create expanded kinship systems that are inclusive of all the people who are important to a child. The children who are beneficiaries of their adoptive and birth parents' willingness to address, support, and nurture these relationships treasure these expanded families. Professionals also have a role in supporting these systems. Families built around sibling needs represent the best of what it is to be "family." These families have transcended individual needs and fears for the benefit of the children. Over time, everyone gains a larger circle of security by constantly deepening healthy connections to other human beings.

CHAPTER 8

The Creation of a False Self: A Survival Strategy for Siblings of Wounded Adopted or Foster Children

Michael Trout

When any family greets a new member, things change. When that new member has experienced neglect, abuse, isolation, or other trauma—even prenatally—the changes experienced in the family he joins are likely to be tumultuous. This transformation is profound enough for the parents, who—while sorely challenged—have resources of language, emotional expression, social support, parenting knowledge, and a sense of mission that carry them a long way.

For other children already in the family, however, a dilemma presents itself: the dilemma of unfairness coexisting with nobility of purpose. The family is doing something wonderful for a child who may be described as needy and without a family. When the other children in the family begin to experience striking shifts in family energies, parental patience, rituals, and standards of behavior—all in the context of general chaos and (sometimes) personal assaults from the new, adopted sibling—it may occur to the child that something terribly unfair is happening. But with a cause so noble, how can one speak out? The perpetrators of such unfairness (from the child's perspective, these perpetrators may be seen as the parents) are usually without awareness, much less intention or malice. So how can one complain, when mommy and daddy can't help it? The results in the family may include improvements in the altruism and empathy of the other children, overt resentment, or development of a false self as a coping strategy.

To discuss the matter pulls observers into the dilemma: How can we even speak of the matter of unfairness, when the results for the children are so varied and when there is such an underlying drive in the family to *do good*?

WHO ARE THESE CHILDREN ABOUT WHOM, AND FOR WHOM, WE SPEAK?

1. *Those caught in the maelstrom:* the children who, while usually asked, often feel as if they have no real vote, with no felt sense of authority or control in the matter, and were asked to open their hearts, maybe their bedrooms, certainly their souls, their parents' wallets, and the family's energy, to accept a child who, just a few minutes before, was not there: a child born somewhere else, an unpredictable child, a child who looks different and certainly behaves differently, a child unaccustomed to the culture of this once-serene family, a tornado that seems to be spinning the house right out of Kansas. We speak in this chapter of, and for, the children who were asked to love someone whom previous parents may have found "unlovable." We speak of the children who found some way to share their space, their toys, and their parent's affection, and who tried to pretend the cost was reasonable. We speak of the sixth-grader who smiles when her adopted brother (whom she begged mom not to bring with her to middle school registration today—but what kind of a mean little girl asks her mom for such a selfish favor, when she knows perfectly well that mom can never find child care, even for a few minutes, for a child like *him?*) screeches at the top of his cute little lungs in the middle school hall, as the little girl wonders if she will ever recover a shred of dignity again. We speak of those who grow up pretending they are not seething with resentment about the adopted sibling whose attachment disorder evokes such sympathy from the ladies at church, but who sneaks into their bedrooms birthday after birthday, breaking the new music box or gutting the new doll.

2. *Those who went through it themselves, once:* the children who are, themselves, adoptees, and who watch as even more "special, chosen children" are adopted into the family. They wonder: "Was I not special *enough*?" Or, "My parents always told me how much trouble they went to in order to find me. They told me they chose me from this huge bunch of children they could have had. Now that they have me, they want to do it *again*? Have I done something to disappoint them? When did I become just another kid in the house?" One adult adoptee, who was raised with two adopted siblings, says she never felt cheated by being in the middle of these two brothers, who were always in trouble. But she remembers how

hard she worked to assure her status in the family, using the strategy of hyper-compliance. She recalls never complaining about anything. Now nearly 40, it is still important that she never upset anyone. "I'm always convinced that I am the problem, so I just try harder to be good....I'm careful to never state my opinion, if it's different from the person I am with at the moment." For this little girl, complaining—perhaps even acknowledging—her worries, her insecurity, her sense of unfairness, would have been impossible.

3. *Those who can't begin to compete with the neediness of the adopted sibling:* the children whose adopted siblings had a particularly rough start in life—in an orphanage far away, or in an abusive American home. The stories about the new child in the family evoke great sympathy from all members of the family, but they also limit the range of acceptable responses from the bystander children when the adopted sibling begins to turn family life inside out. Sometimes the other children manage to stabilize their feelings and can say, "I hate his autism, but I love my brother." Others struggle: "It's like a three-ring circus day to day. There is no way you can ignore somebody who has motor oil for blood, doesn't sleep so nobody sleeps. There's constant turmoil in the house. It's not a healthy way to grow up, but you learn to cope with it. You either accept it or you flail against it your whole life" (McHugh, 2003, p. 69).

The remarkable foster/adoptive mother who coauthored *The Jonathon Letters* thought there would be a great many ways to answer the simple inquiry, "How are you?" from a friend, after the family took Jonathon into their care. She wrote:

In January we took custody of a new foster child. It has been the most difficult time of our lives. We have been to the edge of insanity and back about a million times. He has Reactive Attachment Disorder, and relationships are not very comfortable or easy for him. He has pushed every button we have, and tested every limit. Many of our belongings have seen better days, and so have we. I have been bruised, scratched, kicked and spit upon. This child has caused friction between Paul and I, and there was no peace in our home... We got to a point where we did not think we could handle another day, and were not sure what to do. We came really close to calling the social workers and telling them that enough was enough. Instead, we decided to adopt him.... (Trout & Thomas, 2005, p. 130)

Do the other children in a family such as this get to vote on whether to follow all of this chaos and internal strife with a decision to *adopt* the cause of it all? And if they do vote, is it a real vote, or a vote designed principally to cause as little extra trouble as possible? If depression and early pregnancy begin to show up in such a family, following the decision to invite the whirling dervish to take up permanent residence, are we likely to see a connection?

Not infrequently, in such families, we hear parents saying that the other children in the family love the foster or adopted child "to death," that they look after him all the time, that they proudly think of him as one of their own. Are the other children always *able* to give voice to their full range of feelings about the new foster or adopted child? Can parents accept that these sibling feelings are not mutually exclusive: that resentment may *coexist* with love; claiming may *coexist* with an impulse to reject; joy about what wonderful things the family is doing for the wounded child may *coexist* with profound questions about whether the price is worth it.

Rare is the birth child like Ben, who speaks openly:

Dear Betsy,

I can't believe Mom and Dad ever adopted you. They already had five of us and did not need you. Why couldn't they be happy with us? What did we do to deserve you? You've made my life a living hell. My friends won't come over because of you.

I have to lock up my room because you steal. Mom and Dad are mad every day. Every day at school you cause trouble, and kids say "Is that your sister?" I wish I never met you. I can hardly wait to be eighteen so I can leave and never see you again. (Keck & Kupecky, 1995, p. 148)

WHAT IS THE RANGE OF POSSIBLE RESPONSES TO THE ARRIVAL OF A NEW FOSTER OR ADOPTED SIBLING?

Some siblings may grow up to be more altruistic, to have higher humanitarian sensibilities, or to have a greater sense of closeness to family (Lobato, 1990; Powell & Gallagher, 1993). These children turn out like Tim, whom I interviewed for this chapter, whose parents took in many foster children, and adopted two of them: one when Tim was about two years old, and one when he was about 10. A big, gentle college senior now, Tim said that the biggest impact of all these children moving into (and many of them out of) his life was that his definition of "family" has been broadened. The adopted sibling just two years younger is schizophrenic and pregnant. Tim's facial expression, as he speaks of her, leaves little doubt that he will be an attentive and tender uncle. The adopted sibling 10 years younger turned out to have a host of disabilities and diagnoses, and turned family life into nonstop chaos. Yet Tim's primary feeling, he reports, is awe about this deeply troubled adopted brother. Tim wishes he didn't remain, to this very day, vulnerable to being hurt when his whirling dervish of an angry brother says, "I hate you!" for the zillionth time.

Sometimes the altruism is mixed with other, hard-to-define feelings. Tim's pregnant, mentally ill, adopted sister, now age 21, was also interviewed for this paper. She denies any resentment about her troubled adopted baby brother: "When he came to us, I knew he needed somewhere to go, and that he was in the right place." Later in the interview, she added: "He hits a lot, and I don't appreciate it, especially now that

I'm pregnant. I can't do anything about it, tho', because he's my brother."
As if to reassure herself about her own safety, and that of her unborn
child, she said, "He wouldn't try to kill me or anything." And then, as if
wrapping the topic up into a container of safe feelings, she concluded,
"He has lots of things on his mind that he can't control. It's just something
I had to deal with. His needs are way more than mine... You have to just
get over it, until later..." Just when I thought the interview was over,
she said it again: "It is difficult, sometimes. I just have to get over it."
I suppose we will learn more about this soon-to-be-mom's altruism and
sensitivity as we watch her bring her own child into the world, and take
up the task of loving him.

Some siblings may experience caregiving—especially when it conflicts
with plans with friends—as burdensome. The result may be resentment
(of the adopted sibling, or of whatever it is that makes him exceptional).
Or it may be passive compliance (capitulating to the demands and the
impossibility of effectively resisting them while retaining status in the
family). Or it may show up as depression (feeling trapped in the exceptional situation, with no way to expend the libidinal energy, no way to
express the feelings acceptably). Or it may express itself in acting out, at
school (where it is safe, because the family will not be further disrupted).

There remains a greater likelihood that girls—especially older sisters—
will be given more responsibility for the adopted sibling, especially if that
sibling has a disability (McHugh, 2003). While the data are equivocal about
boys, there is some evidence that they tend to be more confused about their
caregiving role—especially when the adopted sibling has a disability
(Seligman & Darling, 1997), and angrier about the way things work in the
family (Harris, 1994), with greater difficulties, later, in getting along with
people (McHugh, 2003). One 36-year old, interviewed for this chapter spoke
of "feeling maternal, right away," when the family adopted a baby boy,
when she was three. Now, more than three decades later, she recalls the time
when she was bathing him, at his age one, and she turned on the hot water.
It burned him. "It was horrible. I'll never forget it," she said. When Hurricane Katrina came, in 2005, this same adopted brother—now all grown
up—was in Mexico. She was overcome with a sense of responsibility to go
get him, to somehow save this 33-year-old man from the storm.

Some children may respond by trying to achieve, in order to make up
for the inabilities of the sibling. These children try to compensate, and to
restore family joy or pride or harmony with their own elevated performance in school or in community activities or church work. Yet others
may sabotage themselves just at the pinnacle of success, to avoid looking
as if they think they're superior to that wounded sibling.

On the other hand, some children may decide to compete with the
sibling, to become exceptional in their own right, to win back some of
the attention lost to the wounded, adopted sibling. They may accomplish

this by becoming sick, by acting out at school, or by developing difficult-to-diagnosis problems (tics, lethargy, constant coughing). Or they may regress, using "baby talk," or may lose manners or toilet training. This particular expression of their hunger for a place in the family may come back, involuntarily, throughout life, whenever the now-grown child feels momentarily unimportant at work, or unloved at home, or unseen in a group (Trout, 1983).

Some may express resentment openly, but covertly: by disconnecting equipment critical to the wounded sibling, telling the social worker that the wounded, adopted sibling cries in her sleep and isn't happy here, or by arranging for the adopted sibling to get into trouble for an infraction the sibling did not actually commit. Or they may experience a reaction formation, turning these aggressive feelings inside out, expressing them as exaggerated displays of affection for the wounded sib (Trout, 1983).

Some children may respond by becoming the "fairness police": edgy about any real or imagined slight in the family, watchful about how many presents each child gets at birthday time, or whether the wounded sibling is assigned the right number of chores or whether his performance on chores is monitored properly. Such a child may counter the "specialness" of the wounded child by regularly noting, "I *am* your *only* daughter, you know!" while being careful not to say anything that would make her vulnerable to being accused of insensitivity to the wounded sibling's "specialness."

Some children learn to walk on eggshells in the family, trying not to drain the family's already-depleted resources further by making trouble, or by having feelings they imagine the parents could not handle.

Some, like three-year-old Josie, whom I interviewed and observed, with her family, for this chapter, seem unrelenting in their admiration of the older, adopted sibling. Adopted herself, when her brother was almost three, she is the butt of his physically aggressive attacks over and over, every day. She rarely complains. Instead, she picks herself up, laughs (when she is not hurt too badly) and moves gingerly back in her brother's direction, hoping he will be gentler, next time. That he never is (according to the parents) doesn't seem to have much impact on the cycle of approach, attempted engagement, being knocked over, and trying again. That she will eventually develop her own coping strategies—maybe even finding ways to express her own aggression—seems likely. What, exactly, will become of her soul, her feelings about boys, her boundaries, her thoughts about having her own baby, someday? This is less clear.

When both children in a sibship are adopted, the dynamics resemble those in sibship groups of birth children, but there are important differences. When the two adoptees are, themselves, related by blood, they may cleave to each other fiercely, as if they are secure in their membership in their own club, which helps to balance feelings of never being fully qualified to join the club of the adopting family. They may persist in styles of relating to each other that were functional in the family in which they were born, long past the time that those styles, those hierarchies, those little protective pacts, are needed in the adoptive family.

When the adopted siblings are biologically unrelated to each other, they may struggle fiercely against each other, as if individuation must also be made from the other adoptee, not just from grown-ups. They may compete, trying to find out who is *most* special, whose characteristics are *most* attractive to the adopting family, or even to their new culture. Two boys of nearly the same age, adopted from the Philippines at the same time, were treated as twins by the adopting parents, even though the boys were biologically unrelated to each other. They spent the next decade and a half distinguishing themselves from each other. When one showed interest in learning the dialect of his native land, the other resisted. As one became affectionate to the adopting family, the other resisted both the expression of affection, and receipt of it. When one tried sports—soon finding himself on the team coached by the adoptive father—the other mocked him, declaring that sports were stupid.

Some children get caught up in the drama, romance, and even religious significance of adopting a new child into the family. One adolescent girl, interviewed for this chapter, talked about the huge but self-imposed pressure she felt to "not interfere with this once-in-a-lifetime chance for them [her mother and stepfather, who had been unable to have children together] to be happy." A year before the adoption of her baby brother, she found a can of baby powder in her Christmas stocking. She felt the message was clear: "Get yourself focused on this thing that is the most important thing in our family right now, which is to get a new baby." Throughout the year, as papers were filled out and people came to the house to interview the parents, and as dinner-time conversation was about nothing *but* the parents' dream of adopting, she remembers how easy it was to comply with her parents' request that she pray every day that a baby would be found. Her nagging thought—"Why aren't I *enough?*"—was always followed by self-rebuke about having such a selfish question in her heart.

She recalled the awful tension of the interminable pregnancy-that-wasn't. She said, "In pregnancy, things change slowly and predictably. In our situation, tho', we didn't know when—or even *if*—the new baby would join us. It could happen any second. It was nerve-wracking to have diapers and baby clothes sitting around *way* before we even knew if a baby was ever coming." As the time arrived for her parents to travel to Russia to complete the process and bring a new brother home, she became ill, and was hospitalized. Her surgery for an intestinal disorder occurred while her mom and step dad were several continents away. She was discharged on Halloween, and her parents returned with the new family member on November 16. She reports being so happy about him, but then described the feeling of being ignored by her happy-but-distracted parents at the airport. She tried to assert to this interviewer that she understood it was natural for them to be focused on nothing but the baby. But she had been ill, and had had surgery, and they weren't there, and she wanted something—even in the face of the celebrations about bringing home her adopted brother. When I asked her what it was that she wanted, she looked down at the kitchen table, picked at something invisible on the table surface, then began to weep. "I wanted them to wrap their arms around me, and never let go." Now, a year later, she acknowledges that it has all felt "like a tornado," that she cries a good deal, and that her folks are sure tired. But she also says she would like to adopt a child, someday, along with having birth children.

So the range of responses on the part of the "other" children in the family is wide and deep. I propose that a small group of these siblings simply stuff their feelings, deny their resentment, and find no way to say out loud the awful thoughts inside. I propose that we worry about these quiet bystanders, these compliant siblings who wonder why their lives have changed so much since the new adoptee arrived, but who reprimand themselves for having such naughty thoughts, for being so insensitive. I propose that they may reach for a strategy that holds both defensive and survival properties.

The "False Self" As Survival Strategy

It would be risky business, indeed, for a child to express feelings the family might interpret as negative about the wounded sibling.

The observant child already notices the depletion of parental energies. How much sense would it make to deplete them further?

The observant child already notices the status awarded the wounded sibling because of her being exceptional (due to her special needs, or her sympathy-evoking past). How much sense would it make to throw a spotlight on his own wellness, his own history of having been well-loved, by making a fuss over the huge changes in his status since the new child came?

The observant child sees the compassionate looks on the faces of people in the community when they hear the wounded sibling's story, and the attention afforded the parents due to their having taken the child in. How much sense would it make to try to compete with that with a "What about *me?!*" whine?

The observant child already feels to her core the freezing that occurs around the dinner table when the wounded, adopted sibling melts down. How much sense would it make to add to the tension by demanding some structure and peace at mealtime, or saying out loud that she can't breathe anymore?

The observant child does, of course, have a number of choices for adapting to the situation:

- becoming hyper-compliant
- competing on the special needs front
- becoming altruistic
- containing the seething resentment
- overdeveloping a sense of responsibility for others
- expressing hostility covertly
- becoming the "fairness police"
- walking on eggshells
- showing an unrelenting admiration of the adopted sibling
- identifying with the aggressor
- identifying with the protector
- identifying with the drama
- identifying with the religious significance
- acting-in (depression) or acting-out (getting into trouble)

This author proposes that there is an additional adaptive response chosen by a few children, either instead of—or in addition to—one or more of the above: the development of an alternative self, a more-acceptable self, a "false self."

This sort of false self may have some of the characteristics of—but may not be the same as—the "fictive personality" spoken of by Jay Martin in his report on his patient, Terry:

I see myself now as a patchwork collection of defenses, tricks. Illusions, with no dignity. Now, since the defenses are tumbling and we get nearer to me I get more and more concerned: there isn't a me. The sum total of me is in the illusions, and I'm afraid when we strip all these away, there won't be anything there...I was born and my body grew, but I never did...I became convinced I was nothing and so I had to acquire pseudo-characteristics, costumes, whatever it was "they" wanted from me. So every new relation is a challenge to see how long I can confound them—showing images or reflections of things that don't exist. It's like I died when I was a child—but that's my secret. I came back to fool everybody. Everybody thinks I'm still there—but I do it with mirrors. How deep is a reflection? (Martin, 1988, pp. 31–32)

This defense is less pervasive in the makeup of the person than Helene Deutsch's "as-if personality," which is characterized by inner feelings of unreality and relational bonds that are devoid of warmth (Deutsch, 1942).

Nor is this adaptation as mechanical and detached—or as desperate, with respect to the person's struggle to maintain an illusion of reality—as the "false self" described by R.D. Laing (Laing, 1965). And when Ernst

Kris spoke of the "personal myth" as a secret, hidden life based on early, unconscious fantasies (Kris, 1975), he suggested a different defensive structure and purpose than that under consideration here.

When Winnicott used the term "false self," he was speaking of a delusional process, in which a child fuses an identity out of bits and pieces of ideas and emotions, in an attempt at rebuilding a collapsed relational world (Winnicott, 1965).

Anna Freud's description of "altruistic surrender" (Freud, 1966, p. 125) captures some of the function of the adaptive response under consideration here. She describes the child's indirect pursuit of gratification, through projection of his wishes onto another, then identifying with the gratification the other person experiences. Speaking of a patient who was a young governess, she said, "It looked as if her own life had been emptied of interests and wishes...Instead of exerting herself to achieve any aims of her own, she expended all her energy in sympathizing with the experiences of people she cared for. She lived in the lives of other people, instead of having any experience of her own" (Freud, 1966, p. 125).

The false self of which we speak here is one that is created for specific purposes: to reduce chaos in the family, to conserve the energy of the parents (by not causing them further trouble), to attract parental interest in the "non-squeaky wheels." The child observes the behaviors and traits which are most likely to achieve these results, then creates an identity for himself or herself which is most correspondent to those behaviors and traits.

WHICH CHILDREN WILL MAKE USE OF THIS UNCONSCIOUS STRATEGY?

Daniel Stern's research would suggest that the likelihood of a particular child responding with the development of a false self to the extraordinary internal struggles experienced when a new and exceptional adopted child enters the family rests on the child's own infancy experiences with attunement. Misattunements in either direction ("under" or "over") tend to encourage the baby's imagination about what the parent wants, and to orient her in the direction of supplying the parent with the response that seems to produce attunement (Stern, 1985).

Masterson teaches that any formulation of a false self pivots on the child's experiences with his mother's approval for his steps toward individuation, a process most developmentally profound in toddlerhood: "The key is the mother's ability to perceive and to support the child's emerging self, for without that support, he experiences her as withdrawing and disapproving of his efforts" (Masterson, 1988, p. 54). If the mother withdraws approval for separation-individuation, an abandonment depression may arise in the child. "However, since the mother rewards regressive clinging, the child defends himself against the depression by regressive compliance..." (Masterson, 1981, p. 106). From Masterson's perspective, the die is then at least partially cast, as the child has "learned to disregard, even fear, parts of his potential self that he realized threatened his mother" (Masterson, 1988, p. 55). In other words, if the child reads, as a two-year-old, that his primary parent might punish his efforts at establishing himself as a separate person, he may—in order to avoid the punishing abandonment—simply make a decision to never go there again: to not assert the self too much, to be good, to be compliant. When, years later, an enormous stressor challenges the family, that child may be more prone to again set aside his true self, and adopt a false one that he believes likely to restore order and gain parental approval.

When we consider these specific developmental vulnerabilities to the development of a false self, we wonder about what it means to have lost the first mother, oneself. If a child enters the separation-individuation phases of development with a history of sudden and permanent loss of the first parent, does that change the child's readiness to take the risks of rapprochement, to tickle the tail of the dragon by moving away from the second mother emotionally? If so, does being an adoptee, for some children, increase the likelihood of using the false self strategy later in life, when the child encounters the threat of another abandonment? Some have suggested that this is part of the lifelong quest for the adoptee (Brodzinsky, Schechter, and Henig, 1992), even without the unusual stressors of standing by—and trying to respond appropriately to—the family's adoption of another child.

IS THE CREATION OF A FALSE SELF AN ILLNESS?

Virtually by definition, narcissism is involved in the adaptive measures taken by these children. Order has been lost in the family; status has been lost by the child, and the child is trying to restore both. More to the heart of the matter, the child's unconscious may have discerned that the only route to preservation of parental interest—perhaps even parental bonds—is through assumption of an identity which the child understands to be of greatest value and importance to the parents. According to Kohut, "the narcissist is at heart unsure of himself even as he wants to convince others of his supreme value" (Kohut, 1977, discussed in Martin, 1988, p. 137).

So a kind of narcissistic terror may underlie a child's assumption of a "false self," under these conditions. But does this make the child who assumes the identity of "devoted caregiver"—a role which assures her some kind of valued identity in the family—a narcissist?

We worry about the woman in her mid-30's, spoken of earlier, when we see how terrified she became when she momentarily fell short (at her age three) in carrying out this role, when she accidentally turned the too-hot water on her adopted baby brother. And we see how pervasive this clinging to the role of responsible caregiver has become, for her, when we learn how desperate she felt to save him from Hurricane Katrina, several decades later. But she also developed herself as a nurse, as a pianist, and as a thoughtful, intelligent adult. Did she give up too much? When she tells us that, as a grown-up, she still struggles with whether her voice matters, and with her own culpability if anyone else is troubled, we fret about how much energy was stolen from her development of a fully individuated self. Then we wonder: what choice did she have?

So this author does not propose that the struggles of the child with a wounded adopted sibling—especially when disability or "exceptionality" is part of the adopted sibling's portrait—constitute a true developmental disorder. But we also wonder whether it is developmentally and clinically realistic to imagine that such defenses can merely be used when needed, and later discarded.

Winnicott refers to an alternative version of his "false self" as occurring in normal development, as something akin to taking on a social manner. He suggests that it is adaptive (Winnicott, 1965). Can this strategy—and the narcissism that underlies it—be merely temporally defensive, not constituting a personality disorder?

Martin takes the discussion to an even more specific level by suggesting that there are both "bad fictions" (which lead to isolation, denial, or grandiosity, and which block spontaneous experimentation) and "good fictions" (which may be adaptive, because they compensate for loss and tend to prepare us for action) (Martin, 1988). When a child adopts the fiction that all of her feelings for her adopted sibling are warm and positive and that she really doesn't mind when he sneaks into her bedroom and smashes her favorite music box on her fifth birthday, she may be trying to compensate for the losses she has already experienced. She may be fending off additional and inevitable losses that would accrue if she complained too much. That she is being strategically narcissistic may not necessarily suggest that she is becoming ill. It certainly suggests that she has come to know how the family works, and how to get some bare minimum, at least, of what she needs. But is she able to simply pull up her old self, at will, when the stressors end or when she grows up?

Only later may we discover whether she has permanently suspended her own independent perspectives on the world (in favor of whatever ones are most popular to the group in which she finds herself, at the time—including the marital dyad she may enter, someday); or whether she will use the individuation opportunities of adolescence to loudly proclaim what she could never "say" before; or whether she will become physically or emotionally sick, herself, later, to pay her family back and to inspire the devotion that she once saw lavished on her adopted sibling; or whether she will enter adult life determined to find her *own* voice, and more than a little sensitive about whether it is, on any given day, being heard.

CONCLUSION

So, do we have a clinical problem to solve, or simply a family dynamic and a developmental issue to notice? If we begin to take note of such family dynamics, and the developmental issues that sometimes emerge from them for other children in the family, we may find ourselves shifting the focus of the supportive work we do with foster and adoptive families, in favor of making sure we ask about the "non-squeaky wheels" in the family and of not necessarily accepting pat answers to the question. Indeed, if the family is too quick to suggest that all the other kids in the family are "fine," we might take it as a tip-off to look further. Perhaps we will become attuned to just how much energy it must take to be "fine" in a family marked by this much chaos and this much energy heading in one direction, and ask a second time about how the other children are: who they're dating, what their favorite (or most difficult) school subjects are, how much attention they are giving to favorite hobbies (or whether such hobbies seem to have fallen by the wayside lately).

In the noticing, do we become better equipped to offer guidance to foster and adoptive families, about these other children in the family? Perhaps we become more assertive in proposing a slight restructuring of family energies, so that *each* child gets uninterrupted, private time with at least one parent on a regular and predictable basis. When the parent replies that there are just not enough hours in the day to accomplish this, perhaps we help that overburdened parent make the case to the other parent that the other parent's long work hours are taking a real toll on the family. Or perhaps we help the parent find respite care for the wounded child, or mentors for the other children in the family. Perhaps we talk about some of the meanings of depression in children, including the possibility that it implies the turning inward of whatever emotional energies the child has, lest the child express them outwardly and cause trouble for the family. Perhaps we talk about some of the meanings of acting out, including the possibility that the child is trying to get noticed, is trying to "speak," or is even trying to compete with the wounded sibling.

In the noticing, do families gain permission to set firmer standards for fairness, and consider more fully the implications of allowing the new child—for all his wounds, for all his hurts, for all the ways he deserves parents who can go all the way for him—to create pandemonium in the family? Perhaps we inquire about how differences in family standards for different children (the fact that Tommy is allowed to eat his mashed potatoes with his hands, but others must use utensils, for example) then listen empathically as the family explains why the wounded adoptee must be given more leeway, then reiterate what this must feel like to the other children—all the while knowing that the aim is not to even the field for all, but to give understanding to all. Perhaps we propose that the health of the wounded child really does rest in the overall health of the entire family, so that it becomes the caseworker's business to uphold the needs of each member: *both* parents, and *every* child in the family. Perhaps we suggest, indeed, that nobody gains if the family collapses under the weight of the wounded adoptee's behavior and neediness.

And in the noticing, do we, ultimately, become better caseworkers on behalf of the wounded children we placed in foster care and adoption in the first place? Perhaps, when the needs of all members of the family are more equally attended to, the family system does not just survive, but truly thrives.

CHAPTER 9

"Suddenly, Sisters!": Sibling Adjustment in Reunion

Susan Thompson Underdahl

As an adoptee reuniting with my birth family at the age of 25, I was surprised to find that the most overwhelming and confounding aspect of my reunion experience was the relationships with my three younger siblings, all of whom were teenagers at the time I came into their lives. In the years that have since passed, I worked to gain both personal and professional perspective on the dynamics of those relationships: the connections we initially set out to form and the final ones, the *real* sibling-ships that ultimately evolved between us.

Since the mid-1980s, many publications have focused on specific aspects of sibling relationships, including juvenile siblings (Boer & Dunn, 1992), siblings across the lifespan (Cicirelli, 1995), sibling rivalry (Klags-brun, 1992), sibling loss (Fanos, 1996), cross-cultural comparisons (Zukow, 1989), and other aspects of siblingship.

In most adoption literature, however, the focus is on the members of the primary triad: the adoptee, birth parent, and adoptive parents. This is particularly true in literature related to search and reunion. Consequently, in the excitement that often characterizes reunions between birth parent (s) and an adopted individual, the intense emotional responses of siblings may be overlooked. The purpose of this chapter is to explore potential adjustment issues and seek constructive solutions.

No one is surprised when a young child reacts emotionally to the birth of a new sibling; it is commonly expected that he or she might have emotions ranging from love and acceptance to jealousy and anger at being displaced. Yet little research within the adoption literature addresses the reactions of a sibling to the arrival of an adoptee, an arrival that changes the family structure and relational dynamics in profound and irreversible ways. In the face of this dearth of formal studies, much of the information contained in this chapter is the result of informal interviews or contacts made through adoption reunion Website forums, where reunited siblings come together to support each other and work to make sense of their experiences.

For their 1989 book *Birthbond,* Gediman and Brown conducted intensive interviews with 30 birth mothers who were engaged in post-reunion situations of at least six months' duration. They also spoke to the other family members involved in the reunion and made the point that, "Finding a brother or sibling you never knew can be as significant as finding a parent" (Gediman & Brown, 1989, p. 186). Even when they do not reconnect with birth parents, adoptees who learn of siblings they have never met are often driven to meet them. Gediman and Brown suggest that there are several important factors that make for an easier transition between siblings compared to the elder generation. First, the relationship between reunited siblings is less likely to be affected by the circumstances of the adoption itself. Second, siblings tend to be closer in age; not only may they have more in common, but they likely grew up in an era where they are less affected than previous generations by stigma associated with unplanned pregnancy and out-of-wedlock birth. Finally, Gediman and Brown suggest, the intensity of the connection may be more manageable if it is diffused over several siblings, as compared to the emotionally charged primal relationship with the birth parent(s).

While these positive dynamics may certainly impact the relationship between "new" siblings, my own experience is that the road to siblinghood may not always run smoothly; and comments from online contributors seem to agree, according to the following internet forum comments:

Adoptee: I am struggling to make headway with my birth sister; I had a lot of naïve expectations and no real insight into the effects of the adoption on us all. I feel really mixed up about having a birth sister and not knowing how to build a realistic relationship with her.

Sibling: I have so many mixed emotions I don't know what to think or do. I felt out of place. I was no longer the oldest. I was no longer my mother's firstborn. I questioned everything of my childhood.

Adoptee: Does anybody else out there have situations with siblings they have found? How are you handling your relationships, especially if they are really up and down and going nowhere? Sometimes I just wonder if it's all worth it.

In my own reunion experience, I discovered to my great surprise that, a year after my birth, my parents had married, and were still married at the time I reconnected with them. Consequently, my "find" was not only an intact set of birth parents, but three younger full-siblings. As with most adoptees who search, I had prepared as best I could for the emotional impact of meeting my birth mother, but had not even considered the conflicted, confusing emotions my siblings and I would experience while trying to adjust to this new version of "family."

FAMILY SYSTEMS THEORY: THE WHOLE IS GREATER THAN THE SUM OF ITS PARTS

Webster's dictionary (1996) defines a system as "a group of elements that interact and function together as a whole" (p. 685). In the field of psychology, family systems theory applies this concept to the family unit, suggesting that the family must be understood by appreciating not only the individual elements, or members, but also their relationships to each other. The family is a system of interconnected and interdependent individuals, none of whom can be fully understood in isolation from the system. An apt metaphor for a family is a mobile, in which altering the position of one element or adding a new one will shift the balance, and the family may or may not be able to reestablish equilibrium.

Within families, each member carries special characteristics that define him or her in relationship to the other members. One family member might be considered the "moody" or "smart" one, the "complainer" or the "entertainer," but these designations are made in comparison to other family members. Characterizations as elemental as being "the baby of the family" or "the only son" become aspects of our core identities and, if we are to believe birth order studies, may even shape our personalities.

Appreciating the subtle importance of these inter-relational characteristics makes it easier to imagine the impact of finding oneself displaced from one's lifelong role as "the only son" or "the funniest one." If another son, or someone who is more amusing should arrive, what impact might this have not only on the displaced individual, but on the structure of the family as a whole?

SPECTRUM OF FEELINGS IN REUNIONS

In any reunion, siblings bring their own histories, personalities, and insecurities to the table, any or all of which might potentially impact the relationships that evolve. The potential range of emotional reactions is broad and impossible to imagine, but some common ones described by siblings going through reunion include the following:

Excitement—at the prospect of welcoming a new sibling

Resentment—at the intrusion or at the attention paid the adoptee

Anger—at having no control over the arrival of an uninvited sibling

Jealousy—of the adoptee's relationship with the birth parent(s)

Confusion—over ambivalent feelings

Protectiveness—toward the birth parents or other family members

Guilt—about not feeling entirely positive about the reunion, about being "kept," about not feeling wholeheartedly loving toward the new sibling.

Gediman and Brown (1989) found that sibling reactions ran the gamut from "extremely close" to "guarded and perfunctory." Some of these relationships were such emotional roller-coasters that they created crises for the birth mother, who then felt guilty all over again.

RELATIONSHIP STAGES AFTER REUNION

As with any life-changing adjustment, adoptees and siblings in reunion may expect their relationships to progress through a series of stages, as proposed by Turesk (2004), a Texas-based marriage and family counselor in her comments to an online forum. Turesk suggests that not everyone goes through every stage, nor must the stages be experienced sequentially or without expectation that they will occur more than once. Nevertheless, she lists the following:

Honeymoon Stage

- This stage is characterized by euphoria, joy, and a sense of being on top of the world.
- Effort is made by parties to find similarities and common interests.
- Much time is spent together in an effort to "catch up" on each others' lives with exchanges of photos, letters, and gifts.
- Each family member is preoccupied with the other party.
- There may be minor negotiating about relationships.
- Some uncertainty exists about place or role in each others' lives, frequency of contact, how to introduce each other to family and friends.

Time-Out Stage:

- One party may pull back to evaluate and process event, possibly causing confusion, anger, hurt, frustration, or fear.
- Problems in relationship may develop due to lack of information and few societal references to help parties understand what is happening.

Showdown Stage

- There may be a confrontation of parties to address the status of the relationship and its future.
- Fear of rejection may be present in one or more parties.

Disengagement Stage

- Parties not only pull back, but actually move away from each other.
- These actions may create feelings of anger, loss, and rejection.
- This stage is more likely to occur if expectations are too rigid and/or differences between parties too great.

Solidifying Stage

- Earnest negotiations between parties begin as to all aspects of future relationship.
- Increased emotional stability in the relationship results as consensus is reached in many areas.
- New relationship roles emerge, ongoing renegotiation as needed.

In my own experience, virtually every one of Turesk's "stages" has manifested over the many years since my reunion with my birth parents and siblings. The "Honeymoon" was appropriately blissful; "Time Out" was disconcerting; and the "Showdown," fortunately, had a positive outcome. While my brothers and I have slipped into "Solidification" with seeming ease, "Disengagement" has occurred in my relationship with my birth sister, and to date, at least, seems irreversible.

FACTORS THAT MAY IMPACT THE REUNION EXPERIENCE

We are left to wonder about what factors determine whether a relationship with a reunited sibling has a positive or negative outcome. We can begin with the most obvious.

Preexisting Awareness versus 'Have I Got a Surprise for You!'

It can be understandably difficult for a birth mother to tell her other children about the existence of a surrendered child, and the question of *what* and *when* to tell make it a discussion that is easy to postpone...until the prospect of a reunion makes it necessary. Consequently, sometimes birth siblings know about the placement from childhood while, in other instances, they are the last to know.

We all prefer to have our company call ahead; it is easier to accommodate the arrival of an expected guest than one who drops onto the scene unannounced. This dynamic applies as well to the reunion experience, in which the addition of a new family member will restructure the entire family system. Having pre-awareness of the existence of a surrendered sibling allows the others to conceptually integrate that brother or sister into the family "mobile," even if only in an "absentee" capacity. While the surrendered child may have been previously viewed as a remote part of the system, reintegrating him or her will be less of a disruption than adding an entirely new element.

"Shock" was definitely the word I would use to describe my own reaction to learning I had three new siblings and reportedly their response was much the same. Not knowing that we had siblings who were missing from our lives definitely made it more difficult to integrate that idea into our conceptualizations of where we came from and who we were in relation to each other.

Age of Siblings

It stands to reason that a sibling who is still in the home may have more adjustment issues in response to the arrival of a new family member than one who has struck out on her own before contact is made.

Maturity and life experience may allow older siblings to view the reunion as adding something positive to their lives, not taking anything from it. A sibling who has already established a family of his or her own may be less invested in maintaining the historical view of the family of origin and will likely be less threatened when the boundaries change to admit another member. Furthermore, lack of history with the adoptee can allow the opportunity for the new siblings to establish a relationship as adults, without the competitive "baggage" of siblings raised under the same roof.

There are negative possibilities as well—older siblings may react adversely as their view of the family is forced to change. Involvement in their own busy lives can make it inconvenient or difficult for an adult sibling to engage with the reunited brother or sister, and some adult siblings may be reluctant to invest the time or emotional energy necessary to create a bond with a new family member. Additionally, the very lack of shared familial history may make the fact of their siblingship feel superficial and unreal.

I was in my mid-twenties and my three siblings were all teenagers when we connected for the first time. Their lives revolved around friendships, school activities, and where to spend Spring Break, whereas my world was filled with a husband, graduate school, and concerns about embarking on a career. The age difference might not have been much in years, but we were worlds apart in terms of perspective. These dynamics made it more difficult to connect; looking back, I can see now that at moments I felt something like an older cousin who happened to be passing through town.

Gender

Our sexual identity is an important aspect of not only who we are, but of our identification in the family. How many times do we say "I have two sisters and one brother," or "I'm the only girl"? Consequently, there are potential adjustment issues related to whether the returning child is of the same gender as the sibling or not.

The arrival of a same-sexed sibling creates potential for feeling bumped out of one's position as the "favorite son" or "oldest daughter," or competition to be the best. On the positive side, siblings of the same gender at least start out with that in common.

One might imagine, then, that the arrival of an opposite-sexed sibling creates other potential issues. Clearly, research is needed to enable a better understanding of the role that gender might play in sibling reunion.

Birth Order or Position

Oldest, middle, youngest, only...birth order studies tell us that each position fosters unique characteristics in siblings. Issues of identity that relate to birth order may prove important, especially in a family where the reunion removes an oldest child, or an "only," from those unique positions. The following comments from online respondents illustrate the influence of birth order on reunion experiences:

Birth mother: "I think it was helpful that since my birth daughter was coming into a family of all girls, she still had her status as the only daughter in her adoptive family."

Adoptee: "I could tell that my sister has been really affected by my becoming part of her family. Although she wasn't the oldest, she's always been the only girl. I can tell she feels a little funny, even though she tries to act happy."

There is no doubt in my mind that gender and birth order initially influenced the evolution of my relationship with my birth sister. Until she was informed of my existence, part of her identity was that of the only girl in the family, and my arrival on the scene meant that her position as "daughter" had to be shared. To make matters worse, she was an intelligent, goal-oriented, 16-year old who planned to attend college to become a psychologist; imagine the impact on her when her older sister arrived, just completing my PhD in psychology. Not only had I barged in unannounced and elbowed her to the side, I'd already achieved all her goals. Is it any wonder we've had a rocky road?

Full- versus Half-Siblingship

Gediman and Brown (1989) reported no significant differences in relationship dynamics between reunited siblings who shared both parents or those who shared only one parent. It would seem likely, however, that the arrival of a full sibling could potentially feel more threatening to a child's established position. On the other hand, sharing both parents is strong common ground on which to establish a future relationship and gives the siblings an opportunity to bond over shared heritage.

Domestic versus International Adoption

Domestic adoption reunions are complicated enough, but in the case of international adoption, the reunion with biological siblings often occurs across cultures. Hollee McGinnis, MSW, is a Korean adoptee who started life as Lee Hwa Yong and spoke eloquently in 2006 during a presentation entitled "Siblings in International Adoption" about meeting her birth family at age 24 and finding she has five half-siblings:

When I returned home from my first trip to Korea, I was terribly confused. My family had suddenly expanded to include people living thousands of miles away on the other side of the world.(McGinnis, 2006)

Seemingly insurmountable distance is one factor which may make it seem difficult or impossible for reunited birth parents and adoptees to form a relationship, much less siblings. Even though reunited families in the twenty-first century enjoy advancing technology that makes communication easier, those luxuries may not be readily available to all parties in the reunion experience, due to any combination of location, economic, or educational limitations. Issues as fundamental as cultural or language differences may be obstacles to overcome, and American adoptees often find themselves primarily responsible for driving the relationship forward. There may be other challenges, as McGinnis notes:

I also know of one Korean adoptee who had reunited with her birth mother, and had a full biological brother with whom she was committed to building a relationship. Over time, she realized her brother wanted her to bring him and his family to the United States, and to provide financial support.

In Daughter of Denang, the documentary of a Vietnamese adoptee's experience reuniting with her birthfamily, she is similarly repulsed by the financial assistance her Vietnamese family immediately expect from her.

McGinnis goes on to say that in addition to the language barrier, one factor that strains the relationship between her and her half-siblings is her birth mother's poverty.

Reaction of the Birth Parent(s)

Reunions are complicated emotional roller-coasters for everyone involved; the twists and turns for birth parents may include joy, fear, guilt, sadness, loss, and even unresolved anger. Fearful of adding to the birth parent's emotional burden, siblings may feel protective and hide their own ambivalent emotions. Gediman and Brown (1989, p. 190) state, "Some [siblings] protect the mother from their feelings by putting on company manners or by not telling her their complete feelings about having a new person in their midst." Similarly, an adopted person in reunion reported on an online forum, "There are a lot of emotions going through me right now. My parents are on such a high that I don't want to bother them [with my feelings]."

When an intense connection arises between the birth parent(s) and the surrendered child, it may also feel like a threat. Kept children and their parents share history and baggage that inevitably color their relationship, whereas the new arrival enjoys a clean slate as well as, initially at least, unconditional acceptance. This dynamic is illustrated in comments expressed to the author by persons in adoption reunion whom she interviewed:

Sibling: My mom never acted like this before. Doesn't she love me that much?

Sibling to Parent: If you still love me as much, then why do I feel less important?

Sibling: My dad told me that he has already booked his ticket and is flying out to meet her face to face. And I was jealous. I kept thinking, "Would he do that for me?"

Adoptee: As much as I love my birth sister, she does complicate things. My deepest longing is for my birth mother, and sometimes (my birth sister's) jealousy of our relationship makes that a challenge. But I understand that, because jealousy rears its head in my heart too.

My own reunion experience included an intense, raw connection with my birth mother that surprised even me. We were mirror-images of each other, as close as sisters from our first meeting, and I felt disconcerting levels of jealousy toward my siblings when my birth mother was leaving after a weekend visit. Looking back now, I wonder how my birth sister felt. Did she compare her own mother-daughter relationship to the unconditional love and positive regard that grew instantaneously between her mother and a virtual stranger?

Circumstances of the Surrender

The question of why a birth parent or parents relinquished their child to be raised in another family is the most profound issue in the adoption experience and one that cannot help but become important in reunion. Kept children may experience feelings of guilt at being "kept" while their sibling was surrendered, or may feel resentful if they perceive the surrendered sibling somehow had more opportunities than they themselves did.

Family Communication Styles

Family communication style was an issue that became important with several reunited siblings I interviewed. This primarily became an issue in conflict, as family members and the adoptee worked through difficult issues. The worst problems occurred if the family tended to resolve conflict in a manner that was completely unlike that of the adoptee: as we all know, some families engage in conflict resolution through direct confrontation of the issue while others tend to avoid confrontation and uncomfortable dialogue. When a surrendered child has been raised to handle challenging situations in one fashion while the family of origin copes differently, this can pose a barrier to connection between siblings. One birth mother expressed this to me in these words:

The hard part is that my birth daughter was raised in a family that handled problems in a passive-aggressive way, while we are the "yell and get it out, then give each other a hug and be done with it" type. In her family, it is not uncommon for family members to not talk to each other for a month…that is unheard of in our house. So there have been some run-ins over things like that. I've threatened to lock people in a room until they work it out.

Individual Differences

Whatever their similarities, siblings bring their many differences into these new relationships, including their own histories, personalities, strengths, and insecurities. Within the same family, two members may react completely differently upon reuniting with a surrendered sibling. One may immediately accept the reunited sibling as her new brother or long-lost sister, while for others a bond may take longer to form, if it ever does.

ADOPTIVE SIBLINGS' FEELINGS

Siblings reunited after adoption are not the only ones who are affected by the search and reunion of their surrendered brother or sister. Often the surrendered child has other siblings with whom he or she was raised, siblings who are not immune to the fact that their brother or sister now has found "new" family members.

An adoptee's siblings may feel

– angry about the search because they feel it is a disloyalty to the adoptive parents
– confused and rejected by an adopted sibling's desire to search
– threatened by the potential for the adopted sibling to bond more closely with her birth parent's children
– "left behind" when their sibling has reunited with his or her birth parents.
– less inclined to proceed with their own search, fearful of hurting the adoptive parents further.

I was fortunate enough to have been raised in a loving family with three wonderful adoptive siblings, and during the years after my reunion, they asked me many questions about my "need" to search that suggested they had struggled with feelings of confusion, of rejection, and of concern for my adoptive parents. My adoptive brother is also adopted, and although he professes to having never been interested in searching himself, I am now left to wonder whether my adoptive parents' devastated reaction to my own search made *his* less likely. Did I inadvertently take away his choice in this way? I sincerely hope not.

POSITIVE REUNION EXPERIENCES FOR SIBLINGS: GUIDELINES FOR FACILITATION OF SIBLING REUNION EXPERIENCES

Understanding the reactions of adoptees and siblings in reunion is not just an idle exercise; it creates an opportunity for all involved to facilitate these experiences in very real ways. To the degree that we are able to provide support, allow for personal expression of feelings, and assist in the resolution of issues, we can help reunited siblings establish a framework upon which to build positive long-term relationships. The following guidelines are offered to facilitate positive reunion experiences.

Invite Communication about Feelings

The most basic principle of communication in reunion is to acknowledge that everyone experiences a broad and ever-fluctuating range of emotions, both positive *and* negative. As a facilitator or birth parent, this can best be accomplished by the following actions:

- *Initiating discussion* about competing feelings and *acknowledging* that they are an important facet of the reunion process
  - *So, what do you think of all this?*
  - *What is the best and the worst part of all this for you?*
- *Accepting* and *validating* feelings, rather than questioning or disagreeing with them.
  - *Thank you for sharing that with me; I wouldn't have guessed that you felt that way.*
  - *I can understand why you might feel that way.*
- *Creating a safe environment* for the expression of feelings
  - *It's important that you let us know how you're feeling about things.*
  - *I'm interested in hearing more about how this is going for you.*

Message: All feelings, even those that are confusing or difficult to talk about, are acceptable and will not be judged.

Validate and Normalize Feelings

Just as important as expressing one's inner feelings is having those emotions placed into a context that makes them less threatening or confusing. It can be very reassuring to hear that *it is quite common* for siblings to experience ambivalence, jealousy, and even anger when a new family member arrives. For example, statements similar to the following may facilitate this validation of feelings:

- *Most people in these situations feel a little confused by all this. How about you?*
- *Do you feel angry sometimes? That's pretty normal, actually.*
- *It must seem like . . .*
- *Sometimes I feel overwhelmed by everything that's happened. How about you?*

Message: The road to establishing a new family order is going to have some potholes. It is normal to feel frustrated, frightened, or overwhelmed at times.

Remember that the Passage of Time Can Change Things

No matter what the tenor of the early phases of reunion, things change over time. Relationships evolve and perspectives change, as the view of the family adjusts to include the reunited sibling. Recognizing that reunion is a process rather than a discrete event helps reduce the pressure that all parties put on themselves early in the reunion process, when the formation of a "bond" seems to be at a premium.

Adoptee: The best advice I got was to take things slowly.

Message: It is okay to take time to build a relationship. With commitment from all parties, the process will move forward.

Encourage Family Members to Seek Professional Assistance if Needed

When an individual or family in crisis seeks counseling, no one thinks it is strange, and there are few situations fraught with more raw emotion and uncertainty than a reunion of an adoptee and his or her birth family. It would stand to reason, then, that in some circumstances the individual members or family as a whole may need assistance in integrating the experience. In these situations, assistance by a trained professional or facilitator may provide the best chance for a positive outcome.

As an overwhelmed graduate student at the time of my own multifaceted reunion, I sought support from a therapist for the first time in my life. The hours spent in Dr. Doyle's office helped me to resolve feelings of loss and to learn to cope with the overwhelming emotions of unexpectedly finding an entire, intact birth family at the end of my search. I have no way of knowing whether any of my siblings sought out professional support, but I hope that if they needed help in sorting through their mixed emotions, they found it.

Message: We are not expected to resolve everything on our own; sometimes an objective third party can offer new perspectives, help us gain clarity, and assist in forming a vision for the future.

CONCLUSION

It is undeniable that the reunion of separated siblings poses many unique opportunities and challenges, and we are only beginning to learn how to guide siblings in navigating through these unique and life-changing experiences. My own life has been immeasurably enriched and complicated by my relationships with my siblings, and I would not trade the experiences we have shared. Through them, I have learned much that has contributed to my growth as a person, as an adoptee, as a sibling, as a friend, and as a psychologist.

In closing, the words of Hollee McGinnis, MSW (Lee Hwa Yong) convey the hope we all share:

Today I mostly communicate with my birth father's daughter.... I do not know where the relationship will go or how it will all unfold...but I believe we have many rich years ahead.

CHAPTER 10

Practice Strategies to Preserve Sibling Relationships

Deborah N. Silverstein and Susan Livingston Smith

Achieving and maintaining permanence for children who are without stable caregivers can be a significant challenge. This demand is especially daunting for professionals working in the child-welfare system. Achieving permanence for these children when they also come in a bundle of other siblings can be experienced as an insurmountable obstacle. In recent years, child-welfare professionals have met this challenge head on with multiple innovative and creative practice strategies and interventions. This chapter explores a set of core principles that each of these approaches embodies and describes several approaches in depth as illustrations of strategies that each form a different piece of the tapestry designed to preserve sibling relationships.

STRATEGIES THAT PROMOTE KEEPING SIBLING GROUPS TOGETHER IN PLACEMENT

Historically, preservation of sibling ties was not a priority in child welfare. Even today, there are many constraints in the realities of child welfare that make finding homes for large sibling groups and siblings who enter care sequentially very difficult. There is, however, a growing consensus among child-welfare and mental-health professionals about the importance of sibling ties. Concerted and exceptional efforts are now being undertaken to both promote clear policy that reinforces keeping siblings together, except when this practice is clearly harmful, and a system to hold professionals accountable for following that policy. In addition, training on sibling issues for all those who need to collaborate to meet the needs of siblings—foster and adoptive parents, workers, therapists, and judicial personnel—is being implemented.

BEST PRACTICE STRATEGIES FOR PLACING SIBLINGS

Strategies advanced by many in the field to more effectively address the needs of sibling groups include the following:

- Designating specific foster home resources for large sibling groups and offering incentives to hold them open for these placements
- Having contracts with private agencies to offer a specialized foster-care program designed specifically for large sibling groups
- Conducting a thorough social-work assessment of sibling groups as a whole and of each individual child
- Assigning all siblings to the same case worker, no matter when they enter care
- Providing for a review within the first week of placement to plan for reunification if siblings must be separated in an emergency placement
- When siblings are separated, placing them in the same school district and in as close proximity as possible, ideally in the same neighborhood
- Discussing sibling issues at regular case reviews
- Listing the siblings as a group with a picture of the entire sibling group when conducting child-specific adoption recruitment
- Recognizing that a visit with a sibling is a child's *right* and should never be withdrawn as a punishment or used as an incentive

RESOURCES FOR TRAINING ON PRACTICE WITH SIBLINGS

A key prerequisite for maintaining sibling connections is educating workers, child-welfare legal professionals, and foster parents about the importance of sibling relationships and strategies for safeguarding them. Two excellent resources for helping professionals and foster parents understand the child's perspective on the importance of sibling connections and the painful impact of separation from siblings are found in Herrick and Piccus (2005; reprinted in Chapter 3 of this book) and Folman (1998). In addition, The Proceedings of the National Leadership Symposium on Siblings in Out-of-Home Care may be downloaded from the Website of Casey Family Programs (2002). Another excellent resource for agencies is a *Sibling Practice Curriculum* at the National Resource Center for Family-Centered Practice and Permanency Planning (NRCFCPPP), that utilizes materials developed by Casey Family Programs, as well as many other resources that are available on the NRCFCPPP site. Standards to guide workers in placement decisions and other practice related to siblings are included in the *Child Welfare League of America Standards of*

Excellence for Adoption Services (2000). Standard 3.7 specifies

> *Siblings should be placed together both in out-of-home care and adoption unless the serious, specific needs of one or more of the siblings justifies separation. The decision to separate siblings should be based on a carefully documented and reviewed determination that such separation is necessary.*

Separation of siblings in the initial foster placement creates ongoing obstacles to the youngsters' ever being reunited. Therefore, every effort should be made to keep sibling groups together at initial placement or very soon after. During intake, workers need to complete a thorough assessment of sibling relationships and of the individual children, including the experience and feelings of each child. Only in rare circumstances will these assessments lead to substantial clinical concerns that might require further evaluation and decision-making regarding separating siblings. However, if separate placements must be made for very large sibling groups, this early assessment will help guide decisions about which sibling relationships are most essential to the well-being of specific children.

In planning for permanency, families who can accommodate the needs of all siblings need to be recruited. The common belief is that it is hard to find families to adopt sibling groups; however, a study of over 10,000 children photo-listed for adoption in New York found that members of sibling groups on the listing were more likely to be adopted and were placed more quickly than single children. In fact, the time to adoption was decreased by 3.2 months for each additional child in the sibling group (Avery & Butler, 2001).

When siblings are separated in foster placement, workers often are put in the untenable position of having to make a permanency plan for the child that necessitates choosing the lesser of two evils—separating the child from a current foster parent who may want to adopt her in order to reunite the child with siblings *or* keeping the child with a foster parent to whom she is attached, thereby preventing her from living with her siblings. Sound practice dictates that children should not have to lose significant attachments, including those with siblings, regardless of the permanent plan.

A similar dilemma may occur when a sibling group placement is disrupted because the foster parents cannot handle a single child's behaviors, but the caregivers want to continue parenting the other siblings. Unless there is a compelling reason not to keep the siblings together, replacement of all of the siblings should be a priority goal. An alternative would be to have a temporary specialized therapeutic placement for the sibling with behavioral problems and to help the foster parents to work toward reintegrating this child back into their family. Some of the factors that are assessed in making such decisions include the duration, quality, and intensity of sibling relationships and weighing the possible long-term benefits of keeping siblings together *versus* potential attachment damage of separating them from the current caregivers.

HANDLING ABUSE AMONG SIBLINGS

When there is a concern that one sibling poses a safety risk to another, practitioners agree that a thorough assessment needs to occur. Distinctions need to be made between sexually reactive behavior (inappropriate sexual touching or fondling between children close in age who may have been abused themselves) and sexual abuse that is an abuse of power by one sibling over another. In reference to physical aggression, rivalry and hostility within the normal range of sibling relationships needs to be differentiated from physical abuse or victimization of a weaker sibling. Also, the severity of the abusive behavior needs to be assessed and a determination made as to whether the safety risks are moderate and can be managed through closer supervision, therapeutic parenting, and clinical treatment.

If there is significant abuse that does not respond positively to treatment or if the risk of reoccurrence is high, the abusing sibling needs to be replaced. Victimization of one sibling by another should not be minimized. Research indicates that the impact of sexual abuse by a sibling is just as harmful to the victim as sexual abuse by a parent or step-parent (Cyr, Wright, McDuff, & Perron, 2002). If the quality of the sibling relationship is sound apart from the sexual interaction, it may be possible to work toward reunification after a period of intensive treatment.

PRESERVING SIBLING RELATIONSHIPS WHEN THE SIBLINGS ARE SEPARATED

When siblings cannot be or have not been placed together, facilitating regular contact is critical to maintaining these relationships. States vary considerably in statute or child-welfare policies regarding protection of sibling rights to contact.

Two of the *CWLA standards of excellence for adoption services* (3.8 & 6.17) make recommendations for facilitating contact when siblings are in separate placements. They recommend that adoptive families should be helped to understand the importance of ongoing contact with siblings, former foster brothers and sisters, and others, and that the agency should make every effort to promote contact between siblings.

Often keeping up with this commitment becomes burdensome for workers and parents, and the contact lessens in frequency or ends altogether. Sometimes there are value, social, or cultural differences between families or other issues that cause parental discomfort with visits. Such differences need to be discussed and resolved.

Sometimes sibling visits stir up strong emotional issues in children, much like the intense feelings they may experience when visiting birth parents. Children need to be helped to express and work through these feelings; however, this does not mean visits should not occur. Visits may provide some opportunities for joint Lifebook work with siblings. Another suggestion may be to schedule siblings' therapy or other necessary appointments either jointly or back to back. They can be transported together and see each other before and after these appointments. Providing recreational opportunities for children and families also affords them natural opportunities to socialize.

ADDRESSING SIBLING ISSUES AFTER FOSTER/ADOPTIVE PLACEMENT WITHIN THE FAMILY

Facilitating healthy attachments and interactions among all siblings in foster and adoptive families, including all birth, foster, and adopted children, is an essential therapeutic goal. A single family may contain birth and foster children, as well as adopted children coming from different backgrounds or types of adoptions. Often negative interaction patterns can result when children perceive different statuses in their families or have special needs that require a disproportionate amount of parental attention and create stress for other family members. Other dynamics lead to tensions as well; for example, one adopted child may have extensive information about her background as well as ongoing contact with birth relatives, while another may have neither of these.

Two social workers in Minnesota (Mullin & Johnson, 1999) developed a model for supporting other children in families adopting special needs youngsters in the initial adjustment to placement. This model advocates having a separate social worker assigned to the sibling group to meet with them at strategic points. Preparing children for both the positive and negative changes in the family that are likely after a new placement and assisting parents in developing strategies to communicate and cope with all their children's needs is essential to achieving a healthy family equilibrium.

The following goals are important for addressing the needs of all children in the family:

- Encouraging children to share their thoughts and feelings and empathizing, in responding
- Providing opportunities for fun, positive interactions between children to promote and maintain attachments
- Promoting reciprocity among children in the family
- Finding ways to have meaningful one-on-one time with each child

- Teaching children problem-solving skills to resolve their own disputes
- Developing a support group for siblings, either informally or through an agency

Behind each strategy lies a core assumption—that children, however they are connected, deserve to have those connections honored and, if at all possible, preserved in some fashion. The following list of foundational principles, then, has been extracted from the program descriptions that follow:

- Always consider the need of siblings to be connected
- View siblings as vital to the fostered or adopted individual, at times more important than the relationship with birth parents
- Acknowledge sibling attachments as valid and that one sibling cannot be replaced by another
- Consider a broad definition of "kin-sibs," meaning siblings by biology, by fostering, by adoption, by affinity
- Strive to preserve sibling relationships through flexible, creative approaches
- Create opportunities for siblings to spend quality time together, away from adults who may have their own agendas and issues
- Allow for opportunities for sibling attachment to unfold naturally and without pressure

For some programs, these beliefs are clearly delineated in the program's mission, vision, or statement of principles. For other programs, the beliefs are simply inferred.

KINSHIP CENTER®: TRAINING PARENTS AND CAREGIVERS TO PRESERVE SIBLING BONDS

The first program to be highlighted is that of Kinship Center's Foster and Adoptive Placement Program. Kinship Center is a licensed, California-based, multiservice agency specializing in meeting the needs of foster, adoptive, and relative families. At the core of the agency's work is a belief in preserving families and family ties. Founded in 1984, Kinship Center has been at the vanguard of offering quality pre-service parent education and post-placement support, including an emphasis on preserving children's connections to their siblings. The program has a well-developed and field-tested curriculum that is taught by Master's level practitioners to families prior to the family's approval and certification to become a foster-adoptive family. Keeping youth connected to those individuals who have been, are, or may become important in that individual's life is a cornerstone of the agency's philosophy, training, and support. Siblings are defined in the broadest terms possible: someone the child or youth views as a brother or sister. Consideration is also given to siblings of whom the youth may not be aware, as well as future siblings who may be born into the birth family.

In the pre-service training that prospective foster and permanent families receive to prepare them to accept the placement of sibling sets or to remain in contact with families who are parenting other siblings of the set, families are led through experiential exercises to help them develop their own innovative interventions to connect siblings who have been separated from one another. Families are introduced early in their contact with the agency to the importance of maintaining a child's connections and to the broad definition of siblings. Families who are parenting separated siblings make a point of attending family events sponsored by the agency and encouraging the children to reconnect with each other and to enjoy crafts, music, and food. Kinship Center believes that the early and frequent emphasis on the importance of sibling relationships helps families to adopt large sibling groups, to keep siblings connected to each other, and to honor their children's connections.

CAMP TO BELONG: *GIVE SIBLINGS THEIR RIGHT TO REUNITE*

Lynn Price founded Camp To Belong to bring together siblings who are separated in placement, as she and her own sister had been. She describes the benefits of this camp in the examples that follow:

GOOD NEWS. GUESS WHAT? We had court yesterday for Brianna, Leonard and Raymond, and they're all moving in together next FRIDAY with their grandmother. Since camp they are different kids, Brianna especially. In court yesterday she was laughing and telling the judge about the mouse in her cabin and what a great time she had. When the judge asked her what she wants (before everyone was in the court room) she said "I just want to live with my brothers." Jessica Busch, Camp To Belong Volunteer Counselor and CASA—Court Appointed Special Advocate

Founded in Las Vegas in the summer of 1995, Camp To Belong (CTB) Summer Camp was created to offer siblings in foster care and other out-of-home care the opportunity to create a lifetime of memories. The program was the only one of its kind in the country and has since been replicated in other states and Canada. The Camp has reunited over 2000 siblings in its 12 seasons. Price is a staunch advocate for the rights of siblings both to know each other and to spend quality time together. As Price explains it "Brothers and sisters share life's longest relationships... sibling rivalry... sibling connection...siblings matter."

CTB is dedicated to reuniting siblings placed in separate foster homes or other out-of-home care for events of emotional empowerment, sibling connection, and shared memorable experiences. Summer Camps are the flagship of CTB connection. Unconditional accepting and loving havens invite youth 8–21 years old to indulge in spontaneous typical everyday or childhood moments with their brothers and sisters or carefully planned reunion activities. From the time campers arrive until they leave, relationships and emotions take them on a roller-coaster ride through a process that reintroduces siblings, builds acquaintances, and embraces and cultivates their connection.

Price describes the youths' reactions to their camp experience:

Youth of all demographics, ethnicities, religions, lifestyles, shapes, sizes, and geography arrive to a welcoming burst of applause from counselors who are united for the purpose of giving siblings their right to reunite. Some youth shout out loud with joy and enthusiasm as they run into siblings' arms or skip to their sides. With others, silence and hesitation prevail as they consider how to acknowledge a sibling; sharing quality time will bring comfort between them. The children come from the neighboring community or from across the country. They haven't seen each other in a week, or perhaps it's been ten years. They are in awe as they realize there are others just like them. They all have two vital things in common. They have a support team (care providers, social workers, CASAs, teachers, coaches, etc.) who honor their sibling bond. They have the individual courage to give themselves and each other a chance at friendship, sisterhood, and brotherhood.

An Art Therapy Expression experience allows campers to uncover and express their feelings toward their siblings in a creative way through structured arts and crafts projects. Art treasures are created by siblings to express their feelings to, and for, each other. In an environment where they can be themselves, the youngsters put aside their fears and honestly share pure sentiments of love and care. By making personalized sibling pillows, flower boxes, and leather bracelets, brothers and sisters provide one another with cherished gifts that are constant reminders of their week at camp.

"When you look at the stars at night, hug this pillow and think of me," writes one camper to her brother on her specially crafted pillow presented to him in front of all the campers.
    "I am going to share this scrapbook with everyone I know, so they'll know who my sister is," says one brother proudly displaying his book.

The Sibling Enhancement Program is designed as an intervention tool for sibling groups who are struggling to communicate with each other after lengthy separations. With innovative strategies, the experts facilitate positive, open communication and subsequent healing between brothers and sisters whose relationship has been fragmented due to their separation.

The Birthday Party Event is a favorite among campers. Brothers and sisters get to "shop" at a birthday store choosing gifts to give their siblings. They create birthday cards. At the huge camp-wide party, each sibling group receives its own birthday cake as everyone in attendance sings a chorus of "Happy Birthday." Siblings rarely have the opportunity to share this special moment together, so it is an exciting evening for all.

CTB melds camper, counselor, and activity composites for theme nights and inspirational forums. Belonging sets the framework. And, at the closing campfire, it is clear that Camp To Belong has made a difference.

"This is the first time someone has taken care of me," explained an 18-year-old teen mother who took care of her siblings growing up.

"I came here hating my sister. I blamed her because she reminded me of our mother who abandoned us. Now I know I don't have to blame her, and I love her," shared a 13-year-old young camper.

Time and time again, campers thank their siblings. Counselors thank CTB. Independently and collectively they call CTB life altering. Youth go home with a better understanding of the importance of their siblings while care providers and social workers strive for more accountability for placement together or communication when separated. Counselors renew their understanding of the value of sibling relationships and may improve their own sibling relationships.

Member camps are located in Maine, Massachusetts, Nevada, Ontario, and the Pacific Northwest, and new camps are being developed in Washington, D.C., Georgia, Southern California, Hawaii, Australia, and London. More information about Camp To Belong can be obtained by accessing their Website, http://www.camptobelong.org/.

HULL HOUSE: NEIGHBOR TO NEIGHBOR—SIBLING FOSTER CARE

Neighbor to Neighbor, developed by The Jane Addams Hull House Association, is a unique child-centered, family-focused, foster-care model. The program is designed to keep large (four or more) sibling groups together in stable foster care placements while working intensively on reunification or permanency plans that keep the siblings together. Neighbor to Neighbor began in 1994, serving targeted communities in Chicago where large numbers of children came into foster care. The program uses a community-based, team-oriented approach, including foster caregivers and birth parents as part of the treatment team. Trained and supported foster caregivers for large sibling groups are key to the model's success. Neighbor to Neighbor has professionalized this key role by placing these trained foster caregivers on the payroll of Jane Addams Hull House Association, complete with salaries and benefits. Foster families, birth families, and children receive comprehensive and intensive services including individualized case management, advocacy, and clinical services on a weekly basis.

There are four phases to mark the milestones and progress that families make as they move toward permanency. These phases of foster care start from the point of families being admitted to the program, and end with the achievement of some form of permanency for the sibling group. The phases are described in the following paragraphs.

Phase One: Placement and Stabilization

There are several important goals for Neighbor to Neighbor team members to achieve in Phase One, typically in 30 to 60 days. The first goal is to engage, establish trust, and build relationships with the birth families. The second goal is to assess the needs and strengths of the individual, the sibling group, and the family. This appraisal is an integrated assessment process to determine the family's current level of functioning, needs, and strengths. The third goal is to provide stabilization services designed to address immediate short-term needs. In many cases, improvement may require sibling stabilization therapy, clinical consultation for foster care-givers, crisis intervention, and behavior management planning. The fourth goal is service planning with the birth and foster families together. Birth-family services are designed to aid in reunification. The fifth goal is concurrent planning, because reunification is not always possible for every family. Concurrent planning begins at the onset of Phase One during Child and Family Team meetings. Alternative permanency options are discussed with the team members during this phase; however, it is made clear to all that the intent is to reunify families.

Phase Two: Intensive Services

Phase Two is the longest and most active phase of sibling foster care, lasting from two to 12 months. The foster caregiver's position was designed to be a temporary extension of the birth family and not a replacement. The birth parent and the foster caregiver are expected to work together in order to support the adjustment process of the siblings coping with separation from parents. Staff members have specific goals and responsibilities in working with families, and these goals and responsibilities involve teaching, role modeling, and supporting family goals.

Phase Three: Permanency

The ideal time frame for achieving permanency is 12 to 24 months. The amount of time depends on the complexity of the issues for a particular family, the size of the sibling group, and availability of community resources. Phase three is the stage where it is hoped birth parents are making positive progress toward goal achievement through a therapeutic process with their family therapist. For children requiring alternative permanency options, case managers implement the concurrent plan, which includes the introduction of adoption or subsidized guardianship services for the siblings. Children and their families (birth and potential adoptive or guardian) are prepared for the transition through a therapeutic process with their family therapist. For children being adopted or achieving subsidized guardianship, the goal may take longer depending on whether a resource is already identified, the siblings' behavioral needs, as well as the length of the legal process. The majority of the children in the Neighbor to Neighbor program achieve some form of permanency *together* as a sibling group and less than 1 percent reenter the system within 12 months of permanency.

Phase Four: Aftercare

Following reunification, the duration of Phase Four is typically six to 12 months. In many families with large sibling groups, the children may be returned home at different times to allow for a smooth transition and adjustment to reunification. The purpose of aftercare services is to wrap up any final work being done with the family, to solidify the various gains and progress made by the family, to provide services to prevent possible reentry into the system, to provide information and resources as families identify their own needs, and to monitor the safety and well-being of children until the case is fully closed in Juvenile Court.

In summary, Neighbor to Neighbor's phases of sibling foster care offer staff and family members milestones to work toward on their quest to achieve permanency for siblings. The phases of sibling foster care provide a context for this temporary and hopefully short-term life situation for families involved in the foster care system. There are eight handbooks available (http://www.hullhouse.org/) to offer comprehensive and practical guides to this model of sibling foster care.

THE SIBLING TRAIN

Regina Kupecky, therapist and advocate for siblings, suggests that professionals who work with foster and adopted children will soon realize that they are not only working with a child in the current family but with all the families in the past who are also an important part of the child's history, feelings, and issues. Ignoring the past immobilizes the children and family. Professionals often talk about the birth parent but miss the important issue of siblings.

One adopted child, for example, may have full birth siblings, half birth siblings, foster siblings, and adopted siblings—all of whom played a role in the building of the adoptee's identity and belief system. Internationally adopted children often have or will have birth siblings and often have other adopted siblings. Often the "unknown" sibling has a great impact on a child.

Kupecky illustrated the impact of the "sibling train" on children in describing her recent work with a young girl who was the only child in her adoptive home. However, she did have 37 siblings of various types (foster, birth, half, full) in her history, and some of them impacted her greatly.

The loss of her baby sister through the younger one's adoption is a major issue for this young lady who is having trouble attaching to her new family because she feels it will somehow lessen her attachment to her sister whom she has not seen for seven years but is so alive in her heart, mind and belief system. She does believe if she had taken better care of her baby sister (she was 5 at removal; her sister, 3) they would still be together in the birth family. She thinks about her baby sister every day. This is not unusual. Often the adults are waiting for the child to bring up a sibling; "she never talks about her" does not mean she never thinks about her. Often the child is waiting for the adult to bring up siblings. When they do not, the child thinks this means it is a forbidden subject, or that the adult does not care. In trips to five other therapists, no one had ever asked her about her siblings although many were in her Lifebook, and the child was very eager to talk about them.

This omission is unfortunately not unusual. When presenting on sibling issues a few years ago, Kupecky was shocked when several mental health professionals said they had never talked about siblings to their young clients. "I assumed" they said "if they were adopted as an only child, they were an only child." That is not true. It is estimated that a large proportion of foster children lose a sibling in the process of adoption, not always due to adoption but sometimes due to kinship arrangements or guardianships. International adoptees, too, often wonder about siblings left behind, or wonder if they have siblings. Many international adoptees also consider an orphanage or crib mate as a sibling, even if there was no biological connection. This wondering without facts is often more difficult to grieve.

It is imperative that professionals consider sibling issues in every case. The siblings can be historians, transitional objects, playmates, and comforters. They provide nieces, nephews, family, and sometimes, lessons on sharing and love despite dislike. They can also be abusive. Abusive behavior does not mean that the children do not love each other; it may mean they cannot live together. When a separation has happened, helping children grieve these losses is an important part of healing the hurt child. Not mentioning the siblings does little to help the sadness. Unacknowledged sadness is hard to grieve. Most children grieve through behaviors that are usually not helpful or positive. These behaviors are often triggered by the holidays, birthdays, or seeing children who look like the missing sibling. It can also be triggered by the family taking in another child. A child may think, "why take him when you didn't take my brother?" Blaming the adoptive parents for a decision made by social workers, judges, or kin is a common occurrence, and this also may make attachment difficult. Many people in the field have quickly gotten on the "openness" and "kinship" train, but, in embarking on these new movements, siblings are often left at the station. "Openness," occurs along a continuum which might include visits, letter writing, yearly reports, calls, or simply having a picture of the birth family. Seldom, however, is there an openness plan for separated siblings. Workers tell parents "He has two brothers he should keep in contact with," but when the brothers are moved to residential care, group homes, or adoptive homes, no one tells the other families where everyone is. When parents ask, their requests are often put in the "when I get around to it pile" and years go by with no visits because parents cannot locate the other children. Often, no one helps the adoptive parents with the communication, cultural issues, or other obstacles to maintaining contact. Some have even been told by institutions "You cannot visit, as they are no longer brothers since you adopted only one." We need all children's service providers on the sibling train.

Kinship placements are often wonderful resources, but again, siblings somehow may not be considered kin. If an aunt, unknown to a child, wants to provide a home, the child is often separated from his half-sibling with whom he has lived for 10 years. "Kin trumps all" may be a policy that separates siblings as one is adopted by an aunt who is not biologically related to another child in the family. Was the aunt asked to take both children? Was this decision based on the best interest of the child? In this case, adoption with his brother might be more a kinship placement even if adopted by non-relatives. We need thoughtful, case-by-case analysis of the sibling relationship. The children deserve that.

So what is a social worker, therapist, or parent to do? There are many techniques to try:

- The most basic requirement is to bring up the sibling issue throughout the entire process. At removal, look first for a foster home where they can be together. If not available, let the children call or email each other daily.

- Arrange times after a birth-parent visit for a sibling visit. Exchange pictures; invite them to events (like birthdays, plays, games).

- Let them go to the same therapist, so sibling issues can be addressed. Most foster children are reunited with family, so they will live together again.

- If the children are being adopted, bring up sibling issues in the matching meeting.

- Make a reasonable visiting plan. Do the families live far apart? Can the agency use a subsidy to help pay for visits?

- Look at foster and adoption training. How much is there regarding sibling issues, visiting, and sibling group adoption? Agencies may want to rework training for both workers and parents.

- Make sure Lifebooks and other materials passed along with a child have information and pictures of siblings.

When there is a split where children will not visit or siblings are unknown, parents can try the following:

- Mention the sibling on the birthday. "Your sister is 10 today. I bet she can ride a bike. She is probably in 4th grade maybe even 5th." "The other babies in the orphanage with you are six now, too." This helps the child "unfreeze" the sibling, as they tend to believe the sibling stayed the same age as when they last saw them.

- Ritualize the sibling birthday with a once a year "sibling unbirthday." A cake and a mutual talk among current siblings and parents about a missing sibling is the order of the day.

- Light a candle at church or include siblings in prayers to "watch over them." Some families buy holiday ornaments to add to family events.

- Open up some contact. Will the agency contact other families to secure a current picture, a phone call, a letter, a visit? Maybe they said "no" 5 years ago; maybe it will be "yes" this time. Families must not give up! Even if the answer is "no," the child appreciates the effort.

- If visits are allowed, parents should do them even if the child acts up before or after the visit, has not done homework, is disrespectful, or there is a long drive. Sibling visits are a *right* not a privilege, and should not be taken away as a consequence.

- If the child acts up after a visit, just acknowledge it. "I know you are sad to leave your brother. Most people talk about it instead of being mouthy to their mom. Let's talk."

- Once is not enough to talk about siblings. The topic needs to be brought up over and over and over and over.

- Help the child grieve. If the sibling died, go to the cemetery. If they can't visit missing siblings, some children like to plant a tree or bush to remember them.

- If siblings need to be separated, put the information in the file and Lifebook. Tell them why they were separated. Make sure the information is in the files explaining why and who made the decision to separate them. After all, more and more siblings are coming back to agencies to ask "Where is my sibling?" Make sure they have pictures and birth dates. Leave a trail for the future.

- Never say "never." Siblings, who were not "allowed" to visit, may run into each other at a doctor's office, on the soccer field, or at an adoption party.

- Add hope. Someday, the siblings may meet again. Some children like to make a scrapbook or box for the sibling. They put in school pictures, postcards they would have sent, holiday cards, and other mementos. One young lady did that and met her sister after 10 years. She presented the gift to the sister and said "I never forgot you." The sister said "I wasn't allowed to talk about you in my adoptive home (Her sister disrupted from the family). I never made you anything, but I thought about you every day."

Remember because of circumstances beyond the children's control, parents and social workers are making "parental" decisions. Professionals need to put themselves in the siblings' shoes. If something happened to you, would you want your children separated? Would you want someone to take extra time to make a good plan for your children? Do these children deserve less than your children? Until they are settled in permanency, these children are our children. We need to respect them and their sibling rights. The decisions we make for these vulnerable children will be life-long ones. We, as thoughtful professionals and parents, can do no less.

In sum, common themes run through all the highlighted programs—maintaining siblings' connections, whether the children are living together or not. The programs described here are just a few of the established and new programs committed to the preservation of sibling connections. So, whether it is parent education, camping, professionalizing foster care or getting on the Sibling Train, the time has come for a significant shift in social work and mental health to respect and honor children's connections to each other.

CHAPTER 11

Mental Health Strategies to Support Sibling Relationships: Nonverbal Interventions to Process Trauma and Maintain the Sibling Bond

Margaret Creek

Nonverbal interventions and sensory experiences support the processing of trauma and increase connections among siblings in foster care or adoption, whether living together or apart. Anecdotal successes are now being explained and supported by recent brain research focused on memory, trauma, attachment, and the right brain (Hass-Cohen & Carr, 2006). Thus, a basic understanding of the role of the right brain in the areas of memory, trauma, and attachment will help therapists, social workers, parents, and caregivers become more effective in their efforts to assist children in developing and maintaining healthy relationships with their siblings.

It is widely known that the first few years of life are a time of intense and immense brain development. The latest research shows that most of the growth in the first two years occurs primarily in the right brain, which houses the systems that are involved in processing emotion, in modulating stress, self-regulation, attachment, and the origins of the bodily based implicit self (Schore, 2003a). When a baby is born, the brain is full of 20 billion neurons that are not yet connected to each other. With every experience a baby has, a neural pathway is formed until each neuron could be connected to as many as 10,000 other neurons. The key to creating this massive web of connections is "experience." According to Siegel, "experience shapes the developing structure of the brain" (Siegel & Harzell, 2003, p. 34). In simple terms, each experience creates or alters connections in the brain. During these first 18 months to two years, the brain depends on very basic modes of processing using the systems of sight, hearing, touch, taste, and smell because the language centers of the brain are not yet developed. Preverbal, sensory experiences are stored in the right brain hemisphere in the form of "implicit" memory, a type of nonverbal memory. Implicit memories lack the ability to be accessed consciously and cannot be remembered in context (Siegel & Harzell, 2003). However, the experiences remain present in the form of stored emotions, bodily sensations and unconscious underlying assumptions that may come flooding back when triggered, sometimes out of context. This storage of nonverbal trauma explains why a toddler who was frightened by a dog may continue to feel fear years later when approached by a dog, even though no conscious memory of the initial incident exists. Implicit memories can also be formed at any stage of development if stress or trauma blocks the normal processing or encoding, essentially "stalling" the memory in implicit form.

A significant number of siblings in foster care and adoptive placements have suffered trauma and loss, either during their early preverbal years or under extreme stress. Because these traumas are stored in implicit right brain memory, they can be difficult to access, process, understand, and heal. Triggered emotions manifest in behaviors that can severely impair relationships, including difficulty with self-regulation, such as boundary violations, lying, stealing, impulsivity, aggression, and sensory overloads. Somatic complaints, mood disorders, flashbacks, and hypervigilence may also be prevalent. Siblings can have entirely different reactions to identical triggers, dependant on how their body stored a similar event previously.

Healthy relationships are critical to sound brain development. This rapid brain development that occurs in the first few years of life cannot happen in isolation, but requires the interaction of another person. Cozolino (2006, p. 81) describes the brain as having "experience-dependent plasticity," meaning that our brains are "structured and restructured by interactions with our social and natural environments." Primary interactions are typically between child and parent or caregiver, forming the foundation for the child's attachment patterns. However, siblings, especially in the absence of available caregivers, often provide meaningful experiences for and with each other that can build resiliency. In cases of trauma, resiliency is important because "we appear to be capable of coping with just about anything when we are connected to those for whom we care and who care for us" (Cozolino, 2006, p. 229).

Thus, it is the right brain that needs to be engaged to address effectively a myriad of issues and symptoms stemming from previous trauma. Nonverbal interventions are effective in engaging right-brain systems because they are, in essence, using the same "language" that developed the systems in the first place. Each of the five senses—sight, hearing, smell, taste, and touch—has the potential to access the right brain in its own unique way. The techniques presented here are designed to stimulate right brain systems through the use of the senses in the context of the sibling relationship. The interventions are intended to be creative and enjoyable to maximize the benefit to all types of sibling connections and to stimulate powerful nonverbal experiences. Experiential interventions do more than create positive experiences or memories between siblings. Ideally, they access the implicit memories that may be creating barriers to successful relationships and temper them in the moment with the goal of strengthening the sibling bond.

In order to give context to the interventions, I will introduce you to clients who have participated in and benefited from working nonverbally as we explore each of the five senses. My primary focus will be on *Alexis* whom I met when she was three years old. She was referred for family therapy to Kinship Center—a California multiservice foster care, adoption, and relative care agency offering a broad array of supportive services.

Alexis' presenting problems included angry outbursts, defiance, oppositional, and clingy behaviors. *Alexis,* along with five older half-siblings, had been removed from the family of origin because of parental drug abuse and neglect. One older brother was in residential treatment; two other brothers were in a foster-adopt placement in another city, and two sisters were in a third foster-adopt placement. When *Alexis* was eight months old, she was placed in a two-parent foster family who wished to adopt her. In that placement, she had a foster sister just a year older, and they became very close. After two years, the foster mother became pregnant and changed her mind about adopting *Alexis.* Unfortunately, the foster mother severed all ties; *Alexis* lost another sister. Her new parents expressed fear about maintaining contact with the birth parents, but they were committed to maintaining ties with her siblings. Sadly, her brothers' adoptive parents refused sibling contact. *Alexis* and her sisters had regular visits at a nearby park until her sisters moved to another state after their adoptions were finalized.

SIGHT

Visual experiences are some of the most powerful communication tools possessed by children. Researchers believe that the right brain of an infant is "biologically prepared" to be stimulated by visual input (Schore, 2003b, p. 12). Research shows that "visual experiences play a paramount role in social and emotional development" (Schore, 2003b, p. 7). These visual experiences begin with the infant's intense interest in mother's face, evoking periods of mutual gaze that have been described as the most intense form of interpersonal communication. Facial expression is known to be a prominent vehicle for nonverbal communication. Early on, babies become experts at monitoring and responding to many visual cues, including facial expressions, gestures, and body language. While some nonverbal communications are intentional, most of the processing takes place outside of conscious awareness (Cozolino, 2006).

Alexis was together with her birth siblings for the last time on her fourth birthday. Their interactions were not extraordinary (they did not know they would not all be together again), but *Alexis* has photos of herself and her siblings, which she treasures. Art and art therapy can be powerful when working with siblings—together or separately, child or adult. In art therapy, the process of creating and viewing images becomes a language all its own. The adage "a picture is worth a thousand words" holds true and becomes even more powerful when one realizes that this creative process can unlock areas of the brain otherwise closed off to spoken words. In cases where photos are not available, children can draw or sculpt images of their siblings as they might remember or imagine them to be.

Alexis came to therapy after losing all the family members she had ever known. She was too young to draw and may have been too intimidated to begin play with lifelike dolls. Instead, she fashioned tiny modeling clay "globs" which she identified as a family. Initially the globs were nothing more than bits of clay pulled from a larger piece, perhaps representing her experience of being pulled away and feeling small and undifferentiated. At the end of each session, she would put them carefully away in a small box until the next week. Each week the tiny globs played out themes of babies getting lost, separated from siblings and parents. She was very consistent in her representations; she knew which globs represented which family members from week to week, although they were fairly unrecognizable to anyone else. Eventually, the globs became bigger, and she shaped them into simple figures as she grew more comfortable in her placement and maintained some contact with her sisters.

Memories and dreams are often stored as images in the "mind's eye." Sadly, for children who have been traumatized, their minds' eye has stored a wealth of painful memories, easily triggered. Once triggered a child may react to a safe situation as if it were a traumatic one or hold onto the traumatic memory as if it happened yesterday. Guided visualizations can reduce the negative impact of these memories while replacing them with alternate experiences that can empower the child. Guided visualizations start with a series of relaxation exercises and then invite the child to imagine a special place or a person. A good visualization is to start to imagine a "safe place" and bring anything into it that the child desires. It is often helpful to complete an artistic rendering of the safe place after visualization. It is important to document the feeling of the safe place with abstract colors, a collage, or an image held in or by the body. Creating the artwork in a circle can create a "mandala," an ancient symbol of wholeness that is always complete. This safe place is now part of memory and can be accessed when needed. Once the safe place has been established, a child can "invite" an estranged sibling in for visits and healing conversation. The brain will incorporate these positive interactions and images into memory form. Guided visualizations can also be used with siblings who have suffered a common trauma or who have traumatized or perpetrated on each other. Sessions such as these may best be done with individual children at first to shift perspective, with the ultimate healing occurring when siblings get together and can practice their newfound relationships.

Another case illustrates how guided imagery in a group-setting improved the relationship between two brothers. *Mark* and *Carl* were referred to a latency-age boys group to help them process an abusive past in hopes they could move forward together with an adoptive family. *Mark*, age 10, presented as the parentified brother. He had recently returned from residential treatment. Prior to residential treatment, he had tried to jump out of a moving car and attempted to smother his brother with a pillow during a fight. *Carl*, age 8, was borderline in intellectual functioning and hyperactive. *Mark* was constantly watching *Carl*, correcting him and pleading with him to "behave." When *Mark* chastised him, *Carl* became more agitated and anxious; he would often hold *Mark*'s past behavior against him. Together, the two brothers joined the 12-week group. This boys' group, affectionately called "The Warriors Journey," used a combination of guided visualization and art therapy to process personal "journeys" and to build cooperation and teamwork. Each week the group would gather around an imaginary sacred fire, listen to a narrated visualization that guided them along part of the journey, complete an art experience or challenge and process with the group. Guided imagery was used to identify personal strengths, social supports, and losses that the boys had in common. Creating art and processing the experience enabled each brother to express his feelings of fear and hurt underlying the anger and frustration. Slowly, *Mark* was able to let go of his role as the caretaking brother, which gave him the opportunity to become both a stronger individual and a better brother. *Carl* was able to experience his brother in a different context, which reduced his fear and anxiety.

Suggestions for Parents

Children respond to facial expressions and body language far more than to any words. Thus, the more often positive visual interactions can be experienced between siblings, the more effective the interactions will be toward strengthening their relationship. Suggestions include: (1) encourage the use of games that require eye contact, such as "staring" games where siblings look into each other's eyes and the first person to make the other laugh is the "winner"; (2) have siblings participate in games that focus on body language and gestures such as charades; (3) help siblings learn basic sign language gestures or invent their own private sign language to communicate with each other. Photos, lifebooks, and home videos also use visual stimuli to increase a sense of belonging and connection. Even siblings who live apart can share these forms of communication.

HEARING

The sense of hearing develops early in the attachment process as "prosodic auditory signals induce instant emotional effects" (Schore, 2003b, p, 13); that is, the rhythm of the voice causes excitement which induces pleasure. As with body language, children listen more to how the words are said than to the words themselves. When *Alexis* was able to visit with one older sister in particular, she regressed and invented her own version of "baby talk" that she used to communicate at times. Her sister understood *Alexis* completely, and they were able to play out mutual roles of caretaking and nurturing, each providing what the other needed at that time in their lives.

Perhaps the most powerful use of our sense of hearing is creating, listening to, and remembering music. Music can soothe, excite, console, energize, and emotionally transport us with no conscious effort on our part. At the May 2007 Stanford University Second Annual Symposium on Music and the Brain, the keynote speaker, Daniel Levitin, PhD, a former musician and record producer–turned neuroscientist, (*This is your brain on music: The science of a human obsession,* 2006) argued that music may be more fundamental to being human than language. His studies document the activation of neurotransmitters spreading to nearly every area of the brain, including deep into the most primitive brain tied to memory and emotion (Miller, 2007). This powerful tool can be used to connect siblings with their memories and to each other.

Suggestions for Parents

Strive to include music in all parts of the day. Sing or hum "wake up" songs and bedtime lullabies, creating a nurturing routine. Identify or create family songs that will stay with siblings as they grow. Siblings can choose a genre of music for dinner time or housecleaning time in order to reinforce the sense of connection to the household and each other. Music can be an important consideration for siblings who transition from one family to another. Listening to familiar sounds will help the child to feel comfortable and accepted. If a child is separated from siblings, perhaps they can create a "remix" of favorite tunes they have shared together. Music is especially important to teenagers, whose brains are in the midst of a growth spurt accompanied by raging hormones. Levitin (2006) explains that these times of intense social bonding or emotional experience seem to "cement" music in our brains. Encouraging a teen to share his or her favorite music with a sibling is tantamount to sending the message that their relationship with each other is valuable. Foster and adoptive parents help a child connect with his or her siblings and to themselves by exploring their common cultural music.

SMELL

While most people can distinguish only seven to eight distinct types of taste, the nose can distinguish among hundreds of odors. This information is easily stored in our long-term memory and has strong connections to our emotional memory. For example, the smell of mothballs might cause one's heart to beat faster if the odor triggers the memory of a frightening incident in grandmother's attic. Conversely, the smell of yeast bread might activate a saliva response and instill a sense of belonging, if the aroma triggers positive memories of grandmother's bread baking. Products such as shampoo, bath soap, laundry detergent, fabric softener, and cleaning supplies all provide lingering scents that could comfort a child.

Suggestions for Parents

Bring as many of these scents along with a child who is transitioning. If a sibling is having a difficult time with separations, he or she can keep something with a special scent nearby to increase the "sense" of connection. It is best not to rush to wash a child's clothes or linens from a previous home, to reduce the number of changes the child experiences. Also, being aware of any scents (e.g., perfume, powder, bubble bath) that siblings might share can be helpful in maintaining connections.

For example, when *Alexis* attended the going away party before her sisters moved out of state, her mother gave each of the girls a small bottle of the same perfume. When *Alexis* sends a card or letter, her mother puts a dab of the scent on it before the envelope is sealed. This simple act connects the siblings through scent.

TASTE

One only has to look around to understand that food holds a central position in all cultures. Of course, it is primarily the taste that determines which foods we choose to eat. Because increasing pleasure builds attachment, it follows that food, when used appropriately, can be a marvelous tool for building and keeping sibling connections. It is important to acknowledge that not all food experiences are positive or pleasant; siblings may have very negative food associations that should be taken into consideration.

Literature indicates that, contrary to common perceptions, food preferences of parents have little bearing on the food preferences of their children. There is evidence, however, that siblings and peers have substantial influence on food preferences. This influence may be attributed to the fact that cultural forces generally determine food preferences, especially food habits obtained in childhood. Even after most traces of the original culture are gone, family food habits remain, which speaks to the strength and endurance of these food preferences (Kipple & Ornelas, 2000). Siblings will often share a food preference that bewilders adults. The current popularity of "hot" Cheetos, cheese snacks covered with red pepper, comes to mind. Pairing specific foods with positive experiences uses the psychological concept of classical conditioning to form positive connections.

Alexis has positive associations with McDonald's because she had many enjoyable sibling visits there (a neutral location) while separated from her brothers and sisters in foster care. They subsequently can share gift cards with each other, so that when she goes to McDonald's, she remembers happy times with her siblings.

Suggestions for Parents

The following idea comes from Sharon Roszia, national adoption expert and adoptive parent (personal interview 2006). "Every so often," she explains, "we would have a silent meal of finger foods. Here's how it worked: If she wanted something to eat, she would have to ask for it by making eye contact with another family member. Then she would look at the desired food and make eye contact again. She would repeat this process until the family member understood the request, picked up the food, and fed it to her." Roszia says, "The reciprocity of this exercise created attachment. We laughed and had an experience of intimacy that the children still speak of as adults." Roszia also recommends Sibling Cereal: Each sibling contributes his or her favorite cereal to a common mixing bowl to create a unique concoction that represents their relationships. The concept of Sibling Cereal can easily be adapted to Sibling Soup, Sibling Salad, or Sibling Snacks.

TOUCH

Siblings in adoption and foster care may face many challenges regarding their sense of touch. Many children who were neglected in their early years missed nurturing touch. Nurturing touch may have been replaced by physical or sexual abuse. Siblings who experienced negative touch may not know how to respond to positive, nurturing touch and may try to replicate the unhealthy interactions from their pasts. Some children have sensory integration difficulties and may have tactile defensiveness to certain kinds of touch. It is important for siblings to tune into their comfort level with touch, so that they can develop a repertoire of positive tactile interactions.

Not long after *Alexis* was adopted, the family welcomed an eight-month-old baby, *Jenna*, into their household for a brief respite period. This respite was prolonged as *Jenna*'s young birth mother was sentenced to jail. After several months, *Jenna* was deemed "available for adoption" by the courts, and *Alexis*' family jumped at the chance to make *Jenna* a permanent part of their family. By this time, *Alexis* was becoming quite attached to *Jenna*, helping her mother with her care and delighting in *Jenna*'s first words, silly giggles and faltering steps. Eventually, when *Jenna* was about two-years-old, her birth mother was released from jail, and the courts changed to work towards reunification. *Jenna* began having visits with her mother. *Alexis*' parents were very supportive of *Jenna* and her mother, so much so that *Jenna*'s mother would often ask them for advice regarding *Jenna*'s care. Even so, *Jenna*'s mother did not always follow the judge's instructions. Fear and worry began to show up in play therapy sessions with *Alexis*. In one session, a teddy bear became a dangerous animal attacking others with its "spiked shoes." Later, the significance was revealed when I learned that *Jenna*'s mother usually wore "spiked heels." In her nonverbal way, *Alexis* expressed her conflict between nurturing mother (teddy bear) and concerns about *Jenna*'s ultimate safety. When it became clear that *Jenna* would soon be returning to her mother, *Alexis* made a special pillow during a session. She carefully chose soft flannel fabric in colors she identified as their "favorites." We used a "no-sew" technique to tie the fabric together, forming fringe where the two sides connect. With each tying motion, *Alexis* and her mother talked about their ties to *Jenna*. When *Alexis* stuffed the pillow with soft, white fiberfill, she said she was "stuffing it with love." The timing could not have been better because *Jenna* transitioned back to her birth mother in a matter of days. The two girls continued to have visits for the better part of a year, until *Jenna* and her mother moved without leaving a forwarding address. Many months later when *Alexis* grieved her sister, she recalled, "*Jenna* has my pillow."

Suggestions for Parents

Encourage appropriate touch. Nurturing touch can be as simple as a "high five," a pat on the back, an appreciative hug, or holding hands to help each other cross the street. Include games that involve a bit of touch throughout the day; freeze tag and "Twister" are a couple of examples. Siblings can try to walk across the room, side by side, with a pillow between them. Older siblings may enjoy grooming routines, such as hair brushing or nail painting with each other. Special blankets, pillows, and other cuddly items can have positive tactile associations that make them exceptional transitional objects for separations, such as sleepovers and vacations. They can be especially powerful for siblings who do not live together.

Even without the opportunity to actually create a pillow as *Alexis* did for *Jenna*, a similar intervention can be implemented in simple ways by using inexpensive pre-made pillows that can be decorated with permanent markers. "Camp To Belong" (Price, 2004), a camp for siblings living apart, finds volunteers to sew the outside of small pillows with a large white blank patch on one side. During the week at camp, brothers and sisters write notes to each other on a pillow that they decorate, stuff and present to their sibling during a dinnertime ritual.

MOVEMENT AND THE BODY

Creative experiential activities should primarily utilize a multi-sensory approach to accessing traumatic histories, with the goal of facilitating the development of more secure attachments between siblings. To promote the benefits of attachment and healing relationships, children should participate with their siblings in kinetic activities, activities full of movement. Babies' early movements are building neural pathways as they learn how their bodies work. If a child's early experiences triggered repeated "fight or flight" responses, the engaged neural pathways become strengthened until the response becomes automatic, possibly to the point that the child feels out of control. The instinctive nature and strength of this fight or flight response might explain why siblings continue to fight, even with little or no provocation. Memories, both good and bad, become embedded in their bodies in a type of muscle memory. Fortunately, these kinetic memories can be altered by strengthening other neural pathways.

Samantha, age 5, and her sister, *Angelica*, age 3, were adopted by their maternal grandmother. One day in the summer, *Samantha* ran into the street by her home, chasing after a ball; a slow-moving car knocked her down. *Samantha* was terrified but only bruised. Verbally, she understood that she should never run out into the street. With masking tape, I marked off an imaginary sidewalk, curb and street to set up a reenactment. When I asked her what she would do if a ball rolled into the street, she said, "I stop at the curb." So, I rolled the ball across the imaginary sidewalk and curb, into the imaginary street. Without hesitation, *Samantha* ran into the "street" after the ball. She seemed surprised by her response, which had been a conditioned response to follow the ball rather than what she thought she would do. The "thinking part" of her brain knew to stop, but the "muscle memory" had stronger pathways. To reduce the strength of the automatic response, *Samantha* practiced following the ball and stopping at the curb. After several trials, she was finally successful and proud of her accomplishment. In a similar way, siblings can replace automatic unhealthy responses with new behaviors. Purposeful movement modalities, such as yoga and tai-chi, can help siblings increase their body awareness. This recognition, in turn, can help them relate to each other with appropriate insight and self-responsibility.

MAKING METAPHORS VISIBLE

Even the wisest parent's words can have a difficult time reaching a child's right brain directly. For this reason making metaphors "visible" or "able to be experienced" becomes important. Once the input can be processed in the right brain, the information can be transferred to the left brain for verbal understanding and integration.

Books engage the use of language, visual stimuli, and imagination. Coupling the story with art, craft, or another nonverbal experience will increase the brain's ability to integrate and generalize the information. In the following example, the siblings created an "intervention" on their own. Last summer, *Alexis's* older sister *Cassie* was able to visit for a week from another state. *Alexis's* mother had asked *Cassie's* mother for permission for *Cassie* to attend a therapy session with *Alexis* to strengthen their sibling bond. *Alexis* always worked hard in therapy and looked forward to sharing the session with her sister. Unfortunately, *Cassie's* mother refused to allow the meeting. The two sisters took the disappointment in stride; *Alexis* came into the office for her session while *Cassie* waited patiently at a table down the hall. I gave *Cassie* a book called *The Invisible String* (Karst & Stevenson, 2000) to read while she waited. *Alexis* was familiar with the story. In *The Invisible String*, a brother and sister learn that an invisible string connects them to those whom they love, and who love them, even when they cannot be near. *Alexis* took a ball of yarn from my office, gave one end to her sister and unrolled the ball until it ran down the hall, under the door and into my office where we began our session. She immediately picked out several sheets of construction paper and several markers and began to draw pictures of herself with her sister. She did not know how to spell much, but could spell her name and "love." When she finished the first picture, she folded it in half, pushed it under the door and tugged at the "not-so-invisible" yarn. Without a word being said, the picture disappeared and almost immediately another picture was pushed under the door coming from the other direction. *Cassie* had found some art supplies and had been drawing pictures for *Alexis*.

Suggestions for Parents

There are many books—adoption-related, sibling-related, and otherwise—that might be adapted. One resource is *Flat Stanley* (Brown & Nash, 2003). "Stanley" is a boy who inexplicably becomes flat. He realizes that one of the benefits to being flat is that he can mail himself places, which he does. This idea can be adapted for siblings living in different areas. One sibling creates a flat version of him or herself, either tracing the body to create a full-size flat self or simply drawing a small version, "miniature" flat self. The flat self is mailed to the distant sibling who carries it around for a while, as if being visited. Photos can be taken documenting the "adventures" of the flat self as a way of sharing everyday experiences with each other from afar.

Creating traveling books or collaborative art journals are popular with teenagers, traveling from sibling to sibling. Each sibling embellishes a page as he or she chooses, and then passes it on.

An important component of bookmaking is the story itself. Siegel and Hartzell (2003) stress the importance of developing a coherent life narrative in order to make sense of life experiences. Cozolino (2002) points out that narratives aid in supporting emotional security while reducing the need for psychological defenses. Coherent storytelling requires the integration of both right and left brain functions. Left brain processes record sequences and information while right brain processes provide the emotional context needed to give the information meaning. Siblings need shared stories to increase their sense of connection with themselves, each other, and their histories. Caregivers and clinicians can assist siblings in developing an age-appropriate coherent narrative or autobiography that incorporates and explains the previous trauma or abuse including its impact on their relationship.

SIBLING QUILTS

One of my favorite ways to make visible the metaphor of how siblings are connected is through the use of quilt-making. I once facilitated a family quilt-making workshop that was scheduled to last nine weeks, but the siblings became so involved in the project that they did not want it to end. Over a period of 12 weeks, five families pieced together quilts that represented their families. Each member of the group started by choosing a favorite fabric from a large selection of donated cotton prints from which they cut a nine-inch square. This first act alone was ripe with symbolism. Every person is in some way "cut from the same cloth." The simple process of "choosing" one fabric was the first step toward creating something new. Almost immediately the siblings recognized the individual statements made by the fabric choices. In the *Arroyo* family, a boy wanted to choose a camouflage fabric with a gun on it which led to a wonderful conversation as the boys encouraged the father to tell stories about his time in the Army.

Each family member also decorated a solid square of white fabric as a self-symbol. Several techniques for personalizing the squares were introduced, including fabric markers, iron-on appliqué, and photo transfers. Once each family member was represented, the sewing could begin. At least one square had to be sewn to another by hand to represent the patience and struggle sometimes required to piece together a family. Sewing machines were then available to share. Families could add to their quilts as many squares representing anything or anybody they wanted. Many discussions were held to decide on the placement of the squares. The *Arroyo* family created the center of their quilt by attaching squares of their adoptive family (mother, father and the two brothers) together. Around this "firmly attached" center, they added squares to represent extended family members. This design was especially important to the older brother because he was adopted by his maternal aunt and family relationships were sometimes confusing to him.

The *Nichols* family included a square decorated by their daughter's birth mother and a square representing her birth sister, so that they could be seen as an ongoing part of the child's life. The largest quilt was made by a family with two mothers, six adopted children, and two pre-school-age cousins for whom they were caring. This family tried to "mix up" their squares as much as possible so that everyone's squares connected to as many other family members' squares as possible.

Individual quilts can also connect siblings who are separated. *Jill*, age seven, and *Kathy*, age eight and half, are biological sisters placed together in a foster-adopt family. *Jill* was diagnosed with Attention Deficit Hyperactivity Disorder, and *Kathy* was very depressed but tried to hide her feelings. Their 10-year-old brother *Kyle* was placed in a group home after his sister's foster parents could not manage his behaviors. Once a month, all three siblings met together. During their time together, they decorated quilt squares and cut squares of fabrics to represent themselves. This process took place over many months. When enough squares had been completed, the siblings created a ceremony to exchange squares. Each sibling formally presented the others with squares he or she had created for them, as well as squares of "their" personal favorite fabrics. Over the next weeks and months, sometimes together and sometimes individually, each child sewed the gifted squares together with their own to create a quilt with bits of each other in them. Again, this project was very timely because within a matter of months *Kyle* transitioned to a new group home, and sibling visits became much more difficult.

CONCLUSION

Sibling relationships have immense value to children in foster care and adoption, whether living together or apart. Siblings share a unique connection that is different from their relationships with parents or peers and can become very important to siblings in light of the trauma and losses that they share. Often, this connection may be difficult to explain or even describe in words. Thus, nonverbal interventions and sensory experiences become dynamically vital in the process of increasing and supporting connections between siblings. As researchers in the field of neuroscience are beginning to unravel the complexities of how the human brain requires sensory experiences to grow and develop to its fullest potential, my hope is that the information presented here might inspire others to look at sensory experiences and nonverbal interventions in a new expanded way. Every moment of every day, the five senses are actively engaging right brain processes, providing countless opportunities to access what is needed to heal trauma and to build strong healthy sibling relationships.

ACKNOWLEDGMENTS

The author wishes to thank Laura Ornelas for her help and support in the preparation of this manuscript.

CHAPTER 12

Permanency for Siblings in Kinship Families

Carol Biddle and Carol J. Bishop

Relatives play an increasingly important role as permanent caregivers and in keeping siblings together or permanently connected to each other. Informal relative care arrangements are as old as recorded history and common practices in both multicultural and tribal communities. Siblings formerly moved comfortably among their relatives or kin as needed, keeping connected to each other. Only since the 1990s has child-welfare policy in the United States formalized relative placements as a first choice for children who cannot be returned safely to their parents (The *Adoption and Safe Families Act* [*ASFA*], 1997), an arrangement commonly called *kinship care.* A search of the literature shows that kinship care, a logical choice for permanency in a family, is also the least studied, although possibly the most complex in regard to family, economics, and services issues.

KINSHIP CARE AS A PERMANENCY PLAN FOR SIBLINGS IN CHILD WELFARE

To understand the current scope of kinship care, consider the 2002 U.S. Census (U.S. Census Bureau, 2002), which reports that one in 12 children live in a household headed by a non-parent relative. Approximately 4.5 million children are living in a grandparent-maintained family, and 1.5 million live in households maintained by other relatives. There was at least a 19 percent increase in grandparents raising *one or more* grandchildren during the 1990s (U.S. Census Bureau, 1998). Nationally, about one-third of the children in formal foster care are living with relatives (U.S. Department of Health and Human Services, 1997), with percentages varying from state to state.

The literature reports the value of keeping siblings together when possible (Testa, 2001; Chamberlain, Price, Reid, Landsverk, Fisher, & Stoolmiller, 2006). At the same time, surveys of children in foster care highlight their desire to be with their siblings (Shlonsky, Webster, & Needell, 2003). Foster-care studies have shown that children in foster care are more likely to live with their siblings if they are placed with relatives (Wulczyn & Zimmerman, 2005).

Safety, permanency, and well-being are seen as the markers for determining the outcome of child placement and have been examined in the recent literature about kinship care families (Conway & Hutson, 2007). Among kinship care placements, there is emerging evidence of greater stability of placements as compared to non-relative foster care, positive child perceptions of their relative placements, fewer mental health and behavioral problems than reported in the non-relative foster-care population, respect for cultural traditions, and increased stability for children with incarcerated or absent parents (Conway & Hutson, 2007). Significantly fewer children in relative care report having school changes than do children in non-relative or group care (National Survey of Child and Adolescent Well-Being [NSCAW], 2005). In one national survey teachers and caregivers rate children in kinship care as having fewer behavioral problems than do their peers in other out-of-home placements (NSCAW, 2005).

There is no child-welfare policy to establish a preferred path to legal permanency for kin caregivers. In fact, there appears to be some indecisiveness in the existing Federal law. *ASFA* both encourages permanency in kinship care placements and includes specific provisions for long-term foster care for children placed with relatives. The same law also encourages adoption or legal guardianship for children in non-kin care who cannot be reunified and specifically disallows long-term foster care as an option. With limited policy and direction to serve kin caregivers in the same ways non-kin are served, it is not surprising that there exists a variety of approaches in child welfare to serving kinship families.

Early studies reported that relative caregivers did not consider adoption the favored route to legal permanency, with cultural traditions and family relationship issues often cited as the primary factors in those attitudes and decisions. Adoptions have increased as professionals have supported relatives in considering choices that include *both* legal guardianship and adoption.

ISSUES IN KINSHIP CARE OF SIBLING GROUPS

The literature lacks relevant case studies that illustrate the unique challenges and coping skills of relatives raising siblings. This chapter presents information from interviews with two kinship caregivers, *Maria* and *Mary*, raising sibling groups adopted by the caregivers. The authors know the participants through Family Ties, a relative caregiver support program in Monterey County, California. These families are considered broadly representative of the more than 600 unduplicated kinship care families and 1400 children and youth served through the Family Ties program since 2002.

As a grandmother, *Maria* noted, there is not just one way to tell the story about kinship care as each child has a "recipe" that is special to that family. The siblings share their own perspective on the story of how their family was formed. Both caregivers chose adoption over guardianship, after considering both options.

FAMILIES FORMED BY CIRCUMSTANCE RATHER THAN CHOICE

Relative caregivers assume parenting by default rather than by an intentional plan. They may be aware of difficulties in the lives and the parenting of their relatives, but kinship caregivers usually have no control and often no current knowledge of the actual circumstances leading to the children's removal from the birth parent(s) care.

Grandmother, *Maria,* and great aunt, *Mary,* reported scurrying to rearrange their work, social lives, and living situations, each to incorporate a sibling group of young children. Both had no plan or forewarning that their lives would change dramatically and permanently. These circumstances are typical for kinship caregivers. *Maria* has adopted four grandchildren, while siblings *Sarah* (18), *Karen* (16), and *Gina* (12) went to live with *Mary* as preschoolers and were adopted by her two years later.

Maria

Maria worked as an in-home caregiver for the elderly prior to receiving four grandchildren. She needed to be at home with the young children, including an infant and toddler. She used a gift of gratitude from the estate of a deceased client and her modest savings to pay down the mortgage, allowing her to live on a smaller income. Her home is adequate but became crowded as first two, and then two more, grandchildren arrived.

Maria lives on adoption assistance program (AAP) funds and periodic gifts from an adult son. She uses the Family Ties clothing closet and food bank to assist with basic needs. She frequents garage sales to find bargains for children's clothing. She will return to work when the youngest child, a toddler, enters subsidized preschool care. She has Medicaid for the children, but no insurance for herself. *Maria* hopes that her daughter, a chronic substance abuser, has no more children, but is concerned that she might. If so, she expects to raise any future children and to adopt them as well. *Maria* grew up in a migrant family and learned to cope with change at an early age. She is very bright and resourceful, but her own early life experiences caused her to leave formal schooling at about age 12. *Maria* does not see her role as a hardship but as a life experience that she is glad to be able to handle. Although she did not plan this second generation of children, she would now feel "naked" without them.

Mary

Mary had a long career as a teaching assistant. She was widowed and raising a son who was approaching adulthood. First, her life changed when she became primary caregiver to her ailing mother. Soon after her mother moved in, she frequently returned from work to find her niece's young daughters "temporarily" dropped off by a mother unable to cope with a chronic substance abuse lifestyle. *Mary's* brother, the grandfather of the children, was deceased, and so she stepped in to do what she could.

Sarah, the oldest sibling, recalled the day that she and her sisters were taken by their social worker to live with *Mary*. Their birth mother's apartment was filled with people who were stoned on drugs, and there was no food in the house. On one of their many prior stays with *Mary*, she had given *Sarah* a social worker's business card and told her to call if she needed help. *Sarah* used this opportunity when she could not rouse any of the adults in the house, her sisters were hungry, and there was no food. The social worker came, saw the conditions, called *Mary*, and moved the children to her home that day. Court dependency and formal foster care placement with *Mary* followed quickly. *Gina* was too young to remember the move, but *Sarah* and *Karen* report being grateful for the quick response to a call for help. They were able to go together to the person they regarded as a second mother.

Mary's two-bedroom mobile home had been sufficient prior to taking on caregiving to an elder and then, three children. *Mary's* ordered life changed dramatically when the children came, but they have learned to live well in limited space for the past 10 years. Caring for the children, *Mary* quickly went through her retirement savings. *Mary's* mother is now deceased, and her son is fully emancipated and offers some support to his mother and the girls. In addition to the lifestyle changes, she reports the loss of long-term friendships when, unlike her friends, her new life became focused almost exclusively on child rearing. *Mary* is now employed by the Family Ties program as a valued family outreach worker, serving other relatives.

CHALLENGES IN DECISIONS ABOUT KEEPING SIBLINGS TOGETHER IN RELATIVE CARE

With many relatives living on low and fixed incomes, it can be difficult to keep siblings together in placement. Sometimes siblings are split up and placed with several relatives in close or distant geographic proximity. *Mary's* family group has made maximum use of all of the ways in which connections can be achieved in difficult sibling situations. *Mary* believes in continuity in relationships among the siblings.

Mary made the difficult decision to incorporate the three girls who were frequent "visitors" when they needed a permanent family. With her small home overflowing, Mary could take no more children but worked with social services to be included in meeting and establishing an open relationship with the non-relative family who adopted the fourth sibling, an infant boy. A fifth younger sibling is being adopted by *Mary's* sister. The sixth and youngest sibling lives out of state with a paternal grandmother who has cut off contact with the other siblings.

Sarah, Karen, and *Gina* each stated the importance of knowing that their siblings are safe and of being able to be a part of their lives. They now understand that their birth mother is unable to care for *any* child. The fourth sibling is in regular contact and feels like a "real brother." The fifth sibling lives further away and they characterize him as "like a cousin." They lost contact with the sixth and youngest sibling, but they hope someday to reconnect.

POST-PERMANENCY ISSUES FOR RELATIVE CAREGIVERS

Many of the issues in relative placements of siblings are similar to non-relative foster care with regard to early life trauma, separation from birth parents that may impede the development of attachment, and dislocation of neighborhood and school. These stories illustrate how siblings acting together can give valuable information to their caregivers that one child would find difficult to articulate.

Mary was unprepared for the effects of the children's prior trauma to enter their lives so dramatically. Unlike most adoptive parents, relative caregivers usually do not have prior preparation, education, and skills acquisition before the children are placed. They learn "by the seat of their pants" and often rely on their own resources or common sense to weather challenges. They are rarely encouraged to seek out specialized training and support. Such was the case when *Mary* took her three girls to her son's graduation in a neighboring town, the girls' first outing that included staying in a motel. While the girls feigned interest and excitement about the event, the closer they got to the motel, the more anxious and disruptive the girls became in the car. *Mary* pulled off the highway for a family conference about what was going on. For the first time, the girls demonstrated potential distrust of *Mary* and asked pointedly who else would be sleeping in the room. On further questioning, the children asked if drugs would be present. *Mary* quickly intuited that awful things had happened to the children in motels. Instead of interrogating the girls, she said that in her family visits to motels were about vacations and happy events; that they would all be together, and that no strangers would be around. She then told stories about her own adventures in motels when she had traveled with her parents. Calm ensued and continued throughout the weekend as the children experienced her as being trustworthy, and they enjoyed a good family time. This incident caused *Mary* to recognize that, although the girls had appeared to be adjusting well, their early life experiences and trauma would continue to influence their views of the world. It was at this moment she decided that her family needed therapeutic support and that she needed parent education.

Sarah and *Karen* also recalled the motel experience. They recounted having witnessed violence, drug deals, and once being threatened with a gun in order to scare their mother into paying for her drugs while in motels. They recounted how relieved they were to have had a positive and safe experience with *Mary*.

During their growing up, *Sarah* needed to "check in" with *Karen* about things she remembered, not being sure if the awful memories actually happened or if she had dreamed them. The girls validate each other's memories and find comfort in their close relationship. As they have grown toward maturity, they appreciate how hard their early life was and that together they have survived the hardships.

CHALLENGES OF OPENNESS IN KINSHIP ADOPTIONS

Openness in adoption involves choices in most non-relative placements. In relative care situations, the existing family relationships may assist or complicate the family dynamics. Often it is up to the already overwhelmed caregiver to weigh and manage the unpredictable future relationships with birth parent(s). The decisions are complicated by the affinity of family membership and by the loyalty and love for both the birth parent(s) and the children. In the case of sibling placements, each child has had a different journey with the parent, may not share the same set of birth parents, and must learn to trust the safety of the relationship with the relative caregiver. These confusing loyalties may further complicate the burgeoning relationship among the children and the relative caregiver(s).

Maria

Maria spent some time weighing whether her first action would be to bring her daughter home to live with her or to become the primary caregiver for her grandchildren on her own. Ultimately, she accepted the fact that her daughter had not once admitted her own mistakes in mismanaging her life or in neglecting her children. She set about building a family for her grandchildren, although the pain of this difficult decision has never left her. She still believes it was the right decision as her daughter does not visit and continues her damaging lifestyle. *Maria* does not know what the older boys really understand about the situation, but she believes they feel safe with her. Their attachment to her and behaviors in the home and at school show them to be generally stable and well adjusted at this point in their lives.

Mary

Mary has accepted that her niece will periodically be in the lives of her children. The impact of their birth mother's behavior on their lives was intense as exemplified in their lack of success in school and with peers. One child was not able to attend school for an entire year because of emotional trauma. Because of *Mary's* career in education, she arranged for home schooling. All three girls have been home schooled in the past year, and that tactic seems to have met the need for bridging their social-emotional deficits and their educational goals.

Sarah, Karen, and *Gina* spoke of their birth mother by her first name, with a mixture of anger and disappointment. They are sad that she had three more children after losing them and that she cannot raise any of her children. They recalled their hope when she was clean and sober for two years. During that time they visited, slept overnight at her house, and enjoyed time together. In their mind, she "messed up" and "threw it all away" by using drugs again, failing rehab, and finally receiving a long period of incarceration. They have no interest in seeing her or their incarcerated birth father. The girls consider *Mary* to be "Mom."

UNIQUE CHALLENGES FOR SIBLINGS IN RELATIVE CARE

Although many of the challenges facing siblings in relative care are similar to those of any sibling group in foster care, the usual challenges in kinship care are often complicated by role confusion, shifts in established relationships, loyalties and interfamily tensions, among other issues (Roszia & Silverstein, 2005).

Role changes within the structure of the relative family can create confusion about as to where a child "fits" in the family. When a sibling group is placed in a relative's family, they may acquire new "siblings" in the cousins, aunts, or uncles who live in that family. When siblings are separated into different relative families, each may acquire new familial relationships that differ from the sibling living in another home. For the child in one home, a cousin also may become a sister, an uncle may become a brother, but that cousin or uncle maintains a consistent cousin/uncle relationship with the sibling not in the home. Role confusion and conflict can become an issue, along with shifting relationships, and sometimes resentment and feelings of loss, rejection, and grief.

An additional role change occurs when the "parentified" child has to give up the parent role in the new family. *Sarah* admits to having felt responsible for her younger siblings, and says she "fights with Mom" (*Mary*) for control. *Karen* remembers *Sarah* getting meals for her when they lived with their birth mother, and *Sarah* says she always felt it was her job to take care of herself and her sisters, since her mother did not. She recalls an incident at five years of age when she "told" her mother to watch baby *Gina* while she, *Sarah*, went to the back of the house for something. When she came back, *Gina* was scooting onto the driveway and "some man" was backing a car out, causing the tire to scrape *Gina*'s face. *Sarah* remembers feeling guilty that she had not been watching *Gina* and blamed herself, not her mother.

Sarah recalls being more relaxed during the times they spent at *Aunt Mary's*, but once they actually moved in, it took a long time to feel safe letting *Mary* be the mother. Now that *Sarah* is 18, she is leaving home to move out of state. She has a job and friends to live with and is finally confident that her siblings will be okay without her. Her sisters talk about missing her, but plan to use text messaging and phone calls to keep in touch.

The roles are blurred when an older sibling takes on the care of younger siblings. Sometimes, it is not grandma who takes on the responsibility of the siblings, but one of their own—an older sibling. In these situations, there is a special need for services and support from the placing agency or the community-based organizations serving kinship caregivers. The older sibling's role must shift from that of sibling to limit-setter, disciplinarian, rule-maker, and nurturer. Young caregivers must deal with myriad systems, including the schools. They often feel ill prepared and embarrassed. Depending on the ages of the younger siblings, the struggle to adjust to this shift in relationships can be difficult, and the establishment of authority by the older sibling may take a long time to be accepted, if ever.

Siblings who are separated into different relative homes need help with acknowledging each other's rights to a family. Sibling loyalty can interfere with children's giving each other permission to attach to and to become members of other families, acknowledging each other's loss and grief, and exonerating each other of any disloyalty or blame for not staying together. Siblings must also determine how they will maintain their identity as a family, especially if they are separated among relatives (Crumbley & Little, 1997).

Family loyalties and interfamily tensions may interfere with the integration of children into the relative family. Relative family members may be overtly or covertly resentful of the parent whose child has entered their family constellation. This resentment may create additional feelings of loyalty conflict for the child. Unlike children in non-kin foster care, whose foster parents do not have an emotional tie to the child's parents, children in relative care may be subjected to other family members' feelings, positive or negative, about their birth parents and about the reasons for the removal from the birth parents' care. Siblings placed together may have the ability to reflect on shared experiences and validate each other's feelings about their birth parent(s), or if separated, may do so through regular and consistent contact.

When some siblings are still living with the birth parent(s) and others are living with relatives, questions about how those choices were made must be addressed with the children by their caregivers. Maintaining sibling bonds, or establishing them in the case of children born after some children have left the home, can be very important to the ongoing health of all of the sibling members.

Mary's girls know other children who had no relatives and ended up in foster care. Their message to other children who are with relatives is, "Be grateful, because you have family." They thank *Mary* for keeping them in touch with their birth mother when she is clean and sober. They are old enough now to make their own decisions about how much contact they want to have with her, but they never felt that they were kept from her or from extended family. They believe that *Mary's* respect for their relationships with their birth mother, and her guidance about when it was safe for them to see her has helped them to learn to make good decisions for themselves in regard to their birth parents.

RAISING SIBLINGS REQUIRES SUPPORT AND SERVICES

Some states have instituted programs to provide informal supports, such as resource referral, legal assistance for guardianships, and support groups, through programs like California's Kinship Support Services Program (KSSP) (State of California, Kinship Support Services Program). These programs remain financially limited and do not presently provide the depth and breadth of services that are available to non-kin families who are fostering or adopting.

Maria and *Mary* are fortunate to be connected on one of the few comprehensive kinship support programs in California, where they have access to counseling and referral, support and education services, assistance with adoption and guardianship, recreation and respite activities for the children, access to mental health services for the children, and availability of a food bank and clothing closet. They spoke about what supports have been most valuable to their particular families.

Maria

Maria described loneliness and isolation in the experience of taking on an unexpected parenting role. Her first two grandchildren were in foster care for over a year before she found out. She was never contacted as a possible caregiver. Instead of feeling welcomed, she felt isolated. She was filmed without her consent during visits with the children and was required to undergo a mental health exam (her description). Whatever the process was intended to be, it was experienced as an attempt to eliminate her as a resource for her grandchildren. *Maria* prevailed, but wonders if the process could have been more respectful. When a third grandchild was born, he was again in foster care for a year before she found out. A similar difficult journey to gain custody ensued. This time she had support through a staff member at Family Ties, who was also a caregiver. Having the fourth child placed with her was finally easier. Support of other relative caregivers raising siblings was most important to her. She attends education and support groups when she can. She also uses almost every service available to help her to care for her children, including the children's mental health clinic that supports adoptive and relative families.

Mary

Mary appreciates the camaraderie and peer support from other caregivers. She also cites the loneliness that accompanies unexpected parenthood, especially for a group of children whose extensive needs separated her completely from her former life. Of primary importance was gaining access to adoption assistance (AAP) and medical insurance for the children. In addition, there were practical supports from Family Ties that helped, such as donated bunk beds that fit her small home, locating a counseling resource, and a parent support group. Her girls continue to be involved in the many activities, such as camps and recreation trips. The older girls now volunteer in projects that help families with younger children.

Sarah, Karen, and *Gina* report that the Family Ties experiences are important to them, having benefited from children's groups and family group activities they might not otherwise be able to afford. Their early participation in Family Ties helped them to understand that they were not the only ones who could not live with their birth parents. Friendships with others who are living with relatives helped them to feel fortunate, rather than shamed by their circumstances.

KINSHIP CAREGIVER WELL-BEING ISSUES

While formalized kinship care policies have been evolving since welfare reform and *ASFA* in the 1990s, it appears that there may still be a reluctance to develop policy that establishes a clear line between governmental responsibility and family obligation for these siblings. A double standard of support for non-kin and kin caregivers exists that creates an observable disparity in services received by kin and non-kin permanent families.

The physical and mental health of the caregiver is a risk issue in kinship care permanency decisions, especially for the grandparents who are parenting a second generation of children.

If these issues are not addressed through professional support, the stability of the placement and the ability to keep the siblings together can be compromised. Relative caregivers tend to be older, are most often grandparents, are more likely than non-kin to be in unstable or poor health, to have a disability, to be underinsured or uninsured, and to live in households with incomes near or below the federal poverty line. Additionally, relative caregivers as a group have less formal education, are more likely to be single, and are more likely to be caring for large sibling groups (Barth & Needell, 1994). The stress of parenting and abrupt lifestyle changes can take a toll on even the healthiest individual, especially when placement involves sibling sets. For an already ailing adult, these stresses can be devastating and can affect both the physical and mental health of the caregiver.

Financial instability, present and future, affects more than half of relative caregivers, especially grandparents living on fixed incomes and unprepared for the financial cost of raising a second generation of children (Barth & Needell, 1994). The public financial resources available to relative caregivers vary from state to state but are limited in all cases.

DISCUSSION

The complexity of kinship care permanent families defies comprehensive discussion in one chapter. The authors chose to highlight two relative families as examples of kinship care families with siblings who persevere through difficult journeys. The insights from these families are gratifying, but they do not typify the full range of issues. While the literature is currently limited, the interest is increasing regarding the array of clinical, developmental, sociological, and cultural issues represented in siblings living in kinship care and the large numbers of sibling groups benefiting from the arrangement.

While most state policies indicate that kin are generally eligible to receive the same services as non-kin, past research indicates that these families receive fewer services and are offered and request fewer services (Geen, 2006).

Education for caregivers and professionals is needed to support permanency for siblings in kinship care. The trend toward relative placements as the preferred option for siblings removed from their nuclear family may be a generally positive one with promising outcomes for children. However, there has been limited recognition that relatives are often unprepared to make the emotional or financial accommodations to support placements of siblings. Social workers do not receive specialized training to accommodate the unique service needs of relative caregivers caring for sibling groups. Relative caregivers are not offered education and training tailored to their particular family dynamic, the importance of the sibling bond, and the issues faced by children who may have moved many times. Future directions suggest policy and funding to establish: education, training, and support of relatives who are taking responsibility for sibling groups, as well as education and training of social workers through specialized curricula focused on the unique needs of the permanent relative caregiver population in general and especially those caring for siblings in particular.

Organized advocacy at the national, state, and local levels is required for the cause of relatives who are parenting kin, along with coordination of efforts among the many organizations that have an interest in this issue. Limited legislation addressing a few of the needs of relative caregiver foster parents has been proposed at the federal level (*Fostering Connections to Success and Increasing Adoptions Act*, 2008). In California, recent legislation signed by the governor guarantees that permanent placement through legal guardianship with an extended family member will be honored as preferred over adoption by a non-family member (AB 298 Relative Caregiver Bill, 2007). Efforts such as these have begun to raise awareness of some important issues at the state and federal level, and we hope they will pave the way for more far-reaching legislation and funding in the future. Stronger advocacy is needed at state levels, where funding can be targeted to local needs, and the necessary resources can be put in place to support the growing trend toward keeping children, especially siblings, within their extended families. Funding and support programs for relative caregivers commensurate with the need and equal to that given to non-kin families are worthy of serious discussion.

Conclusion: What Have We Learned? Where Do We Need to Go?

Susan Livingston Smith and Deborah N. Silverstein

The content of each chapter has made apparent the immeasurable value of sibling relationships for children entering foster care or adoption and the paramount importance of preserving these connections. For a young child entering care, keeping him or her with brothers and sisters may be the single most important factor in promoting healing and resiliency as the child matures to adulthood. Several elements must be strengthened in policy and practice to provide this protection for children.

First of all, law and policy must clearly provide protection of sibling relationships, establishing a standard of keeping siblings together in placement barring exceptional reasons where this is not in their best interest, and requiring diligent efforts to reunite siblings who are not placed together within a specified time period, such as the 60-day limit in Texas law. The right of siblings placed apart to have regular visitation also needs to be fortified in law and policy, as well as the right of siblings separated by adoption to have ongoing contact with each other, as is a part of Florida law.

Accountability to attain the standards specified in law and policy must permeate all levels of practice, beginning with thorough training for workers on sibling issues, attention in supervision to these issues, and case-review practices that focus on protecting sibling relationships and reuniting separated siblings at the earliest possible time. When siblings continue in separate placements for significant time periods, reuniting them becomes more difficult and more costly in disrupting attachments that have been made within the families where they are placed.

Education about the value of sibling relationships needs to be provided not only to workers, but to other professionals who exercise decision-making in determining the course of these children's lives, such as court professionals and guardians ad litem. Also, educating foster and adoptive parents about the importance of maintaining sibling connections is critical, since their attitudes and commitments are foremost in shaping their children's relationships. The voices of children are our most effective means for cementing the value of sibling relationships in the minds of parents and professionals. The stories of children, as expressed so eloquently by Herrick and Piccus in Chapter 3, and children's voices telling their own experiences in videotapes are powerful training tools.

A myriad of creative-practice approaches need to be broadly implemented, resembling those practice strategies described in Chapter 10. Developing placement resources to meet the needs of large sibling groups (similar to the specialized program at Hull House in Chicago) is a necessary first step to avoid separating siblings when they enter care.

The most common factor linked with separation in placement is when siblings enter care at different points in time. Assigning all siblings to the same caseworker and keeping separated siblings in the same neighborhood and school district are important strategies to preserve the connections of siblings placed separately. Also, programs such as Camp To Belong provide opportunities for separated siblings to spend meaningful time together.

Beyond the world of the child-welfare system, many children join adoptive families and become separated from siblings who currently live with their birth parents or are later born to them. Sometimes these children have open adoptions and cultivate ongoing relationships with birth siblings. In other situations, they may be reunited with these siblings as young adults. Helping adoptive parents to value the child's having knowledge about other full or half-siblings and providing some opportunity to learn about or have a relationship with them honors these connections.

Finally, the single most important element for safeguarding a child's relationship with a brother or sister is our recognition of the primacy of this bond and its fundamental importance in sustaining a child's spirit. We hope this book has served that purpose—to reinforce in each one of us our commitment to protecting and nurturing sibling bonds.

References

AB 298. (Statutes of 2007). *Relative Caregiver Bill, California.* Chaptered 10/12/07, Chapter 565.

Abdel-Khalek, A., & Lester, D. (2005). Sibship size, birth order, and personality. *Psychological Reports,* 97 (2), 387–388.

Adoption and Safe Families Act, 42 U.S.C. § 675 (1997).

Adoption of Hugo, 700 N.E.2d 516, 524 (Mass. 1998), *cert. denied,* 526 U.S. 1034 (1999).

Adoption of Lars, 702 N. E. 2d 1187 (Mass. App. Ct. 1998).

Adoption of Vito, 712 N. E. 2d 1188 (Mass. App. Ct. 1999).

Aldgate, J., Stein, M., & Carey, K. (1989). The contribution of young people and their families towards improving foster family care. In J. Aldgate, A. Maluccio, & C. Reeves (Eds.), *Adolescents in foster families,* 61–76. Chicago: Lyceum Books.

Aldridge, M., & Cautley, P. (1976). Placing siblings in the same foster home. *Child Welfare,* 55(2), 85–93.

Aristotle v. Johnson, 71 F. Supp. 1002, 1006 (N.D. Ill. 1989).

Avery, R.J., & Butler, J.S. (2001). Timeliness in the adoptive placement of photolisted children: The New York State Blue Books. *Adoption Quarterly,* 4 (4), 19–46.

Baden, A.L., & Steward, R.J. (2007). The cultural-racial identity model: A theoretical framework for studying transracial adoptees. In R.A. Javier, A.L. Baden, F.A. Biafora, & A. Camacho-Gingerich (Eds.), *Handbook of adoption: Implications for researchers, practitioners, and families,* 90–112. Thousand Oaks, CA: Sage.

Bank, S. (1992). Remembering and reinterpreting sibling bonds. In F. Boer, & J. Dunn (Eds.), *Children's sibling relationships: Developmental and clinical issues,* Hillsdale, NJ: Lawrence Erebaum Associates, 139–51.

Bank, S., & Kahn, M. (1982, 1997). *The sibling bond.* New York: Basic Books.

Barlow, J.H., & Ellard, D.R. (2006). The psychosocial well-being of children with chronic disease, their parents and siblings: An overview of the research evidence base. *Child: Care, Health and Development*, 32(1), 19–31.

Barth, R.P., & Berry, M. (1988). *Adoption and disruption: Rates, risks, and responses.* New York: Aldine De Gruyter.

Barth, R.P., Berry, M., Yoshikami, R., Goodfield, R.K., & Carson, M.L. (1988). Predicting adoption disruption. *Social Work*, 33(3), 227–33.

Barth, R., & Needell, B.A. (1994). Comparison of kinship foster homes and foster family homes: Implications for kinship foster care as family preservation. *Children and Youth Services Review*, 16(1–2), 33–63.

Beck, E., Burnet, K.L., & Vosper, J. (2006). Birth-order effects on facets of extraversion. *Personality and Individual Differences*, 40(5), 953–59.

Bentovim, A., Elton, A., Hildebrand, J., Tranter, M., & Vizard, E. (1988). *Child sexual abuse within the family: Assessment and treatment.* London: Wright.

Berge, J.M., Green, K., Grotevant, H., & McRoy, R.G. (2006). Sibling narratives regarding contact in adoption. *Adoption Quarterly*, 9, 81–101.

Berge, J.M., Mendenhall, T.J., Grotevant, H.D., & McRoy, R.G. (2007). Adolescents' feelings about openness in adoption: Implications for adoption agencies. *Child Welfare*, 85, 1011–39.

Bernstein, N. (2000). *A rage to do better: Listening to young people from the foster care system.* San Francisco: Pacific News Service.

Berridge, D., & Cleaver, H. (1987). *Foster home breakdown.* Oxford: Blackwell.

Berry, M., & Barth, R.P. (1990). A study of disrupted adoptive placements of adolescents. *Child Welfare*, 69(3), 209–25.

Binn, B. (2004). Focusing on children: Providing counsel to children in expedited proceedings to terminate parental rights. *Washington & Lee Law Review*, 789.

Boer, F., & Dunn, J. (1992). *Children's sibling relationships: Developmental and clinical issues.* London: Lawrence Erlbaum Associates.

Boer, F., Versluis-den Bieman, H.J.M., & Verhulst, F.C. (1994). International adoption of children with siblings: Behavioral outcomes. *American Journal of Orthopsychiatry*, 64(2), 252–62.

Bond, J.C. (2004). *Sam's sister.* Indianapolis, IN: Perspectives Press.

Boneh, C. (1979). *Disruptions in adoptive placements: A research study.* Unpublished manuscript, Massachusetts Department of Welfare.

Boss, P. (2004). Ambiguous loss research, theory, and practice: Reflections after 9/11. *Journal of Marriage and Family*, 66, 551–66.

Bowlby, J. (1969). Attachment. *Attachment and loss.* Vol. 1. Middlesex, England: Penguin.

Bowlby, J. (1980). Loss. *Attachment and loss.* Vol. 3. New York: Basic Books.

Brody, G.H. (1998). Sibling relationship quality: Its causes and consequences. *Annual Review of Psychology*, 49, 1–24.

Brody, G.H. (2004). Siblings' direct and indirect contributions to child development. *Current Directions in Psychological Science*, 13 (3), 124–26.

Brodzinsky, D.M. (1990). A stress and coping model of adoption adjustment. In D. Brodzinsky & M. Schechter (Eds.), *The psychology of adoption*, 3–24. New York: Oxford University Press.

Brodzinsky, D.M., & Pinderhughes, E.E. (2002). Parenting and child development in adoptive families. In M.H. Bornstein (Ed.), Handbook of parenting,

Vol 1. *Children and parenting*, 279–311. Mahwah, NJ: Lawrence Erlbaum Associates.

Brodzinsky, D.M., Schechter, M.D., & Henig, R.M. (1992). *Being adopted: The lifelong search for self*. New York: Doubleday.

Brodzinsky, D.M., Singer, L.M., & Braff, A.M. (1984). Children's understanding of adoption. *Child Development*, 55, 869–78.

Brown, J., & Nash, S. (2003). *Flat Stanley*. New York: HarperCollins Children's Books.

Buchanan, J.P, McGue, M., Keyes, M., Elkins, I., & Iacono, W.G. (2006). Characterization of shared environmental influence on adolescent behavior: Evidence from the sibling interaction and behavior study. *Behavior Genetics Association 36th Annual Meeting Abstracts*, 36, 952–90.

Buhrmester, D. (1992). The developmental courses of sibling and peer relationships. In F. Boer, & J. Dunn (Eds.), *Children's sibling relationships: Developmental and clinical issues*, 19–40. Hillsdale, NJ: Lawrence Erlbaum Associates.

Caija, M.L., & Liem, J.H. (1998). The role of sibling support in high-conflict families. *American Journal of Orthopsychiatry*, 68, 327–33.

California Children's Services Archive. Child Welfare Sibling Placement from CWS/CS 1. (July 2003). Berkeley Center for Social Services Research: University of California. Retrieved August 1, 2008 from http://cssr.berkeley.edu/ucb_childwelfare/siblings.aspx.

California Department of Social Services. (1997). *Sibling groups in foster care: Placement barriers and proposed solutions*. Sacramento, CA: Author.

California Family Code § 8616.5 (2007).

California Welfare & Institutions Code § 317.5(b) (2003).

California Welfare & Institutions Code § 362.1 (2005).

California Welfare & Institutions Code § 366.26 (2007).

California Welfare & Institutions Code § 388(b) (2000).

California Welfare & Institutions Code § 16002(e)(1). (1999).

Casey Family Programs, National Center for Resource Family Support. (2002). *State legislation on siblings in out of home care*. Retrieved August 12, 2003 from http://www.hunter.cuny.edu/socwork/nrcfpp/downloads/policy-issues/state_legislation_siblings.pdf.

Casey Family Programs, National Center for Resource Family Support. (2003). *Sibling in out-of-home care: An overview*. Retrieved August 12, 2003 from http://www.hunter.cuny.edu/socwork/nrcfpp/downloads/policy-issues/sibling_overview.pdf.

Casey Family Programs. (2002). *The proceedings of the national leadership symposium on siblings in out-of-home care*. Retrieved August 12, 2003 from http://www.casey.org/Resources/Archive/Publications/SiblingSymposium.htm.

Center for Social Services Research, School of Social Welfare, University of California, Berkeley, (1998–2002 July 1). *Caseload children in child welfare supervised foster care by placement type*. Retrieved August 1, 2008 from http://cssr.berkeley.edu/ucb_childwelfare/siblings.aspx 57.

Chamberlain, P., Price, J., Reid, J., Landsverk, J., Fisher, P., & Stoolmiller, M. (2006). Who disrupts from placement in foster and kinship care? *Child Abuse & Neglect*, 30, 409–24.

Child Welfare League of America. (2000). *CWLA standards of excellence for adoption services.* Washington, DC: CWLA Press.

Cicirelli, V.G. (1982). Sibling influence throughout the lifespan. In M.E. Lamb, & B. Sutton-Smith (Eds.), *Sibling relationships: Their nature and significance across the lifespan,* 267–84. London: Lawrence Erlbaum Associates.

Cicirelli, V.G. (1995). *Sibling relationships across the lifespan.* New York: Plenum Press.

Clark, M., & Anderson, B. (1967). *Culture and aging.* Springfield, IL: Charles C. Thomas.

Conway, T., & Hutson, R.Q. (2007). *Is kinship care good for kids?,* CLASP (Center for Law and Social Policy); www.clasp.org.

Courtney, M., Skyles, A., Miranda, G., Zinn, A., Howard, E., & Goerge, R. (2005). *Youth who run away from substitute care.* Chicago: Chapin Hall Center for Children.

Cozolino, L. (2002). *The neuroscience of psychotherapy: Building and rebuilding the human brain.* New York: W.W. Norton and Company, Inc.

Cozolino, L. (2006). *The neuroscience of human relationships: Attachment and the developing social brain.* New York: W.W. Norton and Company, Inc.

Crim. v. Harrison, 552 F. Supp. 37 (N.D. Mass. 1987).

Crumbley, J., & Little, R.L. (1997). *Relatives raising children.* Washington, DC: Child Welfare League of America.

Cummings, E.M., & Smith, D. (1993). The impact of anger between adults on siblings' emotions and social behavior. *Journal of Child Psychology and Psychiatry,* 34 (8), 1425–33.

Cyr, M., Wright, J., McDuff, P., & Perron, A. (2002). Intrafamilial sexual abuse: Brother-sister incest does not differ from father-daughter and stepfather-stepdaughter incest. *Child Abuse & Neglect,* 26 (9), 957–73.

Dale, N. (1989). Pretend play with mothers and siblings: Relations between early performance and partners. *Journal of Child Psychology and Psychiatry,* 30(5), 751–59.

Dancè, C., Rushton, A., & Quinton, D. (2002). Emotional abuse in early childhood: Relationships with progress in subsequent family placement. *Journal of Child Psychology and Psychiatry,* 43 (3), 395–407.

Deater-Deckard, K., Dunn, J., & Lussier, G. (2002). Sibling relationships and social-emotional adjustment in different family contexts. *Social Development,* 11 (4), 571–90.

Department of Health. (1991). *Patterns and outcomes in child placement: Messages from current research and their implications.* London: Her Majesty's Stationary Office.

Deutsch, H. (1942). Some forms of emotional disturbance and their relation to schizophrenia. In H. Deutsch (Ed.), *Neuroses and character types.* New York: International Universities Press.

Devlin, B., Daniels, M., & Roeder, K. (1997). The heritability of IQ. *Nature,* 388, 468–71.

Doka, K.J. (Ed.). (1989). *Disenfranchised grief: Recognizing hidden sorrow.* Lexington, MA: Lexington Books.

Drapeau, S., Simard, M., Beaudry, M., & Charbonneau, C. (2000). Siblings in family transitions. *Family Relations: Interdisciplinary Journal of Applied Family Studies,* 49, 77–85.

Dunn, J. (1988). Connections between relationships: Implications of research on mothers and siblings. In R.A. Hinde & J. Stevenson-Hinde, (Eds.), *Relationships within families: Mutual influences*, 168–80. Oxford, England: Clarendon Press.

Dunn, J. (1992). Sisters and brothers: Current issues in developmental research. In F. Boer, & J. Dunn (Eds.) *Children's sibling relationships: Developmental and clinical issues*, 1–17. Hillsdale, NJ: Lawrence Erlbaum Associates.

Dunn, J. (2007). Siblings and socialization. In J. Grusec & P.D. Hastings (Eds.), *Handbook of socialization*, 309–26. New York: Guilford Press.

Dunn, J., Stocker, C., & Plomin, R. (1990). Assessing the relationship between young siblings. *Journal of Child Psychology and Psychiatry*, 31(6), 983–91.

East, P.L., Weisner, T.S., & Reyes, B.T. (2006). Youths' caretaking of their adolescent sisters' children: Its costs and benefits for youths' development. *Applied Developmental Science*, 10(2), 86–95.

Elgar, M., & Head, A. (1999). An overview of siblings. In A. Mullender (Ed.), *We are family: Sibling relationships in placement and beyond*, 19–27. London: British Agencies for Adoption and Fostering.

Fahlberg, V.I. (1991). *A child's journey through placement*. Indianapolis, IN: Perspectives Press.

Fanos, J. (1996). *Sibling loss*. London: Lawrence Erlbaum Associates.

Farmer, E. (1996). Family reunification with high risk children: Lessons from research. *Children and Youth Services Review*, 18 (4–5), 403–24.

Ferraris, A. (2005). Sibling visitation as a fundamental right in Herbst v. Swan. *New England Law Review*, 39, 715.

Festinger, T. (1983). *No one ever asked us: A postscript to foster care*. New York: Columbia University Press.

Festinger, T. (1986). *Necessary risk: A study of adoptions and disruptive adoptive placements*. Washington, DC: Child Welfare League of America.

Florida Stat. Ann. § 39.0001(k) (Westlaw 1999).

Florida Stat. Ann. § 63.022(1) (Westlaw 2001).

Folman, R.D. (1998). "I was tooken": How children experience removal from their parents preliminary to placement into foster care. *Adoption Quarterly*, 2(2), 7–35.

Fostering Connections to Success and Increasing Adoptions Act, Public Law No. 110-351 (2008).

Freud, A. (1966). *The ego and the mechanisms of defense*. New York: International Universities Press.

Furman, W., & Buhrmester, D. (1985). Children's perceptions of the qualities of sibling relationships. *Child Development*, 56(2), 448–61.

Gardner, H. (1996). The concept of family: Perceptions of children in family foster care. *Child Welfare*, 75, 161–82.

Gass, K., Jenkins, J., & Dunn, J. (2007). Are sibling relationships protective? A longitudinal study. *Journal of Child Psychology & Psychiatry*, 48(2), 167–75.

Gediman, L., & Brown, J. (1989). *Birthbond*. New Jersey: New Horizon Press.

Geen, R. (2003). *Kinship care: Making the most of a valuable resource*. Washington, DC: Urban Institute Press

Goffman, E. (1963). *Stigma: Notes on the management of spoiled identity*. Englewood Cliffs, NJ: Prentice Hall.

Goldstein, B.P. (1999). Black siblings: A relationship for life. In A. Mullender (Ed.), *We are family: Sibling relationships in placement and beyond,* 194–211. London: British Agencies for Adoption & Fostering.

Grigsby, K. (1994). Maintaining attachment relationships among children in care. *Families in Society,* 75(5), 269–77.

Grimm, W., & Hurtusbise, I. (2003). National Association of Counsel for Children, Child and Family Services Reviews: An Ongoing Series Placement Stability and Sibling Placement and Visitation. *National Association of Counsel for Children, Children's Law Manual Series: Access to Justice for Children.*

Grotevant, H.D. (1997). Coming to terms with adoption: The construction of identity from adolescence into adulthood. *Adoption Quarterly,* 1, 3–27.

Grotevant, H.D., & McRoy, R.G. (1998). *Openness in adoption: Exploring family connections.* Thousand Oaks, CA: Sage.

Grotevant, H.D., Perry, Y., & McRoy, R.G. (2005). Openness in adoption: Outcomes for adolescents within their adoptive kinship networks. In D. Brodzinsky & J. Palacios (Eds.), *Psychological issues in adoption: Research and practice,* 167–86. Westport, CT: Praeger.

Grotevant, H.D., McRoy, R.,G., Elde, C.L., & Fravel, D.L. (1994). Adoptive family system dynamics: Variations by level of openness in the adoption. *Family Process,* 33, 125–46.

Grotevant, H.D., Dunbar, N., Kohler, J.K., & Esau, A.M.L. (2000). Adoptive identity: How contexts within and beyond the family shape developmental pathways. *Family Relations,* 49, 379–87.

Groza, V., Maschmeier, C., Jamison, C., & Piccola, T. (2003). Siblings and out-of-home placement: Best practices. *Families in Society: The Journal of Contemporary Human Services,* 84, 480–90.

Harris, S. (1994). *Siblings of children with autism: A guide for families.* Bethesda, MD: Woodbine House.

Harrison, C. (1999a). Children being looked after and their sibling relationships: The experiences of children in the working in partnerships with "lost" parents research project. In A. Mullender (Ed.), *We are family: Sibling relationships in placement and beyond,* 96–111. London: British Agencies for Adoption and Fostering.

Harrison, C. (1999b). Young people, being in care and identity. In J. Masson, C. Harrison, & A. Pavlovic (Eds.), *Lost and found: Making and remaking working partnerships with parents of children in the care system,* 65–90. London: British Agencies for Adoption and Fostering.

Hass-Cohen, N., & Carr, R. (2008). *Art therapy and clinical neuroscience.* London: Jessica Kingsley Publishers.

Head, A., & Elgar, M. (1999). The placement of sexually abused and abusing siblings. In A. Mullender (Ed.), *We are family: Sibling relationships in placement and beyond,* 213–26. London: British Agencies for Adoption and Fostering.

Heatherington, E.M. (1989). Coping with family transitions: Winners, losers, and survivors. *Child Development,* 60 (1), 1–14.

Hegar, R.L. (1988a). Legal and social work approaches to sibling separation in foster care. *Child Welfare,* 67(2), 113–21.

Hegar, R.L. (1993). Assessing attachment, permanency, and kinship in choosing permanent homes. *Child Welfare,* 72(4), 367–78.

Hegar, R.L. (2005). Sibling placement in foster care and adoption: An overview of international research. *Children and Youth Services Review,* 27 (7), 717–39.

Herrick, M.A. (2002). *Alumni of foster care focus group.* Seattle, WA: Northwest Institute for Children and Families.

Herrick, M.A., & Piccus, W. (2005). Sibling connections: The importance of nurturing sibling bonds in the foster care system. *Children and Youth Services Review,* 27(7), 845–61.

Hindle, D. (2007). Clinical research: A psychotherapeutic assessment model for siblings in care. *Journal of Child Psychotherapy,* 33, 70–93.

Hines, D.A., Kantor, G.K., & Holt, M.K. (2006). Similarities in siblings' experiences of neglectful parenting behaviors. *Child Abuse & Neglect,* 30(6), 619–37.

Holloway, J.S. (1997). Outcome in placements for adoption or long term fostering. *Archives of Disease in Childhood,* 76, 227–30.

Hollows, A., & Nelson, P. (2006). Equity and pragmatism in judgement-making about the placement of sibling groups. *Child and Family Social Work,* 11(4), 307–15.

Howe, D., Dooley, T., & Hinings, D. (2000). Assessment and decision-making in a case of child neglect and abuse using an attachment perspective. *Child and Family Social Work,* 5, 143–55.

Huberman, A.M., & Miles, M.B. (1994). Data management and analysis methods. In N.K. Denzin & Y.S. Lincoln (Eds.) *Handbook of Qualitative Research,* 428–44). Thousand Oaks, CA: SAGE Publications, Inc.

IJzendoorn, V., Marinus, H., Juffer, F., Poelhuis, C., & Klein, W. (2005). Adoption and cognition development: A meta-analytic comparison of adopted and nonadopted children's IQ and school performance. *Psychological Bulletin,* 131(2), 301–16.

Illinois Adoption Code § 15.1(b)(7) (1999).

In re Celine R., 31 Cal. 4th 45 (Cal. Supreme Ct. 2003).

In re Christina L., 460 S.E. 2d 692 (W. Va. 1995).

In the Interest of David A., 1998 WL 910258 (Conn. Super. Ct. Dec. 18, 1998).

In the Interest of D. W., 542 N. W. 2d 407 (Neb. 1996).

James, S., Monn, A.R., Palinkas, L.A., & Leslie, L.K. (2008). Maintaining sibling relationships for children in foster and adoptive placements. *Children and Youth Services Review,* 30(1), 90–106.

Jean-Gilles, M., & Crittenden, P.M. (1990). Maltreating families: A look at siblings. *Family Relations,* 39(3), 323–29.

Jenkins, J. (1992). Sibling relationships in disharmonious homes: Potential difficulties and protective effects. In F. Boer, & J. Dunn (Eds.) *Children's sibling relationships: Developmental and clinical issues,* 125–38. Hillsdale, NJ: Lawrence Erlbaum Associates.

Jewett, C. (1978). *Adopting the older child.* Cambridge, MA: Harvard Common Press.

Johnson, P., Yoken, C., & Voss, R. (1995). Family foster care placement: The child's perspective. *Child Welfare,* 74(5), 960–74.

Joseph, S.R. (2002). The relationship between adopted young adults and their non-adopted siblings in the perceptions of current family relationships. *Dissertation Abstracts International,* 63(3-B), 1550.

Kaplan, L., Hennon, C.B., & Ade-Ridder, L. (1993). Splitting custody of children between parents: Impact on the sibling system. *Families in Society: The Journal of Contemporary Human Services*, 30, 131–44.

Kappenberg, E.S., & Halpern, D.F. (2006). Kinship Center Attachment Questionnaire: Development of a Caregiver-Completed Attachment Measure for Children Under Six Years of Age. *Educational and Psychological Measurement*, 66, 852–73.

Karst, P., & Stevenson, G. (2000). *The invisible string*. Camarillo, CA: DeVorss & Company.

Keck, G., & Kupecky, R. (1995). *Adopting the hurt child*. Colorado Springs: Pinon Press.

Kempton, T., Armistead, L., Wierson, M., & Forehand, R. (1991). Presence of a sibling as a potential buffer following parental divorce: An examination of young adolescents. *Journal of Clinical Child Psychology*, 20(4), 434–38.

Kentucky Cabinet for Families and Children. (February 26, 2003). Kentucky foster care census phase one: Statewide report. Retrieved September 1, 2003, from http://www.trc.eku.edu/fostercare/documents/statewide%20report.doc.

Kim, J.C. (2002). The importance of sibling relationships for maltreated children in foster care. *Dissertation Abstracts International*, 62(9-B), 4254.

Kipple, K., & Ornelas, K. (Eds.). (2000). *The Cambridge history of world food*. Cambridge: Cambridge University Press.

Kittmer, M.S. (2005). Risk and resilience in alcoholic families: Family functioning, sibling attachment, and parent-child relationships. *Dissertation Abstracts International*, 65(8-B), 4339.

Kitzmann, K.M., Cohen, R., & Lockwood, R.L. (2002). Are only children missing out? Comparison of the peer-related social competence of only children and siblings. *Journal of Social and Personal Relationships*, 19(3), 299–316.

Klagsbrun, F. (1992). *Mixed feelings*. New York: Bantam.

Knipe, J., & Warren, J. (1999). *Foster youth share their ideas for change*. Washington, DC: Child Welfare League of America.

Kohut, H. (1977). *The restoration of the self*. New York: International Universities Press.

Kosonen, M. (1994a). Sibling relationships for children in the care system. *Adoption & Fostering*, 18(3), 18–35.

Kosonen, M. (1994b). Sibling relationships for children in the care system. *Adoption & Fostering*, 18(3), 31–46.

Kosonen, M. (1996). Maintaining sibling relationships—neglected dimension in child care practice. *British Journal of Social Work*, 26, 809–22.

Kosonen, M. (1999). 'Core' and 'kin' siblings: Foster children's changing families. In A. Mullender (Ed.), *We are family: Sibling relationships in placement and beyond*, 28–49. London: British Agencies for Adoption and Fostering.

Kramer, L., & Baron, L.A. (1995). Parental perceptions of children's sibling relationships. *Family Relations*, 44(1), 95–103.

Kris, E. (1975). "The personal myth: A problem in psychoanalytic technique." In *Selected papers of Ernst Kris*, 272–300. New Haven and London: Yale University Press.

Kunz, J. (2001). Parental divorce and children's interpersonal relationships: A meta-analysis. *Journal of Divorce and Remarriage,* 34(3/4), 19–47.

L. v. G., 497 A.2d 215 (222) (NJ Super. Ct. Div. 1985).

Laing, R.D. (1965). *The divided self.* Harmondsworth, UK: Penquin (first edition, 1959).

Lamb, M.E. (1982). Sibling relationships across the lifespan: An overview and introduction. In M.E. Lamb, & B. Sutton-Smith (Eds.), *Sibling relationships: Their nature and significance across the lifespan,* 1–11. London: Lawrence Erlbaum Associates.

Lamb, M., & Sutton-Smith, B. (Eds.). (1982). *Sibling relationships: Their nature and significance across the lifespan.* Hillsdale, NJ: Lawrence Earlbaum Associates.

Lassiter v. Department of Social Services, 452 U.S. 18 (1981).

Leathers, S. (2005). Separation from siblings: Associations with placement adaptation and outcomes among adolescents in long-term foster care. *Children and Youth Services Review,* 27(7), 793–819.

Lee, R.E., & Whiting, J.B. (2007). Foster children's expressions of ambiguous loss. *American Journal of Family Therapy,* 35, 417–28.

Leon, I.G. (2002). Adoption losses: Naturally occurring or socially constructed? *Child Development,* 73, 652–63.

Levitin, D.J. (2006). *This is your brain on music: The science of human obsession.* New York: Dutton.

Linares, L.O., Li, M., Shrout, P.E., Brody, G.H., & Pettit, G.S. (2007). Placement shift, sibling relationship quality, and child outcomes in foster care: A controlled study. *Journal of Family Psychology,* 21, 736–43.

Littner, N. (1956). *Some traumatic effects of separation and placement.* New York: Child Welfare League of America.

Lobato, D.J. (1990). *Brothers, sisters and special needs: Information and activities for helping young siblings of children with chronic illnesses and developmental disabilities.* Baltimore: Paul H. Brookes Publishing Co.

Lord, J., & Borthwick, S. (2001). *Together or apart? Assessing brothers and sisters for permanent placement.* London: British Agencies for Adoption and Fostering.

Marrus, E. (2004). *Fostering family ties: The state as maker and breaker of kinship relation.* Chicago: University of Chicago Legal Forum, 319–60.

Martin, J. (1988). *Who am I this time? Uncovering the fictive personality.* New York: W.W. Norton and Company.

Maryland Code Ann., Family Law § 5-525.2(a) (Westlaw).

Massachusetts Gen. Laws ch. 119, § 26(5).

Masterson, J.F. (1981). *The narcissistic and borderline disorders.* New York: Bruner/Mazel Publishers.

Masterson, J.F. (1988). *Search for the real self: Unmasking the personality disorders of our time.* New York: The Free Press.

McGinnis, H. (March, 2006). *Siblings in international adoption.* Presentation at Biology and beyond: Siblings in adoption and foster care. Claremont, CA.

McHugh, M. (2003). *Special siblings.* Baltimore: Paul H. Brookes Publishing Co.

Mendenhall, T.J., Berge, J.M., Wrobel, G.M., Grotevant, H.D., & McRoy, R.G. (2004). Adolescents' satisfaction with contact in adoption. *Child and Adolescent Social Work Journal,* 21, 175–90.

Meyer v. Nebraska, 262 U. S. 390 (1923).

Miall, C. E. (1987). The stigma of adoptive parent status: Perceptions of community attitudes toward adoption and the experience of informal social sanctioning. *Family Relations*, 36, 34–39.

Miller, T. (Summer 2007). Science and Song. *Oregon Quarterly*. 22–25.

Millham, S., Bullock, R., Hosie, K., & Haak, M. (1986). *Lost in care: The problems of maintaining links between children in care and their families.* Brookfield, VT: Gower Publishing.

Mississippi Code Ann. § 43-15-13(8)(h) (Westlaw 2000).

Moore v. City of E. Cleveland, 431 U. S. 494 (1977).

Mullender, A. (1999). Sketching in the background. In A. Mullender (Ed.), *We are family: Sibling relationships in placement and beyond,*1–18. London: British Agencies for Adoption and Fostering.

Mullin, E. S., & Johnson, L. (1999). The role of birth/previously adopted children in families choosing to adopt children with special needs. *Child Welfare*, 78 (5), 579–91.

National Resource Center for Family-Centered Practice and Permanency Planning. *NRCFCPPP Sibling Practice Curriculum.* Retrieved January 15, 2008 from http://www.hunter.cuny.edu/socwork/nrcfcpp/info_services/siblings.html.

National Resource Center for Family-Centered Practice and Permanency Planning. Policies on Placing Siblings in Out of Home Care (December 28, 2005). Retrieved on August 2, 2008 from http://www.hunter.cuny.edu/socwork/nrcfcpp/downloads/policy-issues/Sibling_Placement_Policies.pdf.

National Resource Center for Family-Centered Practice and Permanency Planning. Policies on Sibling Visits in Out of Home Care (December 28, 2005). Retrieved on August 2, 2008 from http://www.hunter.cuny.edu/socwork/nrcfcpp/downloads/policy-issues/Sibling_Visiting_Policies.pdf.

National Survey of Child and Adolescent Well-Being (NSCAW). (2005). *CPS sample component wave 1 data analysis report,* U.S. Department of Health & Human Services, Administration for Children and Families.

Needell, B., Webster, D., Cuccaro-Alamin, S., Armijo, M., Lee, S., & Lery, B. (2004). *Child welfare services reports for California.* Retrieved from http://cssr.berkeley.edu/CWSCMSreports/.

New Jersey Stat. Ann. § 9:6B-4(f) (West 1999).

New York City Administration for Children's Services. (2000). *First annual placement report.* Retrieved September 1, 2003 from http://www.nyc.gov/html/acs/pdf/placement_report.pdf.

Nickman, S. L. (1985). Losses in adoption: The need for dialogue. *Psychoanalytic Study of the Child*, 40, 365–98.

Nixon, C. L., & Cummings, E. M. (1999). Sibling disability and children's reactivity to conflicts involving family members. *Journal of Family Psychology*, 13(2), 274–85.

Noller, P. (2005). Sibling relationships in adolescence: Learning and growing together. *Personal Relationships*, 12, 1–22.

Palmer, S. (1976). *Children in long-term care—their experiences and progress.* London: Family and Children's Services of London.

Parker, R. A. (1966). *Decision in child care: A study of prediction in fostering.* London: George Allen and Unwin.

Patton, W.W. (2001). The status of siblings' rights: A view into the new millennium. *DePaul Law Review,* 51(3–4), 1–38.

Patton, W.W. (2003) The interrelationship between sibling custody and visitation and conflicts of interest in the representation of multiple siblings in dependency proceedings. *Children's Legal Rights Journal,* 23(2), 18–34.

Patton, W.W. (2006). *Legal ethics in child custody and dependency proceedings: A guide for judges and lawyers.* New York: Cambridge University Press.

Patton, W.W., & Latz, S. (1994). Severing Hansel from Gretel: An analysis of siblings' association rights. *University of Miami Law Review,* 48(760), 745–808.

Patton, W.W., & Pellman, A. (2005). The reality of concurrent planning: Juggling multiple family plans expeditiously without sufficient resources. *U. C. Davis Journal of Juvenile Law & Policy,* 9, 171–94.

Pavao, J.M., St. John, M., Cannole, R.F., Fischer, T., Maluccio, A., & Peining, S. (2007). Sibling Kinnections: A clinical visitation program. *Child Welfare,* 86, 13–29.

Phillips, N.K. (1999). Adoption of a sibling: Reactions of biological children at different stages of development. *American Journal of Orthopsychiatry,* 69(1), 122–26.

Pierce v. Society of Sisters, 268 U. S. 510 (1925).

Plomin, R., Reiss, D., Hetherington, E.M., & Howe, G.W. (1994). Nature and nurture: Genetic contributions to measures of the family environment. *Developmental Psychology,* 30(1), 32–43.

Powell, T.J., & Gallagher, P.A. (1993). *Brothers and sisters: A special part of exceptional families.* Baltimore: Paul H. Brookes Publishing Co.

Price, L. (2004). *Real belonging: Giving siblings the right to reunite.* Portland: Inkwater Press.

Randolph, E.M. (1997). *Manual for the randolph attachment disorder questionnaire.* Evergreen, CO: Attachment Center Press.

Riggio, H.R. (2000). Measuring attitudes toward adult sibling relationships: The lifespan sibling relationship scale. *Journal of Social and Personal Relationships,* 17(6), 707–28.

Rodgers, J.L., & Rowe, D.C. (1988). Influence of siblings on adolescent sexual behavior. *Developmental Psychology,* 24, 722–28.

Rosenthal, E. (August 18, 1992). Troubled marriage? Sibling relations may be at fault. *New York Times.*

Rosenthal, J.A., Schmidt, D., & Conner, J. (1988). Predictors of special needs adoption disruption: An exploratory study. *Children and Youth Services Review,* 10, 101–17.

Ross, C. (2004). The tyranny of time: Vulnerable children, "bad" mothers, and statutory deadlines in parental termination proceedings. *Virginia Journal of Social Policy & Law,* 11, 176.

Ross, P., & Cuskelly, M. (2006). Adjustment, sibling problems and coping strategies of brothers and sisters of children with autistic spectrum disorder. *Journal of Intellectual & Developmental Disability,* 31 (2), 77–86.

Roszia, S. (2006). Santa Ana. CA: Kinship Center. (personal interview).

Roszia, S., & Silverstein, D.N. (2005). Kinship care and the seven core issues in adoption. *Adoption Clinical Training.* Salinas, CA: Kinship Center.

Rushton, A., & Dance, C. (2006). The adoption of children from public care: A prospective study of outcome in adolescence. *Journal of American Academy of Child and Adolescent Psychiatry,* 45(7), 877–83.

Rushton, A., Dance, C., Quinton, D., & Mayes, D. (2001). *Siblings in late permanent placements.* London: British Agencies for Adoption and Fostering.

Ryan, E. (2002). Assessing sibling attachment in the face of placement issues. *Clinical Social Work Journal,* 30, 77–93.

Sanchez, R.M. (2003). *Empowerment through collective action: Foster youth share their personal experiences and perspectives for change.* San Francisco: California Youth Connection.

Sanders, R. (2004). *Sibling relationships: Theory and issues for practice.* Hampshire, England: Palgrave Macmillan.

Santosky v. Kramer, 455 U. S. 745 (1982).

Sants, H.J. (1964). Genealogical bewilderment in children with substitute parents. *British Journal of Medical Psychology,* 37, 133–41.

Schaefer, E.S., & Edgerton, M.. (1981). *The sibling inventory of behavior.* Chapel Hill, NC: University of North Carolina.

Schechter, M.D., & Bertocci, D. 1990. The meaning of the search. In D. Brodzinsky & M. Schechter (Eds.), *The Psychology of Adoption,* 62–90. New York: Oxford University Press.

Schore, A. (2003a). *Affect dysregulation and the disorders of the self.* New York: W.W. Norton and Company.

Schore, A. (2003b). *Affect dysregulation and repair of the self.* New York: W.W. Norton and Company.

Schwartz, J. (2001). Siblings torn apart no more. *McGeorge Law Review,* 32, 704.

Scruggs v. Saterfiel, 693 So. 2d 924 (Miss. 1997).

Seifert, M. (2004). Sibling visitation after adoption: The implications of the Massachusetts sibling visitation statute. *Boston University Law Review,* 84, 1467.

Seligman, M., & Darling, R.B. (1997). *Ordinary families, special children.* New York: The Guilford Press.

Shlonsky, A., Elkins, J., Bellamy, J., & Ashare, C.J. (2005). Siblings in Foster Care. *Children and Youth Services Review,* 27(7), 693–95.

Shlonsky, A., Webster, D., & Needell, B. (2003). The ties that bind: A cross-sectional analysis of siblings in foster care. *Journal of Social Service Research,* 29(3), 27–52.

Shlonsky, A., Bellamy, J., Elkins, J., & Ashare, C. (2005). The other kin: Setting the course for research, policy, and practice with siblings in foster care. *Children and Youth Services Review,* 27, 697–716.

Siegel, D., & Hartzell, M. (2003). *Parenting from the inside out: How a deeper self-understanding can help you raise children who thrive.* New York: Jeremy P. Tarcher/Penguin Group.

Simmel, C., Barth, R.P., & Brooks, D. (2007). Adopted foster youths' psychosocial functioning: A longitudinal perspective. *Child & Family Social Work,* 12(4), 336–48.

Smith, M.C. (1995). A preliminary description of nonschool-based friendship in young high-risk children. *Child Abuse and Neglect,* 19(12), 1497–1511.

Smith, M.C. (1996). An exploratory survey of foster mother and caseworker attitudes about sibling placement. *Child Welfare,* 75 (4), 357–75.

Smith, M.C. (1998). Sibling placement in foster care: An exploration of associated concurrent preschool-aged child functioning. *Children and Youth Services Review*, 20, 389–412.

Smith, S.L. (2006). The nature of effective adoption preservation services: A qualitative study. In M.M. Dore (Ed.), *The postadoption experience: Adoptive families' service needs and service outcomes*, 159–96. Washington, DC: Child Welfare League of America.

Smith, S.L., & Howard, J.A. (1991). A comparative study of successful and disrupted adoptions. *Social Service Review*, 65(2), 248–265.

Smith, S.L., Howard, J.A., Garnier, P.C., & Ryan, S.D. (2006). Where are we now?: A post-ASFA examination of adoption disruption. *Adoption Quarterly*, 9(4), 19–44.

Staff, I., & Fein, E. (1992). Together or separate: A study of siblings in foster care. *Child Welfare*, 71, 257–70.

State of California, Kinship Support Services Program. Retrieved April 3, 2008 from http://www.dss.cahwnet.gov/cfsweb/KinshipCar_343.htm.

Stern, D. (1985). *The interpersonal world of the infant: A view from psychoanalysis and developmental biology.* New York: Basic Books.

Stewart, R. (1983). Sibling attachment relationships: Child–infant interactions in the strange situation. *Developmental Psychology*, 19(2), 192–99.

Stocker, C.M. (1994). Children's perceptions of relationships with siblings, friends, and mothers: Compensatory processes and links with adjustment. *Journal of Child Psychology & Psychiatry*, 35(8), 1447–59.

Stocker, C.M., Lanthier, R.P., & Furman, W. (1997). Sibling relationships in early adulthood. *Journal of Family Psychology*, 11(2), 210–21.

Sturgess, W., Dunn, J., & Davies, L. (2001). Young children's perceptions of their relationships with family members: Links with family setting, friendships, and adjustment. *International Journal of Behavioral Development*, 25(6), 521–29.

Tarren-Sweeney, M., & Hazell, P. (2005). The mental health and socialization of siblings in care. *Children and Youth Services Review*, 27(7), 821–43.

Testa, M. (2001). Kinship care and permanency. *Journal of Social Service Research*, 28 (1), 25–43.

Teti, D., & Ablard, K. (1989). Security of attachment and infant–sibling relationships: A laboratory study. *Child Development*, 60, 1519–28.

Thorpe, M.B., & Swart, M.D. (1992). Risk and protective factors affecting children in foster care: A pilot study of the role of siblings. *Canadian Journal of Psychiatry*, 37, 616–22.

Timberlake, E.M., & Hamlin, E.R. (1982). The sibling group: A neglected dimension of placement. *Child Welfare*, 61 (8), 545–52.

Toman, W. (1993). *Family constellation: Its effects on personality and social behavior.* New York: Springer Publishing Company.

Triseliotis, J., & Russell, J. (1984). *Hard to place: The outcome of adoption and residential care.* London: Heinemann Educational Books.

Trout, M.D. (July/August, 1983). Birth of a sick or handicapped infant: Impact on the family. *Child Welfare*, LXII (4).

Trout, M.D., & Thomas, L. (2005). *The Jonathon letters: One family's use of support as they took in, and fell in love with, a troubled child.* Champaign, IL: The Infant-Parent Institute.

Troxel v. Granville, 530 U.S. 57 (2000).

Tucker, C.J., McHale, S.M., & Crouter, A.C. (2001). Conditions of sibling support in adolescence. *Journal of Family Psychology,* 15, 254–71.

Turesk, Carol P. (2004). Forum contributor, Adoption.com.

Urban Systems Research and Engineering. (1985). *Evaluation of state activities with regard to adoption disruption.* Washington, DC: Urban Systems Research and Engineering.

U.S. Census Bureau, (1998). Available online at www.census.gov/.

U.S. Census Bureau, (2002). Available online at www.census.gov/.

U.S. Department of Health and Human Services. (2004). Administration for Children and Families, Children's Bureau, Adoption and Foster Care Analysis and Reporting System. National Adoption and Foster Care Statistics. Retrieved November 2, 2004, from http://www.acf.hhs.gov/programs/cb/dis/afcars/publications/afcars.htm.

U.S. Department of Health and Human Services: Narrative Report. (June 1997).

van der Valk, J.C., Verhulst, F.C., Neale, M.C., & Boomsma, D. (1998). Longitudinal genetic analysis of problem behaviors in biologically related and non-biologically related adoptees. *Behavior Genetics,* 28(5), 365–80.

van Volkom, M. (2006). Sibling relationships in middle and older adulthood: A review of the literature. *Marriage and Family Review,* 40, 151–70.

Wallerstein, J., & Lewis, J.M. (2007). Sibling outcomes and disparate parenting and stepparenting after divorce: Report from a 10-year longitudinal study. *Psychoanalytic Psychology,* 24, 445–58.

Ward, M. (1984). Sibling ties in foster care and adoption planning. *Child Welfare,* 63, 321–32.

Ward, M. (1987). Choosing adoptive families for large sibling groups. *Child Welfare,* 66, 259–68.

Washington, K. (2007). Research Review: Sibling placement in foster care: A review of the evidence. *Child & Family Social Work,* 12, 426–33.

Washington State Department of Social and Health Services (WS DSHS). (2002). *Department of Social and Health Services—Children's Administration: Strategic plan.* Retrieved September 1, 2003, from http://www1.dshs.wa.gov/CA/pdf/strtgc2003.pdf.

Webster, D., Shlonsky, A., Shaw, T., & Brookhart, M.A. (2005). The ties that bind II: Reunification for siblings in out-of-home care using a statistical technique for examining non-independent observations. *Children and Youth Services Review,* 27(7), 765–82.

Webster's II New Riverside Dictionary, Revised Edition. (1996). Boston: Houghton Mifflin Company.

Wedge, P., & Mantle, G. (1991). *Sibling groups and social work: A study of children referred for permanent substitute family placement.* Aldershot: Avebury.

Werner, E.E. (1990). Protective factors and individual resilience. In E.J. Meisels & S.J. Shonkoff (Eds.), *Handbook of early childhood intervention,* 97–116. New York: Cambridge University Press.

Whelan, D. (2003). Using attachment theory when placing siblings in foster care. *Child and Adolescent Social Work Journal,* 20 (1), 21.

Whiting, J.B., & Lee, R.E. (2003). Voices from the system: A qualitative study of foster children's stories. *Family Relations,* 52, 288–95.

Widmer, E.D., & Weiss, C.C. (2000). Do older siblings make a difference? The effects of older sibling support on the adjustment of socially disadvantaged adolescents. *Journal of Research on Adolescence,* 10, 1–27.

Williams, J. (1995). Sibling rights to visitation: A relationship too valuable to be denied. *University of Toledo Law Review,* 27, 259.

Williams, L. (1998). California Department of Social Services, Adoption Initiative Bureau, Concurrent Services Planning: Resource Guide III-5.

Winnicott, D.W. (1965). *Ego distortions in terms of true and false self. In the maturational processes and the facilitating environment. Studies in the theory of emotional development.* New York: International Universities Press.

Wulczyn, F., & Zimmerman, E. (2005). Sibling placements in longitudinal perspective. *Children and Youth Services Review,* 27(7), 741–63.

YLAT. (2002). *Youth Leadership Advisory Team position paper: Siblings in foster care and adoption.* Retrieved January 15, 2008 from http://www.ylat.org//leadership/policy/sibling position.htm.

Younges, M.N., & Harp, M. (2007). Addressing the impact of foster care on biological children and their families. *Child Welfare,* 86(4), 21–40.

Zukow, P.G. (1989). *Sibling interaction across cultures: Theoretical and methodological issues.* New York: Springer-Verlag.

Index

abandonment, sibling separation and feelings of, 47

abuse, among siblings, 4, 29, 126

abusive homes, effect on children of removing them from, 31, 34–35, 147

Ade-Ridder, L., 32

adjustment, 22, 43–56

Adler, A., 14

adolescents: adoption permanency, 23; loss experienced by out-of-home care, 48, 49; reaction of biological children to adoption, 20; solo placement of, 8

adoption: Attachment Theory as guide to, 9–11, 54; integration of newly placed adoptees, 20; international adoptions, 22, 23–24, 116; legal rights of siblings, 57–68; non-biologically related adopted siblings' experiences with birth-family contact, 69–81; openness in kinship adoptions, 158–159; placement stability, 21–22; reactions of biological children to, 20, 96–102; sibling loss and adjustment to out-of-home placement, 43–56; status loss with, 48; transracial placements, 48–49

adoption agencies, birth-family contact, 80

Adoption and Safe Families Act of 1997, 2, 66

Adoption of Hugo, 62

Adoption of Lars, 66

Adoption of Vito, 65

adoption workers, 80

adoptive kinship network (AKN), 71–72, 80–81

affection, between siblings, 17

African Americans: caretaking in families, 15; kinship, 13; sibling responsibility, 15–16

AKN (adoptive kinship network), 71–72, 80–81

alcoholic families, sibling relationships in, 18

"altruistic surrender," 104

anxiety, of children in foster care, 30–31

Aristotle P. v. Johnson, 62–63

art therapy, 142–143

About the Editors and Contributors

THE EDITORS

Deborah N. Silverstein, MSW, LCSW, is Vice President for Kinship Center's Southern California Division. She has over 27 years of experience, working directly with adopted children and families. She is the codeveloper of the *Seven Core Issues in Adoption,* a theoretical construct for understanding the lifelong impact of adoption on all constellation members. She is a published author and national lecturer. She and her husband are adoptive parents.

Susan Livingston Smith, MSSW, LCSW, is an Emeritus Professor of Social Work from Illinois State University and a leading scholar in the field of post-adoption services. She has published over 15 articles in scholarly journals and coauthored two books on special needs adoptions. The U.S. Department of Health and Human Services awarded her an Adoption 2002 Excellence Award for applied scholarship and research, and she received the Congressional Coalition on Adoption Angels in Adoption Award in 2006.

THE CONTRIBUTORS

Jerica M. Berge, PhD, LMFT, is an assistant professor and behavioral health clinician in the North Memorial residency program at the

University of Minnesota Medical School. She has done adoption research for the past six years, looking at satisfaction with openness in adoption and the adoptive kinship network, which has led to numerous research articles.

Carol Biddle, MSW, is a cofounder and president and CEO of Kinship Center in California. Biddle has led the development of model programs that inspire public and private adoption agencies to collaborate to change and improve practices, including a relative caregiver program that assists grandparents and other relatives. Biddle served as the President of the California Alliance of Child and Family Services and has served on a range of statewide and national boards, promoting innovative adoption practice. She is the author of numerous journal articles.

Carol J. Bishop, LMFT, is a cofounder and Executive Vice President of Kinship Center, California. She is a licensed therapist who has worked as a social worker, supervisor, and administrator since 1965. Carol trains both professionals and parents, and consults in several areas of agency practice and administration. Carol is a nationally recognized adoption expert. Currently, she serves as President of the California Association of Adoption Agencies and is on the Board of Voice for Adoption.

David Brodzinsky, PhD, is Professor Emeritus of Developmental and Clinical Psychology and immediate past Director of the Foster Care Counseling Project at Rutgers University. He is one of the most highly regarded researchers, educators, and authors in the field of adoption and foster care. He is Research and Project Director of the Evan B. Donaldson Adoption Institute and maintains a clinical practice in Oakland, California.

Margaret Creek, LMFT, ATR-BC, works at Kinship Center in Southern California with foster and adopted children and their families using art and other nonverbal experiences to increase attachment and process difficult emotions. She also presents trainings and workshops on the subject.

Kevin M. Green, PhD, CFLE, is the Graduate Admissions Administrator at Brigham Young University. His research interests include adoptive family dynamics, family communication, and parent-adolescent connection. He is also a certified family life educator and teaches courses on family relations, human sexuality, and fathering.

Harold Grotevant, PhD, is Distinguished University Teaching Professor of Family Social Science and adjunct professor of Child Psychology at the University of Minnesota. His scholarly work focuses on relationships in adoptive families and on the development of children and adolescents within their families. He has helped shape the world's understanding of adopted people and adoptive family functioning.

Diane F. Halpern, PhD, is Professor of Psychology and former Director of the Berger Institute for Work, Family, and Children at Claremont McKenna College. She has published over 350 articles and many books. She was 2004 President of the American Psychological Association and has won many awards, including the 2002 Outstanding Professor Award from the Western Psychological Association.

Mary Anne Herrick, MSW, administers the Independent Student Services Program for the Washington Education Foundation and the *Governor's Scholarship for Foster Youth* and *Make it Happen,* the college experience summer program for foster youth. She also has personal experience of having spent over seven years in the foster care system as an older youth.

Ruth McRoy, MSW, LICSW, PhD, is the Director of the Center for Social Work Research and a Professor at the University of Texas at Austin. In addition, she holds the Ruby Lee Piester Centennial Professorship in Services to Children and Families. She has been a preeminent practitioner, researcher, and lecturer in the field of adoption for over 20 years.

William Wesley Patton, J.D., is Professor and J. Allan Cook and Mary Schalling Cook Children's Law Scholar at Whittier Law School. He has written more than 30 law review articles on children's law, and is author of *Legal Ethics in Child Custody and Dependency Proceedings: A Guide for Judges and Lawyers* (2006), and coauthor of *Juvenile Law and Its Processes: Cases and Materials* (2003). He also teaches Forensic Child and Adolescent Psychiatry at the UCLA Medical School.

Adam Pertman is the Executive Director of the Evan B. Donaldson Institute and a Pulitzer-nominated journalist, as well as the author of *Adoption Nation: How the Adoption Revolution is Transforming America* (2000), one of the most influential books written in the field. He also founded the Adoption Nation Education Initiative. He is an adoptive parent.

Wendy Piccus, MSW, works as a Protective Services Worker in San Francisco County. She is an author and advocate to improve child-welfare practice. She is a former foster youth herself and is the proud legal guardian of her three younger sisters.

Cynthia Roe, MSW, LCSW, is a clinical supervisor with Kinship Center's Mental Health Clinic in Santa Ana, California. She herself grew up in and out of the foster care system and has reunited with her birth family. Cynthia has worked for more than 20 years in both public and private child-welfare agencies. She and her partner are adoptive parents.

Sharon Roszia, MS, is a program manager with Kinship Center and coauthor of *The Open Adoption Experience: A Complete Guide for Adoptive and Birth Families from Making the Decision through the Child's Growing Years* (1993). She lectures widely and is a coauthor of *ACT: An Adoption and Permanence Curriculum,* published by Kinship Center (2005). She has worked for over 40 years in the field of adoption. She is an adoptive parent.

Michael Trout, MA, is the founder and Director of The Infant-Parent Institute in Champaign, Illinois, and also maintains a private practice as a psychologist. He is a graduate of the Infant Mental Health Training Program at the University of Michigan under Professor Selma Fraiberg and a nationally known author and lecturer.

Susan Thompson Underdahl, PhD, is a clinical neuropsychologist in private practice in Grand Forks, North Dakota, as well as a member of the North Dakota Board of Psychology Examiners. She is an adoptee and author of *The Other Sister* (2007), a young-adult novel based on her reunion experience.